# HONEY FOR A
# teen's heart

## Also by Gladys Hunt

*Honey for a Child's Heart*
*Honey for a Woman's Heart*

# HONEY FOR A teen's heart

Using Books to Communicate with Teens

# Gladys Hunt
# Barbara Hampton

ZONDERVAN®

ZONDERVAN.com/
AUTHORTRACKER
*follow your favorite authors*

ZONDERVAN

*Honey for a Teen's Heart*
Copyright © 2002 by Gladys M. Hunt and Barbara J. Hampton

Requests for information should be addressed to:

Zondervan, *Grand Rapids, Michigan 49530*

Library of Congress Cataloging-in-Publication Data

Hunt, Gladys M.
    Honey for a teen's heart : using books to communicate with teens / Gladys Hunt and Barbara Hampton.
      p.   cm.
  Includes bibliographical references and index.
    ISBN  978-0-310-24260-4
    1. Teenagers—Books and reading.   2. Books and reading—Religious aspects—Christianity.   3. Christian teenagers—Religious
life.   4. Young adult literature—Bibliography.   I. Hampton, Barbara.   II. Title.
Z1037.A1 H94 2002
028.5'35—dc21

2002000783

*Interior design by Beth Shagene*

*Printed in the United States of America*

*Dedicated to our book lovers*
*Jedediah*
*Austin*
*Jenny*
*Ellen*
*Karen*
*who are always eager*
*for the adventure of a good story!*

# Contents

*Acknowledgments* . . . . . . . . . . . . . . . . . . . . . . . 9

*Introduction.* . . . . . . . . . . . . . . . . . . . . . . . . 11

*A Word to Parents* . . . . . . . . . . . . . . . . . . . . 15

## Part 1—Using Books in Family Life

1. Three Cheers for a Good Book! . . . . . . . . . 19
2. Is Imagination Going Down the Tube? . . . . . . . . . . 33
3. What Makes a Good Book? . . . . . . . . . . . . 39
4. Using Books to Talk About Values . . . . . . . . . . . 53
5. Rejecting the Philistines . . . . . . . . . . . . . . . . 65
6. Building a Christian World/Life View. . . . . . . . . . 71
7. Fantasy in a Real World . . . . . . . . . . . . . . . . 87
8. Getting Teens into the Bible. . . . . . . . . . . . . . . 97
9. Encourage the Best in Books. . . . . . . . . . . . 105
10. A Word for the College-Bound. . . . . . . . . . . . . 115

## Part 2—Book Lists To Help You Choose

11. How to Use the Book Annotations. . . . . . . . . . . . 125
12. Adventure and Suspense . . . . . . . . . . . . . . . 129
13. Contemporary . . . . . . . . . . . . . . . . . . . . . 141
14. Fantasy. . . . . . . . . . . . . . . . . . . . . . . . . 168
15. Historical . . . . . . . . . . . . . . . . . . . . . . . . 191
16. Mystery . . . . . . . . . . . . . . . . . . . . . . . . . 219
17. Nonfiction . . . . . . . . . . . . . . . . . . . . . . . . 228
18. Science Fiction . . . . . . . . . . . . . . . . . . . . . 242
19. Sports. . . . . . . . . . . . . . . . . . . . . . . . . . 254
20. Tried and True . . . . . . . . . . . . . . . . . . . . . 259
21. Quick Reference. . . . . . . . . . . . . . . . . . . . . 278

*Glossary* . . . . . . . . . . . . . . . . . . . . . . . . 287

*Index of Authors* . . . . . . . . . . . . . . . . . . . . 289

*Index of Book Titles* . . . . . . . . . . . . . . . . . . 294

# Acknowledgments

People who call themselves "readers" are keen on sharing books, especially books accompanied with an exclamation, "You just have to read this one!" Teens have enthusiastically shared book title favorites; others have read books for the list and given their evaluations for our consideration.

The Hamptons made a family affair out of producing the booklist for the bibliography, discussing books together, suggesting and reading new titles, and helping with annotations for the bibliography—doing the very thing this book suggests. Thanks to Ellen, Jenny, and Chuck Hampton for this encouragement. What a gift your sharing has been for Barbara in the midst of reading stacks of books!

Teen friends who recommended books are Sarah Feldhake, Cameron Exner, Jedediah Hunt, Catherine Papai, Adrienne Ramsay, Brian Ramsay, and Ben Trube. Their contributions put a teenage stamp of approval on our list. Thanks so much.

Our gratitude to Sandra Vander Zicht, executive editor at Zondervan, who saw the potential of this edition. Our thanks also to Angela Scheff for careful editing and to Beth Shagene, who designed the book's interior.

*Pleasant words are a honeycomb;*
*Sweet to the soul and healing to the bones.*

PROVERBS 16:24

# Introduction

Honey for a Child's Heart has been one of the most satisfying books I have written. It is an inspirational, motivational annotated guide to selecting books for children and, over the course of more than thirty years, thousands of parents have used it to introduce their families to good books. That reality is awesome. I feel privileged to have entered the lives of so many people, and I am especially glad to receive letters like this one from Shirley Woolsey, a mother of five children, who has raised a family of book lovers.

> When your book Honey for a Child's Heart was featured on the magazine cover, I knew that it is what I wanted for our kids: honey for their hearts. Imagine my delight when my husband brought your book home for our family to use. I began marking the books that I wanted for the children and hunted for them in the library. Can you believe that I was the valedictorian of both my high school and college class and had never been in a public library?
>
> We have been reading ever since. We read The Secret Garden during a family vacation in the hill country of Texas. We read Heidi during a camp in the Colorado mountains. We've recently read Where the Red Fern Grows and included another family in the reading. We've read the favorites: the "Laura" books (the kids were indignant that the TV Pa didn't have a beard—and Jack wasn't the right kind of dog), the Pooh books, the Narnia books, and because of you I am finishing C. S. Lewis's science-fiction trilogy, and Craig has read Tolkien. We loved The Good Master and Lamb's Shakespeare for children. And the real version of Mary Poppins.

For me it is more than receiving a positive letter; it's imagining all those parents, children, and teens—having fun with books! I feel connected to families like these, all of whom are finding out what good books can do.

It is time now for Honey for a Teen's Heart. Parents have been asking me about books as their children have grown older, and an explosion of books labeled "Young Adult Fiction" has poured from publishing houses in the last few years—a category of books that

*When people read together, they share something of themselves and know each other in important ways that keep teens respectful and caring.*

hardly existed when I first wrote *Honey for a Child's Heart*. Some of the output is confusing, reflecting sophisticated urban values and lifestyles that add to teenage chaos, rather than helping to resolve the questions teens have about relationships and self-worth. Other parents are concerned that their teens, who were avid readers in elementary school, have stopped reading and use their free time for sports or exploring pop culture movies, television, videos, music, computer games, and the Internet.

Family life with teens becomes increasingly hectic. Hours are spent in the car, taking kids to soccer, hockey, baseball, music lessons, and whatever. Meals are often eaten on the run. Teens get jobs and their schedules keep them away from home or doing homework. Most families hardly have time to talk about important things or relate to each other in meaningful ways. Parental duties narrow down to the management of schedules.

What we are proposing in this book goes against this cultural grain. This book talks about reading and listening to each other, talking about ideas. It gives clues about how to do it. We believe it is possible to have a growing friendship with our children as they mature, rather than a growing alienation. Parents and teens both profit from time spent in *knowing* each other and sharing feelings and ideas.

We present these ideas with enthusiasm because parents need to think about whether they are giving too much ground to cultural pressures instead of establishing their own family culture—one that nurtures the inner lives and values of young adults. All parents need to ask *who is in charge of our family life?* It is too easy to let it get out of hand or simply to go with the flow.

Barbara Hampton and I have found that books open up important areas of life that need thinking and talking about. A book can tear down defenses and build a bond of closeness more easily than anything we know. Stories often leave us vulnerable. We find ourselves sharing our own stories. Families need all the encouragement they can get to keep their members functioning as a family rather than as a group of individuals living separate lives. Don't wait too long to initiate a nourishing pattern of family life, but don't ever think that it is too late to start.

We hope that both the chapter content and the bibliography in this book will help you in establishing this kind of relationship with your teens. I have written the motivational chapters in this book. My book-loving friend Barbara Hampton is responsible for the bibliography. I love her concise use of language in her annotations. She is the mother of three book-reading grown daughters. Barbara has degrees in journalism and English from the University of Michigan and the University of Wisconsin. She is presently a freelance writer, adjunct professor of First Year Seminar, and a consultant at the Writing Center of the College of Wooster, Ohio, where her husband, Charles, is a mathematics professor.

I have a degree in journalism from Michigan State University and have loved writing since I was young and composed rhymes for family greeting cards and wrote productions for school assemblies. After marriage and the early days of parenting I began writing articles about subjects of interest for various journals, honing my skills. Since those days I have written twenty-two books, largely inspired by issues that came from our work with university students in InterVarsity Christian Fellowship. As a mother and grandmother I am seeing the happy fruits of putting good ideas to work—ideas like this book.

The project has been exhilarating. When I think about the richness that books can bring to your life, I want to sound a trumpet and ring bells to get your attention and then shout about the importance of being a lifelong reader. I am convinced about using books in teens' lives—so convinced that when I see families with rebellious, noncommunicating teens, I sometimes remark to my husband, Keith, (who is a great read-aloud story person) that I wonder if that family ever read books together. My experience has been that when people read together, they share something of themselves and *know* each other in important ways that keep teens respectful and caring. Family members bond together over great literature and have a common treasure to draw on in discussing almost anything. Good books can show you your heart and your values. Books can illumine life's choices.

The wonderful thing about books is that while building strong values in us, they are pure pleasure to read. We laugh, we cry, we sit on the edges of our chairs in suspense, we create kings and kingdoms and whole new worlds in our heads. We underline important ideas and share a good story line with our friends. Memorable characters are forever etched in our minds. Language from the story becomes part of our daily idiom.

Our hope—Barbara's and mine—is that reading this book and using its bibliography will spur your family on to even greater treasures of literature.

GLADYS HUNT
GRAND RAPIDS, MICHIGAN

# A Word to Parents

Ever since the 1960s parents have been wondering how to protect their children against the cultural onslaught that has ravished teenage life for so many. Some want to cloister their children and separate them from "wrong ideas" and pressures. Home schooling and parochial schools are ways to try to do this. Others have depended on the church youth program to divert their teens from danger. Sometimes this means that parents are asking youth leaders to do what they can't do. Often this involves generous spending money for whitewater rafting, trips to amusement parks, and all sorts of adventures that keep kids in the right company but apart from the family.

We have let teenage years become the entrance into an alien society. It scares both teens and their parents. Teens are afraid they won't fit and parents are afraid they will. Parents become hostage to their fears and desperate to feed children into another lesson, another advantage, another extra-curricular activity—whatever it takes to raise teens.

What we haven't spent nearly enough time on is making sure that every family member—and that includes parents—understands that God's Truth can stand in the marketplace of ideas. Truth does not need to be protected, not if it is true. The problem is that we don't see what an all encompassing thing Truth is. We haven't talked together about the little niches of life where Truth has something to say to us. In short, we don't talk enough together as a family about what a big thing we are in on when we say we believe in God. We are not people who know all the answers; we are people who are committed to God, who does have the answers. Not every idea in the world can be right—or wrong. We need to talk together about how we decide what is right.

Sharing ideas and feelings about books is foundational to the purpose of *Honey for a Teen's Heart*. The classroom, the living room of your home, around your dining table, riding in your car, eating lunch in the cafeteria, lying on the beach, and talking with friends— what great places to grow close to each other by sharing what touches

*We don't talk enough together as a family about what a big thing we are in on when we say we believe in God.*

our hearts, what causes our mind to grow big with wonder, what injustices anger us, what questions the plot of a story insists upon asking.

Our contention in this book is that reading together provides opportunities for the discussions every family needs. Books are about someone else; that means we can look objectively at the characters' choices and actions and discuss them. In addition, books delight, quicken the imagination, widen our world, and live in our hearts. Reading is not a luxury, but a necessity. We hope you will proft from our discussion.

# Part 1

# Using Books
# in Family Life

The Mountain-path

"The Mountain Path"—one of J. R. R. Tolkien's own illustrations for his book *The Hobbit*, reprinted by permision of Houghton Mifflin Company.

## Chapter 1

# Three Cheers for a Good Book!

Solid food is for the mature,
who by constant use have trained
themselves to distinguish good from evil.

HEBREWS 5:14

We can strip the knight of his armor, to reveal that he looks exactly
like us, or we can try on the armor ourselves to experience how it
feels. Fiction provides an ideal opportunity to try on the armor.

C. S. LEWIS

**D**inner was over at 6:30. We switched off the telephone and went
into the living room to read the next chapter of J. R. R. Tolkien's *The
Fellowship of the Ring*. Just as we sat down, the doorbell rang. It was
Mark's friend from down the street; he was part of our reading adventure. The two of them sprawled their lanky teenage bodies across the
floor, and Father began reading. It took twenty minutes to read the
chapter aloud, and the length of the next chapter was too long to
allow us to sneak in a second one. We all made some kind of noise at
the end of the reading: a sigh, a comment on the adventure, or an
inquiry about the plotline—expressing our pleasure at "words fitly

spoken." Then we got up and left the world of the shire and hobbits and went about our business—homework, a meeting, the dishes.

We began reading aloud the first book of this trilogy, *The Fellowship of the Ring*, as we drove home from skiing one weekend. We knew we had to finish the experience together. The first book hooked us into the adventure of these hobbits and easily wooed us into the second volume. By the time we got to the third volume, *The Return of the King*, summer had come and we were together, canoe-camping on the edge of a lake in Canada. Each evening we read around the fire in the fading light, with the night sounds of loons echoing across the lake. One day rain and a strong wind blew arctic coldness into our campsite. It would not be a good day for exploring, so the four of us huddled into one tent, snuggled into sleeping bags. Only the reader sat upright swaddled in blankets as we took turns reading chapter after chapter, going on an adventure far beyond the one we had canceled because of the rain. Sometimes the reader paused because a lump in the throat stopped up the words. No one felt embarrassed by tears; we were all wet-eyed. Beautiful word choices, raw courage, incredible goodness—it was almost too much to bear.

I mention this favorite memory partly because it warms my heart, but primarily to point out that something bigger than the book was happening as we read together. Feelings of closeness and understanding are woven into our memories of the marvelous adventure of the Tolkien trilogy; we "belong" to each other in some special way. We have laughed together and cried together and wondered together.

More than that, the book told us something about honor and truth, about valor and integrity, about what goodness looks like in a person. The impact of these books was more profound than any teaching we could ever give. Out of the books flowed ideas to talk about, behavior to emulate, feelings to share.

This book is about books—about using good stories in raising healthy teens.

It has never been harder to bring children to adulthood with your family values intact. The world is swirling with ideas and dissonance and our technology brings both into our homes. What is base or immodest becomes the story line of sitcoms on television. Clever writers brew up scenes that evoke laughter over what is offensive and demeaning. Disrespectful remarks and put-downs are the stuff of comedy. The music industry invades the air space with its cacophony and sometimes life-destroying words.

Pop culture "strips the knight of his armor," as C. S. Lewis observed in the quote at the beginning of this chapter. It reduces everything to its lowest level. Teens lose the vision of what they could be, of what they were meant to be, created in God's image. Our thesis (and Lewis's) is that good books allow a young person to try on the armor and see what it feels like to be a knight.

Anti-culture speeches from parents and others have little effect on pop-cultural "cool." Restrictions and rules about behavior in some instances protect our children but, unless parents make some effort to help young people understand the world and how to live in it, they leave an empty place that can potentially be filled with lesser or greater evils. The situation is similar to the one Jesus described when teaching about Beelzebub. A place swept clean is meant to be filled with something positive; otherwise, says Jesus, the empty place is filled with other wrong things.

## If You Like Good Romance

*Rebecca* by Daphne Du Maurier
*Pride and Prejudice* by Jane Austen
*Christy* by Catherine Marshall
*Up a Road Slowly* by Irene Hunt
*Edge of Honor* by Gilbert Morris
*Doctor Zhivago* by Boris Pasternak
*Jane Eyre* by Charlotte Brontë
*Playing Beatie Bow* by Ruth Park

I thought of this recently as I listened to a mother expressing her pain over her daughter's absorption with the teen-culture, pulling away from the family and participating in unacceptable behavior, breaking family rules, and hanging out with the wrong crowd. The daughter's display of anger and resentment is tearing apart the fabric of this family. The mother's anguish caught at my heart.

But I also thought of the complacency of other parents whose teens are outwardly playing by the family rules, but exhibiting a self-centeredness, a disinterest in other family members that frightens me. Some are hooked on computer games and basically anti-social. These parents ignore all the symptoms that should dismay them. They let them go their own way, shrugging their shoulders as they wait for these years to be over. My guess is that the rebellious teen has the advantage of the most prayer. One situation looks more desperate than another, but God is not finished with either of them yet.

All teens need help to transcend their small concept of what it means to be a human being; they need guidance and prayer. How will they get a big look at what life is all about, a concern for the feeling of others, plus a sense of responsibilty for family life? We want to help young people find something deeper on the inside—an adequate world/life view.

Before the 1940s no one thought in terms of *teens*. It wasn't even a word people used. Adolescents were people like the rest of the family, with responsibilities and expectations of growing maturity. The post-World War I culture had its flappers and racoon-coated college students and its music, but for the most part people were too poor to make this a separate culture. These people were on the fringe, not in the middle.

Was it the merchandisers who conceived of making teens a marketing target? They began with way-out clothes and hair fashions and music. The first to participate were set apart as out-of-step, but as the years passed teens were treated as separate from the rest of the human race. Parents began rolling their eyes when they talked about teenage years, as if it were an uncontrollable affliction. The 1960s finished the job of "legitimatizing" *teen* as a separate culture, without the rules adults impose. What most often happens? We abandon them to their own ways; we let them go and hope for the best.

## Sharing Life Through Books

As parents we need to do some fresh thinking about ways to influence the minds of teens—not with speeches or programs—but by living together and sharing life. It does take intentionality. Family unity won't happen without it. Parents have to decide to influence. Maybe they even need to call a family council to talk about family life. Adolescents coming into their teenage years send out two conflicting messages: (1) "Leave me alone and I'll make my own decisions," and (2) "Please help me; I feel very vulnerable." Which message will you listen to?

Having worked with university students for many years, I find common complaint among students when talking about their family life: they don't know their parents. I hear remarks like, "I really don't know my dad. He works a lot and comes home tired and doesn't say much." Or "My mom doesn't like anything I do or anything about me. I am not very close to her and really don't understand her." Or "My dad always wants to do something; we never talk about ideas, so really hardly know who he is."

Somewhere along in their teens as they begin to wonder who they are, they begin to wonder who their parents are—not so much the *what* (outside), but the *why* (inside) of who they are. Parents are people in the management mode, keeping a schedule, getting things done, setting behavior boundaries. At some point teens suddenly realize that they don't know their parents as people. Adolescents also have a weird way of blocking out the humanity of their parents, as if parents were never kids who thought or felt the way they do. Generally, when that is true, it's because we haven't told them about ourselves.

Most families need to talk more together and to live more together. It is too easy to let teens go their own way, to become very involved apart from the family. And worst of all, to have no responsibility for communal family life. The family is a social unit that needs the contribution of every family member—an involvement that goes beyond a list of household chores.

How do you do this—this talking more together, this listening to each other? That's where reading books together comes in. It is perhaps the most enriching idea around—low price tag, a proven idea.

You start by sharing books, preferrably when children are little, before they can read well themselves. Make it a family event. Good books are meant to be shared. A really good children's book has dimensions that affect adults as well as children, older children as well as younger ones. I remember suggesting to a father that he read *Charlotte's Web* aloud with his children and let me know what happened. He called, so filled with gratitude and emotion that I knew he was hooked on reading aloud with his family. "Give me another title," he said. It's best to begin like that. But it's better still to continue to read together and share books as children grow older.

What most parents do, however, is stop sharing books as soon as a child can read alone. That makes reading a solitary happening, with no chance to talk about a book or discuss what it is saying. Read aloud together. Read alone yourself, then say, "Have you read this book? I really liked it." Once you begin to be book-sharers you will have no end of delight in sharing. Our grandson brought us a copy of Brian Jacques' *Redwall* and said, "I think you'll like this. It's a good book." We respect each other's opinions because we have read aloud together and talked about books. That grandson is in college now and recently visited us. He left a book behind, saying, "I'd like you to read this. It tells you some of my thinking about relationships." Sharing a book makes for a delightful companionship. It is sharing yourself.

*Make it a family event. Good books are meant to be shared.*

The bibliography of this book is crowded with book ideas. Here are some immediate suggestions:

If you have a reading-reluctant son, try reading aloud *Holes* by Louis Sachar. The book is a Newbery Medal winner, a strange tale that is so overdrawn and awful that you can't take it seriously. A well-meaning boy is walking along the street when suddenly a pair of expensive sneakers land on his head. They are his size. He congratulates himself on his luck, only to find himself accused of stealing them.

He is sentenced—not to jail—but to a summer camp that turns out to be slave labor where he is assigned to dig a hole of a certain dimension every day. It's a strange combination of the ridiculous and a great adventure tale with mystery and history thrown in. The story becomes a metaphor for everything hard that happens in the reader's life thereafter. One teen wrote from a mission boot camp to say that life there resembled *Holes*. We didn't need to ask any more questions.

For great adventure read Karen Hesse's *Stowaway*, a novel based on the true story of Nicholas Young who stowed away on Captain Cook's ship, *Endeavor*. Or Brian Jacques' *Castaways of the Flying Dutchman*, a gripping story of rescue and task for a young man and his dog.

*A Long Way from Chicago* by Richard Peck is a humorous story about a brother and sister who are sent to live with their eccentric grandmother for the summer. Then read the sequel *A Year Down Yonder*.

The Narnia Chronicles by C. S. Lewis bear repeated readings for children, teens, and adults. It's hard to resist these wonderful stories where good and evil clash, where heroes are so ordinary, and where a golden-maned lion is in charge.

Probably all of us have had the experience of reading a book so good that they could hardly wait to find someone who has read it too. When eighth-grader Tim read *A Day No Pigs Would Die* by Robert Newton Peck, the story evoked deep and even confusing emotions inside him, and he wanted to talk with someone about it. It's the story

## If You Want to Know More about Asia

*Master Puppeteer* by Katherine Paterson
*The Samurai* by Shusaku Endo
*Rebels of the Heavenly Kingdom* by Katherine Paterson
*The Good Earth* by Pearl Buck
*Killing Fields, Living Fields* by Don Cormack
*Lost Horizon* by James Hilton
*Eric Liddell: Pure Gold* by David McCasland
*Into Thin Air* by Jon Krakauer

of a young man's struggle to understand his father, only to have him die unexpectedly. Tim asked his dad to read it. His dad was also moved by the story. He found Tim and said, "Let's go for a walk—just the two of us—to talk about that book." When they recounted this conversation to me, I couldn't be sure who found the walk and the talk most nourishing—Tim or his dad. Obviously it was a significant memory, a building stone for life, and it created a closeness that insured future communication.

Barbara Hampton's family reads aloud as they travel. In spite of differing ages, each person looks forward to a good story plus the closeness of sharing it. The miles pass quickly. One day, reading Arthur Ransome's *We Didn't Mean to Go to Sea* as they traveled, they became so engrossed in the story that they missed their exit and ended up in another city. *They didn't mean to go to Canton, Ohio!* It's one of the family's favorite "Remember the time. . ." stories.

When our son was a freshman in college, he came home for spring break bearing Charles Williams's *Descent Into Hell*—a book that demands discussion—and suggested that we read it together on our trip to Florida. As we drove down Highway 19, we neared the end of the story just as we were nearing our destination. We found ourselves driving more and more slowly so as not to break the spell. That book will always be more than a story for us.

Jim Trelease, author of *The Read-Aloud Handbook*, says that next to being hugged, reading aloud is probably the longest-lasting experience of childhood. Reading aloud together is important for all the reasons that talking together is important—inspiration, guidance, education, bonding, communication, understanding, and sharing. When people read together, they give each other a piece of their mind and a piece of their time, and that says a good deal about human worth. You'll come to know each other in a new way, and prove that life is more than "meat and potatoes."

When the men in our family find the girls they want to marry, a reading-aloud flurry begins in the family room. I think it must be in the genes. We hear these new twosomes reading *Alice in Wonderland*, *The Wind in the Willows*, *Robin Hood*, Tolkien, and all the other books that have been an important part of their past. Then I think they read from her list. It gives them a common cultural heritage as well as a bond of sharing.

Sharing books makes for good companionship. It is the special fellowship of "readers." It opens up a whole new world for those who enter it. If you have never experienced it, begin soon. Share a good book with someone you care about.

## What Do Books Do for Families?

*More than you think.* More than the enjoyment of being transported into another world and meeting the people there, good books evoke feelings and teach us to understand these feelings. We see what selfishness does to a life; we see how necessary compassion is in human relationships; we understand what it means to be honest and have integrity. The story shows us the hard choices that make up life and, because of our involvement with the characters in the story, we absorb more about the real stuff of living than we realize. And because the story is about someone else, I am more open to understanding exactly where the choices may lead. Good books are always about the fight between good and evil. That is the basic story line of the universe.

### Books Widen Our Worlds

Books put us in places and take us on adventures we may never have. No one in our family has ever experienced the racial hatred of the south during the Depression. When we read *To Kill a Mockingbird* by Harper Lee we began living in a different world from any we had known. We felt outrage and shame and fear as Atticus, the lawyer, defends a black man accused of assaulting a white woman. The book gave us a vicarious experience of what it was like to be black *or* white in the south during the 1930s. Robert Louis Stevenson's *Treasure Island* can be read from youth through adulthood—read repeatedly because of the skill the author used in portraying his characters and details of life at sea. We feel richer having seen Jim Hawkins' courage in action and facing his choices with him. And besides that, it is our best experience on a pirate ship. *My Antonia* by Willa Cather puts readers inside the life of early pioneers on the prairie, and their love for the land becomes contagious. The struggle, the hardships, the perserverance—Cather's descriptions and word choices make us glad that we know how to read.

### Good Stories Put Flesh on Abstract Ideas

It is difficult to fathom what it means to be noble, valiant, courageous, or even unselfish, unless we meet people in stories whose actions show us what these things mean. What would you understand about "beauty" if you had never seen or heard anything beautiful? A young woman once wrote to J. R. R. Tolkien, "You have made truth and honor more meaningful to me." If you have read *The Lord of the Rings* and followed the courageous Sam Gamgee and Frodo on their adventure, you already know why she wrote to Tolkien in this way. All of us face choices that involve honor and truth. Especially when it comes to moral issues, it helps to think in terms of stories, rather than abstract concepts.

Once, while reading one of George MacDonald's stories, I came across this description of a person, "Never suspecting what a noble creature he was meant to be, he never saw what a poor creature he was." This seemed to me to be an apt description of a person, maybe a nonreader, who has never looked beyond his own small life to see the possibilities that human beings have. Good books show us our potential.

*When it comes to moral issues, it helps to think in terms of stories, rather than abstract concepts.*

## Reading Teaches Us

We learn how to use the English language when we read good writing. It's a by-product. We come to admire the right word in the right place—and we are amazed at what it can convey. Reading from Tolkien's trilogy, our family found what has become a favorite description of joy. After Sam Gamgee's return home after his experience of victory on the Mount of Doom, someone asked him how he felt. He said, "I feel like spring after winter, and sun on leaves and like trumpets and harps and all the songs I ever heard."

Slowly and imperceptibly we develop our language skills and learn to choose the right words when expressing ourselves. We learn spelling and punctuation too. Words help us shape what is happening to us. The use of language enables us to drop verbal crutches (like "you know" or "he was like. . .") that plague teenage conversation, demanding that the listener fill in the blank spaces. All of which makes our personal life more interesting and contributes clarity and precise thinking to the world—which is not a bad contribution, when you think of it.

We are, after all, word partners with God. He has given us these shining symbols known as "words" and lets us communicate with each other and with him, which is nothing short of amazing when you consider all the possibilities for not understanding each other. In one of her lectures on children's literature, Katherine Paterson said,

> Words are humanity's greatest natural resource, but most of us have trouble figuring out how to put them together. Words aren't

cheap. They are very precious. They are like water, which gives life and growth and refreshment, but because it has always been abundant, we treat it cheaply. We waste it; we pollute it, and doctor it. Later we blame the quality of the water because we have misused it.

I can use words to tell you truth, to help you find the way when you are lost, to make you understand who I am inside, to make you feel loved and understood, and to tell you why I feel uneasy about the telephone call one of the children just received. It's a great side benefit of reading—this learning to use words well. Like Paterson said, they aren't cheap. Sitting before a piece of blank paper with an assignment to write an essay convinces any student of this. Books show all of us the awesomeness of words.

## What If I Don't Read Particularly Well?

Reading is like other skills. The more you do it, the better you can do it. The less reading you do, the more difficult it is. Kids who say, "I hate to read," may really be saying, "I read so poorly that I don't feel good about myself when I do it, so I don't read." It takes some honesty to admit to lack of reading skills, but it's not an insurmountable problem and the quicker fixed, the better. Practice. The ability to read is one of the greatest gifts we have been given.

In the months following my initiation into motherhood I hardly read at all. I was so into "doing" that I rarely sat down to read anything significant. When I realized what I was doing I thought to myself, *What good is being able to read if I never read?* I decided to again become a reader. And I have to admit that when I first began again, I was impatient with myself. It was as if I had fogotten how to read a book, to follow a plotline and let the story develop. But we don't forget that easily; we just get out of practice!

The willingness to read and the skill to read are tied together. Every child by third grade (and usually earlier) knows how special it is to be able to read and begins to feel like a second-class citizen if he can't read well. Then begins the big cover-up. The student reads less and less instead of more and more. We can think of all kinds of strategies to cover up for not reading whether we are adolescents or grown-ups. We can always use the "no time" excuse, except that *we always make time for what we think is truly important.*

Reading is one of the most complex tasks a person can undertake. And one of the most important. Reading is a way of defining a civilization. When we give statistics about a nation, we talk about its "literacy rate"—the percentage of its people who can read. That is the way an individual's cultural level is judged as well.

I had been substitute teaching in an eighth-grade English class and was not yet fully acquainted with the students I was teaching. We were reading a story aloud in class, and I called on a student named Joe to read aloud the next paragraphs. He did not refuse, but he was so intimidated by the words on the page that he made no attempt to read them. He had been listening, so he simply made up some words. I could feel the eyes of the entire class on me, waiting to see what I would do. When he finished, I went on with the class as if nothing unusual had happened. Later, I saw Joe after class and apologized for putting him on the spot. We talked about his reading. He wanted to read; he was incredibly embarrassed that he was fourteen years old and could not read well. We went to work on some ways for him to improve. One of these was to be tutored. It was costly, but well worth what this did for his self-esteem.

*Make sure your children know how to read as they grow into adulthood.* Young men make up most of the students in remedial reading classes—as many as 75 percent. What does this say to parents? Boys don't make up 75 percent of the poor readers in Japan or Germany or Nigeria. Boys account for 80 percent of high school dropouts and attention deficit disorder diagnoses. What has happened in our culture? And where are the fathers to model reading habits? If Dad sits in front of the television every night, claiming that he is too tired to do anything else, he not only stunts his own growth but his children's as well. Fathers need to let their sons know that athletics and reading are not mutually exclusive interests. In today's world we are living with a cultural liability because too many mothers and fathers simply do not read at all.

## If You Want to Understand Life Behind the Iron Curtain

*Nicholas and Alexandra* by Robert Massie

*Doctor Zhivago* by Boris Pasternak

*Night Journey* by Kathryn Lasky

*Long Walk: The True Story of a Trek to Freedom* by Slavomir Rawicz

*One Day in the Life of Ivan Denisovich* by A. Solzhenitsyn

*The Endless Steppe* by Esther Hautzig

*Red Storm Rising* by Tom Clancy

*Last of the Breed* by Louis L'Amour

*Stories are for magic, for grand adventure, for making readers feel and see things, and for taking them to places they've never been.*

## The Environment for Reading

Make books part of the furnishings of your house. Entice family members to read with interesting books on the coffee table or by the lamp. Subscribe to magazines that contain interesting articles, magazines that feature more than pictures of pop-culture figures. If you don't want the television or computer games to be a first choice for a teen, provide something to compete with it.

Make going to the library a family practice. Go often enough so that you recognize it as a friendly place. Libraries have all kinds of people ready to help. I have never yet met one who acted as if my questions were dumb. Librarians don't guard the books to keep them away from you; instead, they are shouting "Look at what you can borrow for free! Let me help you find something good." Sometimes we learn by trial and error what we want to read. The secret is not to give up. Look for books that compel reading because they are so good. It would be strange indeed if in a library with thousands of books you didn't find one that you or your teen couldn't put down once you've started reading it.

A good story is meant to be a *treat*, not a treatment. Stories are for magic, for grand adventure, for making readers feel and see things, and for taking them to places they've never been. A book is the greatest learning device ever invented. You can take it with you, loan it to a friend, put it on a shelf, and pass it on to your children years later. Books offer sheer enjoyment. They give the reader remarkable new insights, even if it is only learning to laugh a bit harder at what is ridiculous in life. They nourish the inside of you, speak to your fears and dreams without your knowing it, and give you a wider look at the world. Books become friends. You get so you can't wait to meet up with a new one, hoping it will be the best you have ever read.

Self-absorption probably is the chief foe to teenage reading. Here is a prayer for teens, adapted from a prayer written by Richard Peck.[1] Posting this on the refrigerator door might promote some discussion.

---

[1] Published in *Horn Book Magazine* in 1986.

## A Teen's Prayer

*O Supreme Being, and I don't mean me;*
*Give me the vision to see my parents as human beings*
*    because if they aren't, what does that make me?*
*Give me vocabulary, because the more I say "you know,"*
*    the less anyone does.*
*Give me freedom from television, because I'm beginning*
*    to suspect its trivial plots.*
*Give me homework to keep me from flunking Free Time.*
*Give me a map of the world so I may see that this town*
*    and I are not the center of it.*
*Give me a love for books so that I can understand*
*    the choices facing me.*
*Give me understanding that nobody ever grows up in*
*    a group so I may find my own way.*
*Give me limits so I will know I am loved.*
*And give me nothing I haven't earned so that my adolescence*
*will not last forever. Amen.*

"It hung upon a thorn, and there he blew three deadly notes"—painting by
N. C. Wyeth as an illustration for *The Boy's King Arthur* (1917) by Sidney
Lanier; reprinted with permission of Charles Scribner's Sons.

# Chapter 2

# Is Imagination Going Down the Tube?

Television has become our imagination, and in a sense, almost eliminates the necessity of thought. Television has many of the properties of an addiction.

DOROTHY A. SINGER AND JEROME L. SINGER

Television is like a drug," someone once said. "A little always leads to more and it dulls the mind, the body, and the soul." It's the "Plug-in" drug.

A television in a room ought to be simply that: a television. It has no life of its own. People are in charge, not the television. To willingly become a slave of something with an "off" switch is failure to control life.

When asked why they didn't do more reading, a group of teens unabashedly gave two reasons: the television and the computer. Both become addictive. Both become a substitute for relating within a family. Neither needs to be addictive; we are the ones who decide if it will be. Neither is totally negative. In fact, our technology is amazing. But technology is not in charge of our lives; we are.

In its relatively short life television has led to more dumbing down than any other gadget invented. It has betrayed its potential. Research estimates the average young person has watched over 15,000–18,000 hours of television by age seventeen. That cuts out a lot of living. TV requires little of its viewers and tends to make them lonely and lethargic. Like skywriting, it gets a lot of attention but doesn't last long.

I would put video games in this same category—an amusing distraction with no long term value, consuming literally hours of time. In his acceptance speech for the Newbery Award, Richard Peck referred to video games as "the pornography of the pre-pubescent, a violent virtual reality that eliminates the parent who paid for it."

Television may be a passive activity, but what you see *does* affect your values, especially if you are not used to questioning what you see or read. If you think of your mind as a pad of paper with blank sheets, what are you writing on its pages? It uses up time; it takes space in your life. We need to decide how we want to fill up the pages of our minds.

Television is the direct opposite of reading. Reading lets us use our imaginations; television does it all for us. The action in most television programming consists of rapid transitions. Instead of holding our attention, allowing us to think, it constantly interrupts our thought processes. We can't ask questions of a television program; it allows for no interaction. Education leaders believe that this is why children are restless and have short attention spans. Television simply doesn't teach you to think, nor will it enhance your verbal skills. Again, it is the opposite of reading.

One of television's worst offenses is its portrayal of antisocial behavior all in the guise of humor. Even cartoon characters are constantly bopping each other over the head. After so much exposure to violence, the average person is desensitized and can even accept violence as "normal behavior." Human life is devalued. Oddly, if animals die, the story line is often full of pathos, whereas humans are gunned down with hardly a second thought.

Even the so-called humorous barbs in sitcoms are like arrows shooting down another human being. They don't model much that is good for human relationships. The constant flow of crises and deviant behavior in afternoon soap operas gives a skewed view of life and is not good training for a happy home life. One young woman told me "the soaps" were her main source of information about "sex and stuff." I hardly knew where to begin to unravel all that misinformation.

I make no claim that books are free from violence, antisocial behavior, or inadequate sex-information. But you would have to read a stack of carefully chosen books to get as much violence as you get in two or three evenings of prime time television (unless you are read-ing Stephen King). Obviously, you have to be as careful about what you read as what you watch.

Videos have made all kinds of movies available for inexpensive and relaxing evenings at home. The great movies of the past—the classics—are available for those who missed them the first time around or who want to see them a second time. A good drama is worth seeing more than once. That's the good news. The bad news are the ones you thought might say something but end up a large cipher. What a waste of time! How come things that seem so cool can end up so empty?

Other movies are thumbs down all the way. I don't have to elaborate the behavior they incite or the feelings they evoke. It's the kind of stuff that exploits its viewers, that influences thought-life and behavior in a neg-ative way. Some teens always have a video on hand to watch, and most of them are either negative input or timewasters.

Every parent knows that these observa-tions are true, but in many homes there is an awesome parental power failure. It's simply easier not to stem the tide in the busyness of everyday life. While we may not be able to control all a teen sees, some conscience-raising family conversations about how our minds work could help. Visual images are powerful and stay around in our heads for a long time. They can reappear to spoil some of the most important moments in our lives. The rating system on movies and videos lacks consistency, so it is hard to make rules.

But we can talk about the courage it takes to walk away from what is gross or demeaning. It may take as much courage to do this in a peer group as meeting a bear in the woods. How to get out of tight situations ought to be part of family discussions. We all need to be our own persons and make decisions about values and behavior, based on something more than prevailing culture.

If it is true that television and video games make people think less, feel less, speak less, and imagine less, we need to ask teens why they let themselves be hooked on them. You don't have to throw out

## If You're Interested in Africa

*Things Fall Apart* by Chinua Achebe
*Cry, the Beloved Country* by Alan Paton
*A Girl Named Disaster* by Nancy
    Farmer
*The Ear, the Eye and the Arm* by Nancy
    Farmer
*The African Queen* by C. S. Forester
*The Return* by Sonia Levitin
*The Baboon King* by Anton Quintana
*Born Free* by Joy Adamson

the television, you just have to *control* it. A good rule is this: However much television you watch, watch less. What kind of person do you want to be? You decide. To arrive at the end of life and realize that you didn't use even a fraction of your potential is incredibly sad. It makes being created a human being seem pointless. Talking, not preaching, about this in a family circle has the potential for strengthening choices.

In the story of the remarkable Ben Carson called *Gifted Hands*, Dr. Carson tells of growing up black in a poor neighborhood with his older brother, Curtis, and a determined mother who worked two jobs to keep her fatherless family together. She was constantly challenging her boys to do better in school than their grades showed. When Ben brought home a D in math, she drilled him on his multiplication tables night after night until he could answer without hesitation, but still his mother was not satisfied.

"I've decided you boys are watching too much television," she said one evening, snapping off the set in the middle of a program. She was not swayed by the protests of her sons and stood by her firm decision that they would watch only three programs a week.

Then she added another demand. "You boys are going to the library and check out books. You're going to read at least two books every week. At the end of each week, you'll give me a report on what you've read." Ben thought that the rule was impossible; he had never read a book on his own in his whole life. But he and Curtis did what their mother asked, reluctantly at first. As time went on, he and Curtis discovered the treasures of the library. Ben checked out books on nature and became a fifth-grade expert on things of a scientific nature. The librarians noticed the boys and began to recommend books to them. As they read, their vocabulary improved. Their schoolwork improved; their self-images improved; their attitudes toward school changed.

There is much more to the story. Curtis Carson graduated from the University of Michigan as an engineer. Ben Carson went to Yale,

## If You Want to Explore the Middle East

*A Beacon at Alexandria* by Gillian Bradshaw
*The Robe* by Lloyd Douglas
*A Hand Full of Stars* by Rafik Schami
*If You Love Me* by Patricia St. John
*Blood Brothers* by Elias Chacour
*The Plague* by Albert Camus
*The Singing Mountain* by Sonia Levitin
*The Return* by Sonia Levitin
*Tales of a Dead King* by W. D. Myers
*Masada* by Gloria Miklowitz
Zion Chronicles series by Bodie Thoene

then went on to medical school at the University of Michigan, and now has a worldwide reputation as a pediatric neurosurgeon at Johns Hopkins University. He was raised in inner-city Detroit by a mother with a third-grade education. His future did not look bright. His mother, Sonya Carson, had twenty-three siblings and had married at age thirteen; she determined her son's future would be better than her own. Again and again she said, "Bennie, if you read, honey, you can learn just about anything you want to know. The doors of the world are open to people who can read. And my boys are going to be successful in life, because they're going to be the best readers in the school."

*Gifted Hands* is a fine, inspiring biography; put it on your list to read aloud as a family. But as I read the story of Ben Carson's life, it occurred to me that the story might have been very different if Ben's mother had not insisted that the television be controlled and that her boys learn to read.

Why this sermon about television? Because I am talking about books and reading and enriching your teen's life, and I know that probably the biggest enemy to personal growth is sitting in a prominent corner in a room of your house. All chairs are facing it—as if this electrical box were the source of a message from on high. Few families are taking action to control its impact. Besides, you need an encourager to cheer you on to action.

The human imagination is one of our greatest gifts. Don't let it literally go down the tube.

## Confronting Computer Habits

Obstacle number two is the incredible computer! We have become so used to what it can do that we hardly realize how this technology has changed our lives. The world of carbon paper is gone! So are the erasures that made the carbons unreadable. What a change the computer has brought to writing anything at all, what with spelling and grammar checks plus the ability to move sentences or paragraphs at will. The wonderful copy machine lets us make multiple copies without cutting a stencil. (What's a stencil?) I sing the merits of technology.

The ease with which people keep in touch by email is a thing to wonder about. One of my teenage friends emails her mother from school when she has something important to share. I treasure every handwritten note or letter I receive because they are so rare, but I keep in touch with more friends than ever before by computer mail.

*Real life beckons us to reach for the highest.*

Nonetheless, the downside of the computer-life in our homes needs discussion. Some parents spend too much time—not tending to family issues, not talking to each other—at this wondrous machine. Searching the Internet is more important than knowing your family. Teens admit to hardly saying hello when they come home, heading straight for the computer to check their email and then log on to spend hours in a chat room with their friends. After that come the computer games—all kinds of them. If this uses up family time, reading time or whatever, it is not the fault of the computer. It is still a question of priorities and making decisions about what builds the best kind of life. I tell myself that every time I play too many games of Free Cell on my computer before going to bed!

Parents need to keep computers in the center of traffic, so that people walking past can see what is happening. The Internet, a tool meant for good, also has an evil side. Parents need to know what is being accessed and to be disciplined enough themselves to not court disaster with what is bad. The ten-year-old son of one my friends was wide-eyed when he pressed the wrong key and pornography came up unbidden on the screen, but curious enough to look at it. When his mother came past he hastily deleted, but was so obviously filled with shame that she guessed what had happened. You can believe there was an unplanned discussion about values at a family council in that house that day.

If communal family life is important—if family members must feel some social responsibility to talk together as a family about life, ideas, and values—then we have to make a decision to have it happen. We can't afford to let either the television or the computer run our lives. If we are dumbing-down our lives by not reading, we have some decisions to make. Real life beckons us to reach for the highest.

This chapter may miss the street you live on completely. Maybe you have super high-achieving teens who have a handle on math and science and the world in general. If so, you hold a commendable place in a minority. You still need to ask questions about family time. How much do you talk together about things that matter? Are your teens getting grades only or are they growing on the inside into thoughtful human beings? Have they read any good books lately?

## Chapter 3

# What Makes a Good Book?

A book is good if it permits, invites or even impels a good reading, one in which the reader has submitted himself to the text, entering the "made" experiences, and been taken beyond himself. While good books can be read badly, bad books cannot be read well. The question is not whether it is a good book, but whether the book compelled a good reading.

C. S. LEWIS

Something happens inside you when you read a good book. Sometimes I say about a book, "This novel won't let go of me," because the author has written something of substance that is staying around in my head and heart.

When I shared this sentiment with a friend and we began talking about the lingering effect of books, she said, "I don't know how to say what happens when you read a good story: it's not TV and it's not reading the papers. It's not the movies, because you get into them faster, but you're out real fast; you forget what you've seen because the next flick has come and you're looking at it. With a novel . . . you take things slowly and get your head connected to what you're reading. Then the story becomes yours." Maybe you relate to that experience.

## What Good Books Give Us

We read for many reasons, mostly for the pleasure and entertainment it offers. We read to know we're not alone. Good books help us shape and express our own feelings; they also help us understand ourselves. We don't read for long unless the story is interesting. Books give us insights and sometimes answers. Stories show how complex life is and the possibilities of being a human being. Francis Bacon once remarked that "Some books are to be tasted, others to be swallowed, and some few to be chewed and digested."

How does one identify a "chewable" book? Do we know how to identify a good book, a book that compels good reading? Without insisting that we all like the same books, we do have some standards.

### Short But Meaningful

*North to Freedom* by Ann Holm
*Holes* by Louis Sachar
*Make Lemonade* by Virginia Euwer Wolff
*The Magic Circle* by Donna Jo Napoli
*Cezanne Pinto* by Mary Stolz
*The Snow Goose* by Paul Gallico
*Night* by Elie Wiesel
*The Middle Passage* by Tom Feelings

### The Realities of Life

A good book has life; it releases something creative in the mind of the reader. The author has captured reality, the permanent stuff of life, and something enduring is planted in the heart. It may be fantasy, mystery, historical fiction, or whatever, but a profound morality comes out of the story. Many books come to mind. In Ann Holm's *North to Freedom* young David, who has lived his whole life in a prison camp, tries to put together his thoughts about freedom and the meaning of life as he wanders north to Denmark hoping to find his mother. The reader gets inside David to see how he handles concepts of conscience and responsibility and what he concludes are foundational truths about life. It is haunting. As you read, it releases ideas in your head that keep coming back.

### An Enduring Theme

The idea behind the book will determine something of the value of the story. What is the author trying to say about life, about the people in the story? That is the theme of the book. A weak or superficial theme means a weak story. Many books written today exploit the natural curiosity of adolescents about the facts of life; such books have shallow plots and superficial characters. The theme behind the story is not compelling enough nor sufficiently significant to give the books a long life either on the shelf or in the heart. A large and enduring theme handles the large and enduring truths or choices that make up the human experience.

## Language Well-Used

A good writer has something worth saying and says it in the best possible way and respects the reader's ability to understand. Language is used well. The word choices make us see, feel, hear, taste, smell, decide. The action of the story and the descriptions have a crisp leanness because strong verbs and simple descriptions are used. The Bible is a model for this kind of writing. With an economy of words, lasting pictures are painted. Consider, for example, what pictures are painted in your mind from a short story that the prophet Nathan told David, after David had stolen the affections of Uriah's wife.

> There were two men in a certain town, one rich and the other poor. The rich man had a very large number of sheep and cattle, but the poor man had nothing except one little ewe lamb he had bought. He raised it, and it grew up with him and his children. It shared his food, drank from his cup and even slept in his arms. It was like a daughter to him. Now a traveler came to the rich man, but the rich man refrained from taking one of his own sheep or cattle to prepare a meal for the traveler who had come to him. Instead, he took the ewe lamb that belonged to the poor man and prepared it for the one who had come to him. 2 Samuel 12:1–4

Notice that the story doesn't say, "The poor man really loved his lamb and had made a pet of it." Instead, you are led to that conclusion from the description of actions taken by the poor man. It is not only that he was poor that made the rich man's action unjust. A whole layer of emotion and feeling, of hope and encouragement, are latent in the description. What would the fact that it was a "ewe lamb" have meant to the poor man? The story doesn't need to use many adjectives to describe the rich man. His action shows what he was like. That's the mark of good writing.

## Memorable Characters

A good story has characters of depth, not superficial stereotypes; they inspire the inner life of the reader. The characters—whether

*Fiction is not untrue just because it is called fiction. Good fiction contains truth.*

animals, people, or creatures created by the author—must be believable, not one-dimensional actors who deliver a thinly disguised message or react with some unreal heroism. Heroes we like, but let them resemble someone we know, at least be a little human—like Charlotte, the spider in *Charlotte's Web*, or Toad in *The Wind in the Willows* or Jody in *The Yearling* or Dicey in *Dicey's Song* or even *Mrs. Pollifax*, secret agent par excellence.

## A Well-Conceived Plot

The plot of the story is part of its genius. Plot does not primarily answer "what happened next?" It tells you *why* it happened. Plot is the design of the idea behind the story. Good plots grow out of strong themes, the quality of the idea. The plot holds the story together in such a way that the story takes on meaning. Add to that memorable characters and good use of language, and you have a winner. These are the ingredients of a good book.

No one has produced a magic formula or set of rules that produce a good story. The quality of the writing comes from the quality of the writer. Add to that the quality of the reader, and you have the right combination. *Good stories have an excellent spirit about them.* They are an experience—imaginative, intellectual, social, spiritual— and a sense of permanent worth surrounds them.

All of these characteristics are also found in books that make us laugh. Everyone profits from a well-written story that brings laughter. Consider James Thurber. We used to read aloud his *The Thirteen Clocks* every Halloween night for fun. Farley Mowat's *The Dog Who Wouldn't Be*, along with his other books, relate such believable, ridiculous incidents that you will find your family chuckling all the way through the book. Books like *I Remember Papa, Cheaper By the Dozen, The Voyages of Dr. Doolittle*, and others of that genre should be part of family reading-aloud. Life can become too serious. A good laugh can often do more for us than anything else.

## Literature Presents Human Experience

Fiction is not untrue just because it is called fiction. Good fiction contains truth. It is not the Truth, but it serves as a signpost to the Truth, to the reality of God, and of our need for redemption. Like John the Baptist crying out, "Prepare the way for the Lord," literature focuses on our deepest needs, and that is why it moves us so profoundly. We see reality in what we read. Read Mollie Hunter's *A*

*Sound of Chariots* and its sequel *Hold on to Love* and see if they meas-ure up to this description.

The story may take us on adventures or introduce us to people not remotely related to our lives. Nevertheless, because people are the same on the inside and have to make the same kind of choices, the story teaches us truth, both about the differences in God's created world and the commonalities of human experience. Good fiction does not always have a happy ending, but it always shows possibilities of how to act or resolve the conflict. It ends with *hope*, with some pos-sible good in sight, some redeeming vision.

Because this is true, good literature helps build self-esteem. I think of this every time I read *Anne of Green Gables*, the story of a girl who did not let her adverse circumstances define her. Reading books, she saw a different kind of life than she was experiencing, and she chose to live in that. Stories gave her a vocabulary that allowed the dramatic expression of her feelings that kept her open and healthy. She could even pretend to be the lovely "Lady of Shalott" and float away with storybook drama, even though a leaking boat kept her swamped in reality. (There always seems to be enough reality around to keep our feet in this world.)

Oprah Winfrey, the popular television host, tells of her own experience of keeping her self-esteem intact by reading, even though her family was torn apart by divorce and there was little in her life that was hopeful or beautiful. She got affirmation for herself from books. They became her entry into another world that had more hope and goodness than the one she came from. No wonder she now spon-sors a book-reading program.

Teenage years are years of insecurity. I have no doubt that good literature has kept many young women and men out of the destruc-tive insecurities of the teenage culture. In the larger world of reading good literature, some of pop culture looks like what it is: fragile and false. The in-crowd, the way one looks or dresses, all the fads seem less important. Bigger truths give stability and perspective.

## What About Realism, Tragedy, and Despair?

Immediately following the cultural upheaval of the 1960s, authors and editors decided that young adult readers wanted *realism* in their literature. The output of books on problem issues was enormous. In doing so these authors redefined realism. Their realism was adult betrayal, violence, sexual encounters, alcoholism, and the Big Ds: death, divorce, disease, and drugs. One teen called such problem-oriented books "those gray, heavy stories."

When commenting about these books, Isaac Bashevis Singer said, "It is tragic that many writers who look down on stories of the supernatural are writing things for young people which are nothing but sheer chaos." No uplifting moral, no heroes, just the turbulence of adolescent life.

Some contemporary writers depict their own meaningless world and foist it on the reader instead of wrestling with life to give it order and meaning. Some of these writers delight in depravity, snicker at morality, and throw bits of pornography into the story line that appeal to baser values. The end product reveals their life view: meaningless-ness. It leaves the reader empty. A constant diet of this kind of reading gives us neither insight nor understanding. When we read the literature of despair, our best response is compassion and pity for those caught in this trap.

Librarians refer to Paul Zindel's 1968 book *Pigman* as the first "young adult novel." Almost immediately every seventh grade class had this book as a reading assignment. From the first I thought *Pigman* a questionable choice because it has so little exemplary behavior in it. But that was only the beginning. *Outsiders* by S. E. Hinton was assigned to eighth grade students, because teachers were convinced that this kind of book, pitched according to the violence of the eleven o'clock news, excited students to greater discussion than the books that reveal values that the reader can build on.

Jim, the seventeen-year-old protagonist in Richard Peck's *Father Figure*, cries out, "Why do I have to know all this just because it happens to be true?" Peck's story has a mugging, the suicide of the boy's mother, a forced reunion with the father who abandoned him, and the boy falls in love with his father's girlfriend. Writers like Robert Cormier, Brock Cole, Margaret Mahy, Harry Mazer, M. E. Peck, Norma Klein, and Judy Blume all produced what New York editors were looking for— grievance-laden, egocentric teenagers, usually alienated from adults, confessional first-person accounts with colloquial and raw language, the problem as the theme with few solutions in sight. They called these "coming of age" books or "slice of life" stories. Even Madeleine L'Engle got caught in the current with her *House Like a Lotus*.

All of us can relate to some degree to this chaos in society. We have seen a good bit of abnormal behavior. School shootings have taken away whatever innocence we may have had. It is a rough and violent world; adults do betray their families; sexual abuse is more common than people want to admit; incest and homosexuality are no longer hidden. People live with all kinds of pain. Editors said, "This is no longer the 1950s. Write about the *real* world." In doing so, however, they created a depressing world that seduces young people into cynicism, a hopeless kind of place where you can't trust anyone. Teen suicides may well relate to this depiction of the world, but a world with no hope is a dismal place indeed.

I have always thought it an unmerciful act to give teens (who are trying to figure out their mood swings, their identity, and their self-worth) a book about someone as mixed-up as Holden Caufield. *Catcher in the Rye*, written in 1951 and often assigned for seventh graders, is written with J. D. Salinger's sensitive ear, acutely sympathetic for Caufield, but it is not a picture of adolescent life so much as a picture of the human condition. Should Holden Caufield himself read *Catcher in the Rye* at age thirteen? Golding's *Lord of the Flies* is written for adults, not young adolescents. It is a story about evil in human nature as the cause of evil in society, not about children. Why are adults pushing cosmic problems onto their kids?

I want to be careful to say that I don't think your children are going to be scarred irreparably if such books are assigned and read in school. They have already seen and heard enough in the movies and on television to know what the world is like. If the book is problematic, read it yourself so you can talk about it with your teen and thus defuse the difficult parts. Just make sure that those kind of books aren't the only input in their lives.

*But good news:* Stories that leave anxiety on our doorstep—like an abandoned baby—may have run their course. A good story *should* represent what is real and true, but *real* means presenting something a reader can build on. Despair is a hard commodity to build on. Real stories don't hide what is wrong, but focus on greater truths. The

## Caught in Hitler's Evil: World War II Stories

Zion Covenant series by Bodie Thoene
*The Ark* by Margot Benary-Isbert
*The Endless Steppe* by Esther Hautzig
*A Bell for Adano* by John Hersey
*The Wall* by John Hersey
*Torn Thread* by Anne Isaacs
*The Long Walk* by Slavomir Rawicz
*Journey through the Night* by Anne De Vries
*Guns of Navarone* by Alistair MacLean
*Anne Frank: The Diary of a Young Girl* by Anne Frank
*Lest Innocent Blood be Shed* by Philip Hallie
*Never to Forget* by Milton Meltzer
*Night* by Elie Wiesel
*The Last Mission* by Harry Mazer
*The Hiding Place* by Corrie ten Boom

*Good stories have hope, but it may not look like the happy endings of fairy stories.*

characters live and grow. Like Rat and Mole in *The Wind in the Willows*, one hears "the thin, clear, happy call of distant piping," an insight into deeper truths.

I was glad to see Richard Peck forsake his depressing books to write winners like *A Long Way from Chicago* and *A Year Down Yonder*, one a Newbery Honor book, and the other a Newbery Medal book. Brian Jacques has created a world of staunchly courageous heroes in his Redwall series that are very popular with teens. The list could go on and on.

A story of despair is different from a tragedy. Some facet of human values, some meaning is always present in the great tragedies of literature. Shakespeare, who wrote many tragedies, always showed the moral result linked with the deed itself. In *Hamlet*, eight tragic deaths take place because of one murder. *Romeo and Juliet*, his best known play, is incredibly tragic. Whenever I read it or see it portrayed on the screen, I want to stop the action and tell them how they could put this whole situation right. Threads of human values and choice run through the tragedy. It is cause and effect at work. The fact that it has a sad ending does not indicate lack of meaning. Many situations in life do not have happy endings, but we learn from tragedy. And, in contrast to the literature of despair, people in tragedies are "choosers, not hapless victims."

Readers have written to Katherine Paterson, expressing disappointment about the ending of her story *The Great Gilly Hopkins*. When streetwise Gilly has been moved to another foster home and made the responsibility of frumpy Maime Trotter and her son William Ernest, she is drawn into a circle of love. However, she lives with dreams of her birth family and plans her own rescue by getting in touch with her real mother. When her grandmother (Nonnie) gets the mother to come home, she doesn't turn out to be the wonderful and responsible mother that Gilly had dreamed about.

> She had come because Nonnie had paid her to. And she wasn't going to stay. And she wasn't going to take Gilly back with her. "I will always love you." It was a lie. Gilly had thrown away her whole life for a stinking lie.

She calls her foster mother, Trotter, to tell her she was coming home. Trotter hears the underlying pain and anger in Gilly's voice and wisely tells her,

"Sometimes in this world things come easy, and you tend to lean back and say, 'Well, finally, a happy ending. This is the way it is supposed to be.' Like life owed you good things. And there is lots of good things, baby. Like you coming to be with us here this fall. That was a mighty good thing for me and William Ernest. But you just fool yourself if you expect good things all the time. They ain't what's regular—don't nobody owe 'em to you."

All of us need hope; people can't live without it. Good stories have it, but it may not look like the happy endings of fairy stories. At the end of Gilly's story we aren't sure whether she will stay on with her grandmother or return to Trotter, but somehow we know that Gilly will be all right. Her pain is not trivialized or erased, but you feel deep in your heart that she will grow up to become a wise and compassionate woman even though she will forever miss the mother she wanted.

Paterson, in an article called "Hope Is More Than Happiness," writes that this world looked at squarely does not allow optimism to flourish. Hope for us cannot simply be wishful thinking. Paterson says,

Hope is a yearning, rooted in reality, that pulls us toward the radical biblical vision of a world where truth and justice and peace do prevail, a time in which the knowledge of God will cover the earth as the waters cover the sea, a scene which finds humanity ... walking together by the light of God's glory. Now there's a happy ending for you. The only purely happy ending I know of.

## What About Books and God?

In a paper read at a literature conference at Syracuse University School of Education, Charlotte Huck from Ohio State noted nine changes in books for children and young adults. There are fewer strong male characters in comparison with female characters. There is less humor and joy, and when we do laugh it is so we won't cry. Another was that religion seemed to be the only taboo left in literature for children or young adults. Authors may write on child abuse, sex, and death but don't mention belief in God.

Commenting on a list of touchtone books given in *The Children's Literature Association Quarterly*, Perry Nodelman commented on the omission of the Bible as a vital part of our literary heritage. He wrote,

"The list ignores the one book that most clearly underlies contemporary culture and that has had the most direct influence on the history and characteristics of our literature: the Bible." He writes that those who teach literature have become fearful of the Bible and have given it a sinister reputation that it doesn't deserve. Why? He tells us,

> Many of those obnoxious people who want to keep good books out of the hands of children because they think children are weakminded enough to adopt every dangerous idea and attitude they read about often use the Bible as the authority for their narrow-minded bigotry.
>
> However, there is a vast conspiracy of silence about children's literature with a spiritual emphasis. The books available don't get reviewed or recommended for public libraries or even discussed in journals like this one. We simply act as if this massive body of literature did not exist at all. Now I am not myself a Christian, I have no special axe to grind. But this reveals a common form of intolerance by theoretically tolerant people, an intolerance that amounts to censorship. It seems to be based on the peculiar assumption that, in order to have true religious freedom, we must never express a religious idea. . . . This is an act of intense bigotry.

Nobel-prize-winning writer Isaac Bashevis Singer writes,

> No matter how young they are, children are deeply concerned with so-called eternal questions: Who created the world? Who made the earth, the sky, people, animals? If I had my way, I would publish a history of philosophy for children. Children, who are highly serious people, would read this book with great interest. In our time, when the literature for adults is deteriorating, good books for children (and young adults) are the only hope, the only refuge.

There you have it. Book editors and writers have admittedly felt uncomfortable about books that mention God. It is still prejudice and fear on the part of the editors that prevent books from addressing the spiritual issues young people wonder about. With the increase of cultural pluralism, it is not likely to get better. However, a book that does not mention God may have a profoundly positive spiritual impact. A book that tacks God onto the plot may have the opposite effect. The best written books are full of opportunities to talk about this very question. Good fiction can't help having an ethical dimension. Everything we do *means* something. Fiction should teach us on many levels. At least it should help us evaluate truth in the context of life.

What the book publishing industry needs is more skillful writers who can write the kind of books that expose children, young adults, and adults to a biblical worldview. Decades ago T. S. Eliot pled for writers who could forge a relationship between religion and literature, a literature that should be unconsciously, rather than deliberately and defiantly, Christian. Read these words again: "unconsciously, rather than deliberately and defiantly." What is needed is something like the writings of Chaim Potok, who, in the course of his stories, exposes the reader to the Jewish worldview. Too often the Christian worldview is packaged as propaganda, rather than a well-written story that engages the mind and asks questions rather than giving answers.

Sometimes our standards are not high enough; we are content with books that don't say anything really important but seem safe. Readers could profit from comparing books like the Clearwater Crossings series by Laura Peyton Roberts with the more secular Sweet Valley High series. In *Get a Life*, the first of the Clearwater Crossing series, a Bible verse graces the first page and the teens have grouped together to help Kurt, a football player who has leukemia. Each book also has a minority person in the story. Perhaps this gives a touch of purpose, but as the story develops the characters think about little but their looks, their clothes, and their social status. When Kurt dies Nicole prays, "Please help me remember that life is bigger than parties and clothes and diets and dates." But the books do nothing to help the characters or the readers do that! There is little to distinguish this series, which seems to please conservative readers, from the Sweet Valley High series. Does having faith make so little difference? Barbara Hampton comments that these books are as nourishing and stimulating to spiritual growth as cotton candy.

I was interested to see how readers responding to books on the Internet had evaluated the popular and sometimes controversial Left

## If You Want to go to the South Seas

*Ash Road* by Ivan Southall
*Tomorrow, When the War Began* by John Marsden
*A Town Like Alice* by Nevil Shute
*The Pearl* by John Steinbeck
*Lord Jim* by Joseph Conrad
*The Proving Ground* by G. Bruce Knecht
*Dove* by Robin Lee Graham and Derek L. T. Gill
*Moon Dark* by Patricia Wrightson

Behind series by LaHaye and Jenkins. Obviously people felt strongly about these books. Amazon.com had almost 2000 reviews. About 60 percent of the readers wrote positive reviews, some recounting how these had affected their spiritual lives, some of them making new faith commitments. About 40 percent had trouble with the concept that Christians could be glad that some were left behind and felt the books were exploiting fears of the end times. One reviewer complained that the books were not well-written, talked down to the reader, seemed too shallow (plus other complaints) but ended up with "But they are about God, so they must be good books." Quite apart from your evaluation of that series, it is important to underscore that believing in God, or writing about him, does not necessarily assure a standard of excellence. (I wish it did!)

If you want to follow through on the kind of writing that makes for good readers, try reading books like *Saint Ben* by John Fischer or *Byzantium* by Stephen Lawhead or *Firebird* by Kathy Tyers. By discussing the quality of the writing, the story line, and the worldview of these books, you will encounter good stories along with increased understanding of what makes a good book.

## Reading What You Can Understand

It is important to encourage children and/or teens not to read books beyond their understanding. This is not the path to maturity so much as the path to confusion. Both parents and children get caught in the intellectual snob-appeal of reading beyond their age. School-testing tells parents that their ten-year-old reads at grade eleven level. That's not an invitation to read books written for adults. Just because you can read it doesn't mean you "get it."

Teens need a life context for processing what they read. Because I had read good reviews and noted it was on the list of the best ten books for young adults, I asked my mature fifteen-year-old friend Sarah to read Irena Gut Opdyke's *In My Hands: Memories of a Holocaust Rescue* for a possible inclusion in the bibliography of this book. It is Opdyke's true story written by Jennifer Armstrong, author of many fine books for younger readers. Both Sarah's mother and I read it after Sarah finished the book, and we all agreed that the book contained material that was too heavy to recommend for teens. Opdyke, a brave and courageous woman now in the later years of her life, is still haunted by terrible images of cruelty and horror of her experiences in Poland during the war. While teens need to know the realities of this terrible time, we need to balance the realities with the age of the reader. It didn't hurt Sarah to read it; it just introduced an unnecessary discussion of problem issues that might have a more helpful focus at nineteen rather than fifteen. That does not say that it is not a well-written account of reality; it just says that it is better read by a more mature person.

I remember a twelve-year-old boy telling me in detail how much he enjoyed *Doctor Zhivago*. I remember feeling impressed—which is what he wanted me to feel. I should instead have asked him more questions and suggested that he read it again as an adult. This past year I heard of a homeschool mother who read Mildred D. Taylor's *Roll of Thunder, Hear My Cry* to her six- and eight-year-old children. She said they loved it. It takes more life experience than an eight-year-old has to really comprehend this multilayered story. I know that these children didn't get half of what is there, and the sad part is that they will think they have really read the book.

Actually it often works the other way. Some picture books are best appreciated by grown-ups. In fact, they are adult children's books, and some of them pack a wallop felt keenly by grown-ups. My husband, Keith, often reads the stories of Winnie-the-Pooh aloud at family conferences. Because Walt Disney has made Pooh characters the stuff of every day, parents bring their younger children to hear Pooh read the way Milne wrote it. Little children—at least most of them—don't get it. The stories are funnier the older you are, not the younger! When publishers rate a book 9–12 years, if that book is well-written, it will be a good read for older readers. It's a big mistake to push readers beyond their understanding; it is not taking either the children or the book seriously.

*It's a big mistake to push readers beyond their understanding; it is not taking either the children or the book seriously.*

## Quality Control

It is hard to describe a good book. Once a book leaves the author's hands, it becomes the property of the reader. Each person who reads it will see different things in it—often, things that the author didn't necessarily intend. What is a good book in one person's eyes may not be so in another's. That's fair enough. It is important not to weigh books down with, "You must like this." At the same time, we do want teens to learn to discriminate between the awful, the good, the better, and the best—not just in reading but in all of life.

The best hope of promoting quality lies in the better education of the reader. When we give a child a taste for what is really good reading, I don't think that child will acquire an appetite for what is not. I've had years of observing teenage readers. The ones who read the most have learned to choose the best. Excellence has a way of eliminating inferior products. That is true in reading, at least for thoughtful people, and we need more thoughtful teens to help save our world from "the mud."

Some children have been put off from reading as they grow older because they have been fed simplistic plots, mediocre writing, and thinly veiled sermons in their younger years. They have grown up without knowing what makes a really good book.

When all is said and done, a good book is a good book. Teens will have to find the ones they like by some degree of trial and error. But the point of this book is to spare them from some of that. The entries in the bibliography will give you some ideas. The annotations show how we evaluated the books with age brackets for each book.

For every teen to like all the books in our bibliography would be expecting too much. But there are good ones for nearly everyone to try out. Some will love books that are not on our list and ask, "Why did you leave this one out?" That question would be indication of an enthusiatic reader. Share that book with someone else and thus supplement our listing.

# Chapter 4

# Using Books to Talk About Values

Stories are a way of teaching. Our own lives are mirrored and intensified by stories. We learn the connection between things by reading stories.

ROBERT COLES

We had been watching together a dramatized version of a poem by Robert Browning, called *The Pied Piper of Hamelin*, one story in a series for public television called "Long Ago and Far Away." The Pied Piper, hearing that rats have taken over the city of Hamelin, offers to "pipe" them out of town with his flute—for a price. As he plays his pipe, the rats rush out from every nook and cranny in the city to follow the piper to their destruction. Afterward, the town fathers refuse to pay him the agreed-upon price. The Pied Piper warns that he might use his pipe another way if they delay. And when they do, the Pied Piper sounds his pipe and all the children of the village run out to follow him. Singing, laughing, and dancing, they follow him up the mountain path, when suddenly the mountain pass closes like a door behind them and they disappear forever. Only one small boy on crutches, who couldn't keep up with the crowd, is left in the village, where people are mourning the loss of all their children.

It was an absorbing, effective production of a story that raised many questions. When it was over, James Earl Jones, the program's host, asked, "Was the Pied Piper good or was he bad, or was he both?" We discussed it among ourselves. Pre-adolescent Jedediah made a quick judgment based on getting rid of the rats and then changed his mind. One of us mentioned the injustice of the town fathers; they hadn't kept their word. Austin, who was six, felt sorry for the moms and dads who were missing their children.

Jedediah came to me later and asked if we could read the poem from which the story was taken, hoping that he could get some more clues. After we read it, we talked more about the story. Finally, he said, "The children followed him without asking him where he was going. It was like someone fooling you with promises of adventure and excitement, like taking drugs. The children didn't know they could never come back to their parents. I think the Pied Piper fooled the children." He has since watched the tape of this story many times and is still asking himself questions about the story. Is the Pied Piper good or is he bad—or both?

I wonder if he would have questioned the story if the host hadn't asked that one single question. Stories often touch us deeply, leaving us wondering, sometimes feeling pain inside, or confusion. (That's when it is good to know someone else who has read the same story or seen the same film.) We need to be aware that stories do affect us profoundly. They can change the way we think or feel and even the way we behave. When we ask questions about the story and our feelings, we begin to understand more clearly.

I don't mean that you should weigh stories down with the baggage of moral lessons so that the fun of the story sinks and disappears. Stories should be read for the enjoyment they bring. Reading should not be a chore, a drag, or just another lesson. A good story is sufficient in itself. It is complete as it stands. But when you were younger, whatever point the story was making was right out front. No one recom-

Malcolm X

### If You Want to Understand the Complexities of Race

*Black Like Me* by John Howard Griffin
*The Autobiography of Malcolm X* as told to Alex Haley
*Dangerous Skies* by Suzanne Staples
*Monster* by Walter Dean Myers
*Roll of Thunder, Hear My Cry* and its sequels by Mildred Taylor
*White Lilacs* by Carolyn Meyer
*Cezanne Pinto* by Mary Stolz
*Go Tell It on the Mountain* by James Baldwin
*To Kill a Mockingbird* by Harper Lee
*Huck Finn* by Mark Twain
*Fallen Angels* by Walter Dean Myers
*Safe at Home* by Bob Muzikowski

mends analyzing *Peter Rabbit.* To my knowledge, none of the other stories on "Long Ago and Far Away" had such a weighty question about the main character—is he good or is he bad? After all, the point of *Saint George and the Dragon* is pretty obvious. He is called Saint George because he killed the dragon and saved the people. However, Saint George, and others like him, did not "pack the emotional wallop" that the Pied Piper did.

The *Pied Piper of Hamelin* is adult poetry made into a fairy tale. The story demands a question. As more complex novels and stories are read, the reading demands a question so that it can make sense. It is not an "unwanted lesson"; instead, it is the exhilaration of getting the point. That is the "double fun" of reading. You have the enjoyment of a good story, plus the inner delight of understanding what it is about. It is somewhat like getting the point of a joke.

Questioning the story is one way of describing what is done in literary criticism. (Our experience watching the *Pied Piper* was more like reading a book together than most television programs because the host asked a question about what we had seen.) No one will really be a good reader without learning how to ask questions about what has been read. A young person may read the words flawlessly, but *reading* is getting the meaning behind the words. It is not so much learning to read as it is *learning to think.*

## Learning to Think

Everyone is a philosopher. All people have some life view, even if they don't know how to express it. By life view I mean the things people believe that give life meaning and help it make sense. A person's world/life view gives that person the values he or she lives by. It is a belief system. It determines not only what people value but how they think and act.

Long John Silver in *Treasure Island* has a life view as much as the boy Jim Hawkins. Long John Silver is clearly the bad guy of the story, but he is living out his own limited view of the world, a confusing one that he probably hasn't thought out with any clarity. The reader waits to see how this affects the story. The immature Jim is in the process of forming values, making decisions to live by. We give him the space to do this, realizing that what he learns will also affect the story. When people fail to think through their values, they often hold conflicting views and never realize their inconsistency.

*Truth is never destroyed by questions; it still remains the truth.*

Whenever people open their mouths to speak, some element of their belief system is evident. All the films you see, the books you read, the way friends talk, the hit songs that kids listen to over and over, even the way news stories are presented—all of them tell you something about the worldview of the producers. All of them are "philosophical statements" to some degree. That gives a family a lot to talk about. Young adults need to be "clued in" so they can begin to observe this truth. After watching a film or a television program together, try asking *What do you think these people base their lives on? What do you think the character thinks is important in life? Why did he act that way?*

Most adolescents are in the process of forming a worldview or a belief system. They are inevitably influenced by the worldview of their parents. As they grow on the inside, they may begin to affirm certain values of their parents and sometimes choose others of their own. Often they are easily swayed because they don't carry through to the logical conclusions of their beliefs. *If I believe this is true, how does that affect my decision to do this?* Teens aren't the only ones with that problem. Many older adults are still being tossed about by every new idea that comes along because they don't have a framework for evaluation. People of all ages need a measuring rod by which to measure their values, to see if they are on track.

Parents of teens need to get their children thinking. Too many people have a collection of half-baked ideas. (I like the phrase "half-baked" because it indicates a soft, mushy, undone state that is neither tested nor seen to conclusion!) Many ideologies produce "group-think" but not necessarily informed thinking or consistent people. Christian parents can do this to their children. You can get a child to recite back a string of truths and behave in a certain way. However, as that child grows into teen years, unless those truths are processed and personally owned, they will not form a solid base for building a life. A teen needs to be convinced of truth; otherwise he will be a robot instead of a thinking person.

Life presents us with questions that need to be asked. Truth is never destroyed by questions; it still remains the truth. That's important to understand because we sometimes offend our children by not allowing questions nor any answer different from our own. Some adults, including ministers, are so aggressive in defending the faith that they either talk down to teens or give them "group think" in huge doses. I sometimes have a sneaking feeling that people who do this may still be working hard to convince *themselves* about Truth. They may be at war with their own doubts and don't want questions.

Questions can lead to truth. Read the gospels and notice how many questions Jesus asked. He answered questions with another question. The trick is to ask the right questions, and to do so gently, rather than offensively. Anxiety-ridden defense of the faith seems only to raise the hackles of hearers and stops thought processes. When the apostle Peter talked about defending the faith he gave instructions for certain behavior and manners. He said, "Do this with gentleness and respect."

What is a parent to do? A teen can be overprotected from ideas that are unacceptable or perhaps even dangerous. At its worst, this is what censorship is all about, although censoring may sometimes be a safety factor in protecting children from encountering ideas they cannot handle. The downside is that overprotection can keep a teen from thinking. It can make a person suspicious of everyone who has a slightly different idea. Or it can work another way, making a person naïve enough to accept any idea. Look at what happened to the children who followed the Pied Piper. They didn't ask where they were going and have never been heard from since.

## Learning to Ask Questions

A book is a story about someone else. If it is a good book it gives perspective on what life is all about, about ways to act, ways to think, choices to make. What we are looking for is the ability to ask questions about what we read to discover what is true. It is not only naïve but downright nonsensical to think that we can consume any idea, without question, and that it won't hurt us. (Some people have thought that about pornography and low-level movies and have been surprised at what a strong hold a vulgar, indecent mental image can have on them.)

Probably the biggest hurdle with teens is not arguments about faith, but the sheer indifference to truth of any kind. Commenting on the consequences of this laid-back mind-set, writer James Morris comments, "In the age of 'whatever,' we are becoming slaves to the new tyranny of nonchalance. 'Whatever.' The word draws you in like a plumped pillow and folds around your brain . . . leading toward a universal shrug."

This makes teens reluctant to think that something can be "true truth" for everyone. The age of "whatever" means that whatever anyone wants to believe is true for them. It is a kind of individualized faith, a tribal faith, perhaps. We can't begin too early to underscore that Christian faith is not "whatever." It is not "whatever I think it is"; it is revealed truth from God. As a family, look for ways to answer, *What questions about life and about the world does Christian faith answer? What evidence do we have that those answers are valid?*

## How Books Help Define Values

Books are full of ideas to question, problems to solve, injustices that produce anger, and the harsh consequences of choices. In that sense, a book can become a microcosm of reality. You might think that the sheer enjoyment of a good story is enough for a reader; many stories are just plain delightful to read. But novels are always saying more than what is on the surface. That's why reading aloud together is so stimulating. We talk about what the story is saying, we learn to ask questions—like the following—about what we are reading:

### 1. Let the story answer questions

Why did this book tug at me?
What is this story really saying about life? Is this story true to life as I know it?
What tests (physical, moral, mental, or spiritual) do the characters in the story face?
How do the characters change or develop?
How did the characters know (and choose to do) what is wrong or right?

In an excellent essay on literary criticism, the poet T. S. Eliot says that you cannot judge literature apart from theology, that the "greatness" of literature cannot be determined solely by good writing but must include an evaluation of what is Truth. We are not reading stories well if we keep our religious beliefs in a separate compartment. Especially today, when there is no common agreement on what is true or right, it is more necessary than ever for readers to scrutinize their reading, especially the reading of novels.

For some people that's reason enough to avoid reading novels, but our thesis is that reading provides not only for the pleasure of the story, but opportunity to learn to exercise the discernment needed for properly handling personal life.

An author whose belief system is very different from ours may tell the truth by portraying the world and people in it so accurately that he is saying more than he knows. A story tells the truth when we understand that this is the way things may happen, when it exposes the consequence of choices. It tells a greater truth when it gives us new insights into *why* things happen that way and shows us what we may have believed to be vaguely true but had never put into words. Then the story qualifies as great literature and helps us clarify and interpret life.

### 2. Question the story with your theology or belief system

> Does this story tell the truth about the human heart?
> Does the story unmask evil (show it for what it really is) or does it encourage it?
> Where does hope come from in this story? Who is in charge of the world?
> Is this story (which may not mention God) compatible with biblical values?

*A story tells the truth when we understand that this is the way things may happen, when it exposes the consequence of choices.*

People who are trying to develop their literary tastes need to read widely. Everyone goes on reading "binges" at some time or another. Remember reading all the Hardy Boys or Nancy Drew books? Some teens read everything Janette Oke writes. Some teens have at least fourteen or more Redwall books by Brian Jacques on their shelves. The craze over the Harry Potter books shocked the literary world. One author can almost take possession of us for a time, and we end up feeling an affection for certain writers because we have read so much of their writing. As we read more widely, we are affected by one writer after another and are no longer overly influenced by any one of them. This allows us to better arrange and define our own life view. But there are other questions we need to ask of the books we read.

### 3. Question the writing style of the book

> Is the writing good prose—strong, clear word choices?
> What metaphors or imagery have left a lasting picture in your mind?
> How does the book help you to see, feel, hear—and use other of your senses—to make the story more real to you?
> In what ways did this book inspire you?

Language well used is a delight. It has a beauty and a rhythm that makes us say to ourselves, *This is what words were meant to do.* Chaim Potok's books are examples of excellent writing for adults and teens alike. I read his *My Name is Asher Lev* while on vacation one year, thoroughly enjoying every page. I could hardly wait until my husband—and then two teens—finished it. We talked about it over our dinner with great delight at each other's insights. I read other books that same week and had trouble getting into them because of the great contrast in the quality of the writing. Potok's writing is great *literature*. It will be around a long time.

Another question to ask of any book: Is it easy to read? That may be misleading. Many of the best books take at least fifty pages to get into. By "easy reading" I don't mean large print or a limited vocabulary. By my definition, easy reading means that without a struggle you get the gist of what the author is saying. That does not mean that the ideas in the book are simple and meaningless; it means that they are presented with clarity. Some contemporary authors deliberately fill their stories with dissonance, making it hard to figure out motives and even what is happening. That represents their view of the world and makes for anxious reading. At the same time, some of the "easiest to read" light-weight stuff does not add anything to our lives. For example, too many formula-written novels can skew the reader's understanding of real life and are only shallow entertainment.

## Should We Censor Books?

Whenever we decide not to read certain books, we are censoring for ourselves. It is a personal decision. We have to recognize that some writing is good and some is not. At the back of this book you will find hundreds of book annotations—books that we consider good writing and reading for teens. If there is something questionable about the book, it will be obvious in the annotation.

Some books listed in the bibliography are by popular contemporary authors that are on school reading lists. Sometimes parents get uptight about what books are chosen by schools. Some teachers opt for the more avant garde "issue" books, overlooking what may be better ones or the classics. However, most teens will not be corrupted by what the teacher requires, especially if they have discussed worldviews with their parents. Most often, legitimate parental complaint will be that the book is too "adult," beyond the reader's experience level and therefore not fully processed. Read books together, talk about them. Try to encourage a teen to see books for what they are— an expression of the worldview of an author who thinks this is the way the world is. Asking questions about books as we read together sets a child in gear to keep on asking questions and making evaluations about what is true and good.

Most school libraries try to carry the really worthy books for young readers. Sometimes librarians get taken in by liberal reviewers who use descriptions like "tender" and "poignant" for questionable books—which are usually called "coming of age" books, dealing with some aspect of sexuality. The standards of what makes a worthy book will vary according to contemporary worldviews. The old favorites will be there, along with some excellent new books. Not every book the library chooses is appropriate for every reader. But that is precisely why it is so important to learn how to critique what we read. If we ask the right questions, there may even be some books that we may not want to finish. Good readers often say, "This book isn't for me. I don't like it."

Sometimes we read books even when we do not value them. I call these the "shrug your shoulders" kind of books. No book will hurt you if you know how to evaluate it and have developed a principled and moral life view. If teens lack the principles to protect themselves, then no rules can keep them safe, because there is too much "out there" with destructive potential. Rules like "Don't read that; don't go there; don't do that"—are never as effective in guarding life as an inner decision to choose what is good.

In the end, the only discipline that really works is self-discipline. Parents can help set up situations in which children learn how to choose, to decide from themselves between good, better, and best— and often between good and evil. And choose we must. Only the garbage can accepts everything put into it. It reminds me of the man who said that he believed in an open mind, but not so open that your brains fall out.

C. S. Lewis, author of the wonderful Narnia Chronicles, said that the best antidote to evil and falsity in fiction, as in life, is saturation

## When Nature Is a Character

Almost any book by Gary Paulsen
*Ring of Bright Water* by Gavin Maxwell
*Pilgrim at Tinker Creek* by Annie Dillard
*To A Wild Sky* and *Ash Road* by Ivan Southall
*A Girl Named Disaster* by Nancy Farmer
*The Animals of Farthing Wood* by Colin Dann
*Incident at Hawk's Hill* by Allan Eckert
*Where the Red Fern Grows* by Wilson Rawls
*Last of the Breed* by Louis L'Amour
*Shipwreck at the Bottom of the World* by Jennifer Armstrong

in the good and genuine. The bibliography at the end of this book will help you learn to have discriminating taste in reading and saturate your reading with the good and genuine. The reader bears the responsibility for judging any work of art—novel, play, or poetry. We need to expand our reading experience to know how to judge.

## Reading on Two Levels

There are two ways to read even the best of writing and to hear what it is saying. If you have read C. S. Lewis's *The Lion, the Witch and the Wardrobe* from the Narnia Chronicles, you already know it is a ripping good adventure. It is enjoyable on that level alone. But Lewis gives us more than adventure. The book is even better when it is read on a second level—as an allegory of life. As you read, you learn something about the clever enticements of evil and what evil does to the world—and about the necessity of redemption from evil. It is true that the book can be read only as an adventure, but think what the reader misses when it is read that way.

The Narnia Chronicles are relatively simple illustrations of reading on two levels. The more complicated the novel, the more readers need to judge what they are reading. *A Tale of Two Cities* by Charles Dickens is often read as preparation for studying the French Revolution. The social structure of French society, the poverty, the injustice, the abuses of power are the obvious message of the book. But it is also a story about good and evil. It too is a story about redemption, about the kind of love that leads one to give his life for another. The thoughtful reader finds significant themes running throughout the book.

When teens read novelist Aleksandr Solzhenitsyn in *One Day in the Life of Ivan Denisovich*, they know that the author understands the nature of evil even if he doesn't refer to the "Fall." When they see moments of generosity, heroism, integrity in Solzhenitsyn's characters in the prison camp, people living above their demeaning surroundings, they will understand new things about what it means to be made in the image of God.

## To Be a Slave

*Slave Dancer* by Paula Fox
*Uncle Tom's Cabin* by Harriet Beecher Stowe
*Anthony Burns* by Virginia Hamilton
*To Be a Slave* by Julius Lester
*The Middle Passage* by Tom Feelings

The input from books is far more profound than we can detail. By asking questions and identifying themes in a book, it is surprising how we can begin to comprehend how a story undergirds basic truths. In a really good book, readers are profoundly gripped by spiritual truths and enjoy heightened understanding of God's character and the nature of evil. But this takes looking for more than what is on the surface, and it takes experience.

Many well-intentioned people want to protect their children by giving them only books in which the message is flatly and firmly evident. Many of these books have thinly veiled plots whose primary purpose is propaganda. Some of these may serve some moral or spiritual function but, for the most part, they do not qualify as literature. However, religious or morality lessons are not the only issues packaged this way. Expect to find messages about environment, lifestyles, gay rights, and political issues laid on top of stories. Most often, this kind of writing lacks beauty or substance. In good writing, the morality of a story is not laid on top of the narrative; it is woven into the fabric of the story so that whatever is true comes out of the characters' actions and the plot of the story. In a fallen world people are mixtures of good and evil, not one or the other, and the plot of any story should reveal this complexity.

If we are free to read, then we must show a willingness to think, to evaluate, to examine. Above all, we must be honest in our reading.

## The Reason We Read

John Milton, the fifteenth-century English poet, believed that in our long-term reading we are collecting "bits of perfection." By that, he meant insights that reveal reality. What we want teens to do is to collect, to judge, and to select those bits that truly belong to God and make use of them in their lives. They will enrich both life and faith. A phrase, an idea, or a situation will suddenly catch the reader's attention and magically illumine life. These bits of truth point to the Truth that holds life together.

If we as readers already know what is good and right, part of maturity will be shown in self-censorship. Quality life always comes from making the right choices, of choosing what we consider valuable. What do you want to put on "the pages of your mind"? That's the question.

It is good to have parents reading books their children are reading so they can talk together about them. This not only gives them a

*In good writing,
the morality
is woven into the
fabric of the story.*

sounding board for evaluating but enlarges understanding on both sides. Sharing is enriching, and neither teens nor adults have enough of it. Teens *can* make value judgments, recognize truth, and make good decisions.

Our children have more "smarts" than we sometimes credit to their account. Asking questions is much more effective than negative harangues. A question can provide a barrier to the sponge-like acceptance of pop-culture, because questions have a way of echoing around in our heads.

All of us need to learn to ask questions of life, of the books we read, of the sermons we hear, of the television programs we watch, of the commercials, and of the newscasts. Don't be a sponge. Instead, ask yourself, "Is this true?" Remember the Pied Piper.

# Chapter 5

# Rejecting the Philistines[2]

It is commonplace that what shocks one generation is accepted quite calmly by the next. This adaptability to change of moral standards . . . is only evidence of what unsubstantial foundations people's moral judgments are.

T. S. ELIOT

I had just finished reading a well-written science-fiction book, a favorite among teens and adults. The subject was imaginative and mind-expanding, the plot developed in a way that set one's own creative energies to work. The problem was that the author put a series of four-letter words in the mouths of his characters. The language added nothing to the story; in fact, it detracted from the otherwise good in his characters. Annoyed with the author I hotly remarked to our son that I was going to write a diatribe about "It's a four-letter world." He was quiet for a moment and then said, "You mean four-letter words like love, hope, good, and Hunt?" I must confess that stopped me cold and made me laugh.

We do have to be careful with our overreactions. The crude use of language, particularly describing body functions, is a fact of life in

---

[2]The Philistines, enemies of neighboring Israel, tried to foist their lifestyle and idolatrous practices onto the people of God.

today's world. Teens can hardly avoid it. The movies are full of it; television scriptwriters push cultural acceptance of such language as far to the edge as they can, music groups hide their obscenities behind rock sounds, and the halls in school resound with words that would make our grandmothers blush. Actually grandmothers have no corner on blushing; we all resent the coarsening of American life.

Profanity and crude speech are in the air around us, and both are in books. In teenage books coarse language seems more common than profanity. Some people talk that way from habit. Remember all the deleted expletives in the Watergate tapes? It seems to have nothing to do with education or social status. The more we hear it, the less offensive it may seem—which maybe is the goal of the Evil One.

I object on two levels. First, it is a misuse of the gift of language. It is no small thing that we are able to take these shining symbols known as words and communicate with each other. We have this ability because we are made in the image of God. He created a world with his own speech. He said, "Let there be light," and there was light. And that was only the beginning of the story of creation. He communicates to us with language, and allows us to speak to him and to each other with words. This is a sacred trust. Just as God created a world for us to live in, so with our speech we also create a world for others to live in.

Our children need to understand something about the importance of language, about the God-given giftedness we possess. Careless words are an affront to our Maker. *What are we saying about ourselves, our view of God, and other people by our language?* In the course of raising children all parents have opportunities to talk about that question. That applies to unkind jibes, to put-downs, to anything that demeans humanity. We traditionally call crude language *dirty talk*. Why? It merits family discussion. *Why does Jesus say we will have to give an account of careless words?*

My second objection is based on the first. Crude language demeans human life. Our bodies are not a joke. Neither are their func-

## If You're Ready for Intellectual Stretching

Any of the Tried and Trues (pages 326–353)
*Ishmael* by Daniel Quinn
*Chris Chrisman Goes to College* by James W. Sire
*Father Elijah* by Michael O'Brien
*Red Shift* by Alan Garner
*A Wizard of Earthsea* by Ursula LeGuin
His Dark Materials trilogy by Philip Pullman
*Descent into Hell* by Charles Williams
*Pilgrim at Tinker Creek* by Annie Dillard
*Defeating Darwinism* by Phillip Johnson
*Eva* by Peter Dickinson

tions. The body serves as an elegant house for a soul that will live for-ever. In the beginning the man and his wife were naked and unashamed. The Fall or the entrance of sin stripped away that inno-cence and now we know shame, all of us. There is nothing wrong with our body functions; it is only shameful when we exploit them and demean them in one way or another. Some ways of speaking about what is private can only be called coarse and degrading.

Our enemy is an expert at twisting what is most valuable. Two great gifts come from God's hand: language and sex. In Satan's per-verse way he has led people to misuse both gifts. What should be holy is made common and crude. People use each other sexually, often without a thought that this is something God created for quite another purpose.

## What's a Parent to Do?

Both sex and coarse language are issues that demand parent-teen dis-cussion. If you avoid these subjects, what are you saying to your chil-dren? How would your teen answer this question, *Why did God make men and women with different body forms? Why did he create sex?* You may find out that they never knew that sex was God's idea; they may think teens discovered it at puberty. *How do we show respect for bod-ies created by God?* Reading books together can introduce these sub-jects in the best possible way so that the discussion originates from the story and is thus less personal and less defensive.

It shouldn't surprise us that what is so obviously a part of our cul-ture is also in books. The use of profanity and crude language is increas-ingly common in young adult literature. In good literature a writer may use "bad language" as a tool or technique to make a character come alive, to be more authentic; it is entirely believable for some characters to use profanity. However, when language of this kind is used only to proclaim, "This is a four-letter world!" it's a different matter. It reflects the author's acceptance of this language as part of the real world. The reader needs to learn how to discern and how to reject.

What should a parent do with bad language in culture and in books? One option is to react with horror and ban the book. That may keep a teen from reading the words, but it doesn't take them out of his hearing in the culture. We need to talk about it openly. *Why do people talk that way?* Get at motivational questions. Is it cool? Is it right?

*How do you handle the bad language in books?* I asked one teen. He gave me a healthy answer. He said he knew that people used words like that, so he just read over them, skipped them. They weren't important to the story. He determined that these words were "bad" and he didn't intend to use them. He had already made a decision about the words because he and his dad had talked about the way they degraded human conversation.

One young reader in our family covers all bad language in a book by saying that a book has "swears" in it. He says it as a fact, not as an exclamation mark. Reading aloud makes it essential that the reader skips over the "swears" because he already has decided this is not acceptable language.

Some popular authors depend on explicit sex scenes or overuse of profanity to give some thrill to their readers. The details add nothing to the value of the story; in fact, they almost become the point of the story. There is no second level of meaning except that the reader realizes the degradation that comes when one lives without rules. Some movies do the same, exploiting people. These may be R-rated on purpose to attract viewers and bring one's thought life down to the level of that of the writer. Let your kids know that it is demeaning to be manipulated like this by an outside force. I, for one, don't want some scenes or kinds of language rattling around in my head.

We reluctantly rejected several otherwise good books for our bibliography because of language that was pervasively foul, making it impossible to skip over it. In many cases, we try to warn you that language (or violence or improperly expressed sexuality) might be a problem in a particular book.

Parents need to give some help on this issue that goes beyond censorship. Our tolerance level is being tested. Young people are not helped by parents who react with shock and outrage. (One mother tore the pages from a book and sent them to me, upset by a father in the story who didn't believe in God and shouted, "Hells bells!" when he found the hamster in the refrigerator. How did this help her son?) It is best dealt with as a fact of life—another area where choices are necessary. Shock doesn't deal with the root problem. To say something is wrong is one thing; to say why it is wrong is another.

One way of dealing with questionable language is to focus on the author's intent. Why does the author use this technique in writing? Does it add to the point of the story? We need to help our reading children not to stumble over this. Ask, *What do you think makes a person talk that way? Does that necessarily make him a bad person? How should you treat the person or the story?*

Reading together and talking about books helps everyone better judge between right and wrong. No one can ever blame a book for one's own bad behavior or language. It is always a challenge to keep one's integrity. A person can read something and become "earthy" by thinking unworthy thoughts or using bad words, but it is by choice. That's what happens when people don't ask questions like, *What is the point of this story? What is it really saying?*

We live in a fallen world. Good literature does not avoid that fact. But it does not revel in it either. In good writing, the author portrays evil behavior as a way of exposing it for what it is. *Les Miserables* by Victor Hugo is a prime example. Javert is a pathetic creature bent on revenge and cruelty, a powerful contrast to the humble Jean Valjean. Sometimes evil properly portrayed exposes the real character of evil. The biblical details about King Ahab and Queen Jezebel in the Old Testament leave no doubt about evil and its results.

## If You're Feeling Left Alone

*The Great Gilly Hopkins* by Katherine Paterson
*Slake's Limbo* by Felice Holman
*Homecoming* by Cynthia Voigt
*A Door Near Here* by Heather Quarles
*Sweet Whispers, Brother Rush* by Virginia Hamilton
*Dave at Night* by Gail Carson Levine

In Tolstoy's *Anna Karenina* the reader is confronted with the terrible folly of Anna's choice to leave her husband and son for an affair with another man. She loses everything. Questions pour out of the story with powerful impact. It's Exhibit A on the consequence of wrong choices.

It is part of becoming a mature adult to recognize the difference between what demeans and what inspires noble action. Words can build, can expand a person's world to make it more beautiful. Unless you talk about it with your children, they may accept the obscenities and destroying words of rap stars and rock bands without your knowing it. All of which makes reading books seem like a tame endeavor.

Maybe you are a parent who wants to exclude all reading except what you know is safe. That becomes more and more difficult as a child becomes a teen and moves further out of your control. Now is a good time to confront the issue of choices: Whose values will be adopted as our own, the Philistines or the people of God?

# Chapter 6

# Building a Christian World/Life View

The greatest danger of truth is not falsehood, but diversion and indifference.

JOHN SEEL

He who begins by loving Christianity better than truth will proceed by loving his own sect or church better than Christ, and end by loving himself better than all.

COLERIDGE

Books provide a great environment for talking about ideas. Since our premise is that in the rush of living we often don't do enough talking about values and truth, how do we begin in helping our children build an adequate world/life view for themselves? We want truth to shape their lives on every level.

We begin by asking ourselves basic questions like, *What are our intentions for this child? Have we ever spelled out our goals?* We have to face the possibility that our ideas are vague and have to do with trouble-free acceptablity. Maybe we simply want them to "believe" enough to get them to heaven.

Our natural tendency, if we have a belief system ourselves, is to indoctrinate our children—tell them what to believe. That is good and it is bad. It is good because we are hopefully recounting great truths; it is bad because it may only give a Christian veneer. A second option is to explore ideas and truth through books, asking questions to lead them into Truth. That offers building material for a life view and should produce more than a veneer. The downside is that we may fail to be specific enough to build a belief-system that instructs all parts of their life.

In our desire to teach our children we may be only "christianizing" them on the outside without changing how they think. Conformity to please others is not the same as inner conviction. Yet conformity pleases us; it meets our emotional needs as parents. Conformity isn't bad; we simply need to know what it is and what it is not.

Sadly we often recognize "Christian veneer" too late when we realize that our good intentions have gone astray. A veneer is fragile in the rough and tumble of a hostile world and often rubs off, leaving little recognizable Christian belief underneath. Indoctrinated children don't always know *why* they are doing or believing *what* they do. Children learn to parrot back truths and earn a reward for doing so. (Children are not the only ones who do this.)

Actually indoctrination goes beyond conformity. Indoctrination is an idea word; it tells people what to think. It gives all the anwers. It does not welcome questions. It has a distinct point of view. Cults are specialists in indoctrination. They don't want their adherents to reason; they want them to repeat what they are told.

## The Problem with a Christian Veneer

All of this says that raising teens to become thoughtful adults is not a "piece of cake." Let me tell you about some teens I have known.

Amy was your average good-kid teenager. The fervency of her participation in the church youth group made her a daughter for others to envy. Mention a Bible study and she was there. Plan a mission trip and she raised the money to go. Have a job you wanted a teen to do for the church, Amy was asked. Amy loved hanging out with her youth group from church—the pizza parties, the after-game gatherings, the backpacking trips, the being together. Looking at it from the outside, anyone would guess that Amy had it all together.

After high school Amy chose a Christian college, and reports about college life were only slightly less enthusiastic than those of her high school youth group. Her parents beamed their approval of her when we talked together.

After graduation Amy moved back home while she came to terms with the hard facts of working life, namely, that a major in philosophy and psychology didn't impress many prospective employers. Her minimum-wage job kept her going while she made further plans to flesh out a career for herself. One day when her mother put Amy's sweater back in her room, her eye caught words on a pad of paper on Amy's desk that looked rather strange. It looked like she had been asked to write "I will not talk in school" fifty times for a teacher. Only it wasn't that. Amy had been writing over and over

> I am part of the divine.
> I am part of the divine.
> I am part of the divine.

What in the world did that mean? Her mother noticed a stack of books on the floor next to the desk. All of them were about Native-American views of the meaning of life and new age religion. She began putting the evidence together, evidence confimed by later conversations with Amy. She was into shamanism. That explained several things: her cavalier attitude toward church, her bizarre choices of clothing and jewelry, the people she was hanging out with, and other strange behaviors. Deeply shaken, her parents asked, "How could this happen?" Given the best of every opportunity, Amy suddenly acted as if none of it mattered. She labeled herself "a contemporary spiritual person," caught up in dialogue with a guru.

While her parents were weeping over Amy, Ryan's parents glowed over his success. Ryan's growing up years were much like Amy's—church, Sunday school, youth group, good college. His attractive personality made him popular and as he grew older he looked pretty successful—good job, pretty new wife, nice car. But those close to Ryan noticed some other traits: having wrong priorities, being

## When Life Isn't Perfect

*Joni* by Joni Eareckson
*All Together Now* by Sue Ellen Bridgers
*Flowers for Algernon* by Daniel Keyes
*Stuck in Neutral* by Terry Trueman
*Lord Foul's Bane* by Stephen Donaldson
*Hang Tough, Paul Mather* by Alfred Slote
*Comeback* by Dave Dravecky
*Saint Ben* by John Fischer
*One Child* by Torey Hayden

enamored with things, being self-centered, playing to the audience, loving positions of prominence. Ryan networks to his advantage and has never been known to do anything for anyone—including his young wife—that costs him anything personally. He has a lot to say, but not about God. He is likely a secular man hiding in a Christian sub-culture because the dividends are good.

"How did this happen?" their shocked parents ask. Amy's parents have concluded that they did not talk enough about ideas as a family; they didn't have conversations about Truth. They feel now that they "christianized her." Ryan's parents try to pretend they aren't disappointed and hope he will grow up.

## Indoctrination or Life-Building

No one can guarantee that what parents or the church program provide will produce Christian offspring—people who give both heart and mind to God. People come into God's kingdom one by one, based on a personal commitment, a response to God. Parents who seem to have done all the right things have wayward children, and that defies all the platitudes we have heard about parenting. John White, a Canadian psychiatrist, has written a helpful book titled *Parents in Pain* that offers comfort and insights for those who are hurting over this dilemma.

However, building a life is different from being indoctrinated. Indoctrination is instruction in the fundamentals of a certain point of view. It does not necessarily mean learning how to think or even how to act. Instead it may mean conforming to a standard.

What happens on the outside is not necessarily what is happening on the inside. Remember the little boy who resisted the discipline forced on him by declaring, "I'm sitting down on the outside, but I'm standing up on the inside." At least he knew what he was doing.

Question: *To what extent do we indoctrinate our children rather than teach them how to think about life's big questions?* Are we tellers instead of listeners? Are we specialists in one-way conversations with our children?

It feels good to give our children all the answers. It can make a person feel superior—having children make public professions of faith or completing confirmation, or whatever makes a parent feel sure their children are outwardly on the right track—but unless this translates into the way a child thinks, it won't stand the test of life. It will only lead to a disagreeable smugness or ignorance when a person bumps into the world of ideas.

Smugness is one of the ugly fruits of indoctrination. Remember the Pharisees. They were not bad people. They were sincerely concerned about orthodoxy; they believed they were protecting truth. They didn't like questions; they already had all the answers. Nor were they seeking truth; they lived by their traditions. When Jesus asked questions about their beliefs, they ran him out of town.

Some people want a system in which all the ducks line up in the right way. It feels safe; they can relax and trust the system. That's what we do with Christian truths some times. We put what we are told in a box, never question it, and end up trusting the box instead of God. The box is not the Way, the Truth and the Life; Jesus is.

Because we are the ones who line up the system, we avoid questions. Is this because we have an uneasy feeling that it wouldn't be true if we questioned it? The reality is that what we claim to believe only becomes true as we think about it. Truth is strengthened, not weakened, by asking questions about it.

Often instead of allowing it to become something that grips the whole person—mind, heart, will—we have made truth into a sub-culture, a doing things in a certain way, believing a list of propositions. The profoundly great truths about God, the world, evil, rescue, human choices—which ought to ignite a fire within our inmost being—hardly faze us.

Amy's problem is that she sees Jesus as one of many options. She likes options; our society has assured her that choice and options are her right. Her parents have one sub-culture; she is interested in another. She does not see this as an issue of Truth with a capital T. She does not see it as a matter of life and death. She has never learned to think christianly. She was indoctrinated, yes; she was never fully convinced about Christian truth.

Ryan isn't interested in issues of Truth. He is a spectator. He has always gone along with what is comfortable. He would be hard-pressed to tell anyone else what he believed in a convincing way. He is interested in heaven; he likes security. He is less interested in

## Sent Out By God

*Peace Child* by Don Richardson
*Shadow of the Almighty* by Elisabeth Elliot
*Killing Fields, Living Fields* by Don Cormack
*Eric Liddell: Pure Gold* by David McCasland

*The person with a Christian mind measures everything in life by the word of God.*

relationships that demand anything from him. Ryan does not have a Christian mind anymore than Amy does.

## What Is a Christian Mind and How Do You Get One?

Having a Christian mind is about thinking; all of this is not unrelated to reading, the subject of this book. Our premise, remember, is that books can help us think about life issues and choices. We want to train young people to think about these "life issues and choices" in a Christian way.

Having a Christian mind means thinking like a Christian. The person with a Christian mind measures everything in life—not by the opinion of others, but by the word of God. Everything in life is seen through the framework of revealed Truth. It touches all decisions, all goals, all value-systems, all relationships. It cares about what God cares about.

We don't manufacture our morals or beliefs. In other words, we could know nothing of spiritual importance apart from God's revealing it to us. Truth, therefore, is objective, not subjective. It isn't determined by how I feel about it.

You can understand why young people come to think more highly of their own ideas than the ideas warrant. Reporters choose people randomly off the street, stick a microphone before them, ask their opinions—opinions that may not only be dead wrong, but totally irrelevant—and then broadcast them across the airwaves or in the newspapers. We live in a world where all opinions seem of equal value.

How do we help a teen see through the folly of this? How do we demonstrate that "my idea of God" is not worth talking about? It's God's revelation of who he is that is important. If I can perfectly define God, then I am greater than God! We don't vote on God. God is not an idea; he is a fact. He is the Supreme Lord of the universe. Minority opinions have nothing to do with Truth.

*How does a person learn to think like a Christian?* First we have to talk about what it means. Second, we begin to monitor our family conversations and behavior to see how we're doing. Third, we learn how to ask questions. Ask, don't tell. Keep asking questions that go beyond easy answers and make our children think about Truth with a capital T.

If teens are free to think and ask questions, they may challenge our own beliefs as parents. This could even feel dangerous and threatening. But if our attitude creates an environment of loving acceptance

that says, "Let's find truth together. . . ," we will find ourselves growing along with our teens.

   We dare not let a skeptical mind throw us off track. John Seel,
headmaster of Logos Academy, writes that Christians are often suspicious of questions. "We don't doubt well," he writes in *Critique*. "We
tend to prefer compliance and conformity. The net result is that we
tend to prefer ignorance. We say we are concerned about truth, but
we do not pay the dues truth demands." Why did Jesus ask so many
questions? He was trying to make his followers come to logical conclusions about what they believed to be true. His method is one to
emulate: *Ask, don't tell.*

## Where to Begin?

The book of Genesis is a good place to begin; it is a foundational study
for what we are discussing here. It is the story of human beings and
the beginning of the world. You will be amazed at the possibilities for
family dialogues if you ask questions about the text. Read Genesis 1
and 2. The first thing to notice is the information about who God is,
about his activity in creating the world. Although the Bible is not a science text book, you can discuss how the world was created from a
biblical point of view.

> *How are human beings different than the rest of creation?*
> *What does it mean to be created in the image of God?*
> *What do you think God had in mind for human beings?*

   A jumble of confused thinking complicates our view of ourselves
and our view of nature. One group of eager conservationists can dis-
tort a worthy cause by seeming to love plants and animals more than
human beings. Animal rights groups do more than love their pets;
they believe animals have the same value and rights as human beings.
Other groups think the natural world is to be used by human beings,
but think of it as *their* natural world, not God's. Within those groups,
some are diligently protecting it from abuse, while another group
thinks it is on its way out anyway, so use it up. The situation is complicated by industries who wantonly abuse natural resources for the
sake of dollars, but the success of their industries makes jobs for
people who need them. One way or another our children have heard
these points of view. How should Christians think about all of this?
Do animals and people have the same value?

Ask your children to decide which of these models is biblical, based on Genesis 1–2.

| A. God (eternal) | B. God | C. God |
|---|---|---|
| Humans | *GAP* | *GAP* |
| *GAP* | Humans | Humans |
| Nature | Nature | *GAP* |
| | | Nature |

The gaps are meant to indicate a whole other level of being. Are there two gaps or one? Or do you think all gaps should be eliminated? Why?

> *How is God separate from all that is created?*
> *In what ways are human beings made in the image of God?*
> *What difference does this make in our thinking?*

That's more than enough for one day, but keep going. Genesis has a lot to teach all of us. Read chapters 3 and 4.

> *What did God provide for the first man and woman? Did they lack anything?*
> *What tasks did God give the man and the woman?*
> *Why did God place restrictions on one tree?*
> *From what happened here, how would you define sin?*
> *Why is this event called The Fall?*

Questions about human relationships, about God's purpose for sexuality—you won't run out of ideas to talk about. These are questions adults should wrestle with, but they are also questions our children need to begin to think about.

It will cost you time and effort to do this. It will come from convictions about the importance of sharing ideas, of discovering truth, of listening to where your teens are coming from. If you squelch every shaky idea they present, you will get only "christianized answers" back. If, instead, you take every question seriously and look for answers together, you will find young people opening up and maybe truly thinking for the first time.

Life presents so many ideas to talk about. Books are about life and ideas. Having a Christian mind means thinking about life and ideas in terms of God's point of view. The secular mind can consider all opinions valid, especially in a multicultural world. It may parade as *compassion* or call itself *understanding others*. It prides itself on being open-minded. For the Christian, obeying God includes having a compassionate and understanding heart, but the Christian mind is God-minded, not open-minded.

Recently in a high school group students were asked how many believed that the gospel is the way for people to come to know God, to be "saved from their sins." More than 75 percent of the students raised their hands. Then the question was asked, *How many of you believe that Jesus is the only way to God?* Only a few tentatively raised their hand, most not realizing that they were contradicting their earlier response. In another group the question was raised, *Are Allah and God the same? Do Christians worship the same God as Muslims?* Adults were as confused as the teens. When someone remembered that Muslims don't believe Jesus is God, another replied, "But they do believe in the same God as we do. It's just Jesus that is the problem." Christians believe in one God in three Persons (the Trinity), not three separate gods. Now how do you answer the question?

We must ask questions like these if we would think like Christians. It is so easy for us to absorb the open-minded, tolerance-inspired thinking of our culture without knowing it. That is why teens need help to think like Christians, to know what they believe and why. As they begin to do this, you are going beyond indoctrination and into life-building.

Reading books together provides fodder for discussions like these. Don't expect earth-shaking discussions about every book you read. An idea here, an idea there; relating one idea to another. It's what growing is all about. We need to learn how to do this.

I remember an important discussion we had one day in the middle of reading together. In the course of the sailing adventure in C. S. Lewis's *The Voyage of the Dawntreader* no one learns more than Eustace, a nasty, opinionated, and very lazy boy. When the ship named *The Dawntreader* survives a terrible storm that lasts for days, it comes to rest in a small bay of a mountainous island. The mast is broken and the ship is in need of many repairs. The crew all sets to work, except Eustace who decides to hike up into the mountains. In a cave he finds an enormous cache of jewels and decides to keep it a secret and have

## Civil War Stories

*Jubilee* by Margaret Walker
*Gone with the Wind* by Margaret
   Mitchell
*Edge of Honor* by Gilbert Morris
*Stranger in Savannah* by Eugenia Price
*The Civil War* by Bruce Catton
*Friendly Persuasion* by Jessamyn West
*Killer Angels* by Michael Shaara

*Teens need to be able to verbalize what they believe not only so they can share it with others, but also to see how their beliefs are shaping in their own lives.*

the treasure all to himself. He falls asleep and awakens to find a dragon in the cave with him, breathing out fire and clanging on the hoard. It takes a while, but after a frightful time he discovers he is the dragon! "Sleeping on a dragon's hoard with greedy, dragonish thoughts in his heart, he had become a dragon himself." It's a hair-raising account, and I have told you only the basics. But what a discussion we had about how what we treasure affects what we become! And that was only part of the story, but you'll have to read the rest yourself. How Eustace is changed back into a boy makes it a necessary reading.

*Shiloh* by Phyllis Naylor is the story of Marty Preston, who has a tender heart for an abused dog he finds, and rather than send it back for more abuse he hides the dog, taking the situation into his own hands. Out of the story pour questions about his actions: *What were his options? Is it ever right to lie? What do you think of his Bible-quoting grandmother? What do you admire about Marty?* These two stories are written for pre-teens and early teens, but read so well that the story makes a good discussion with middle teens, as well.

Try reading aloud *Cezanne Pinto* by Mary Stolz. It's the story of a former slave boy, now free, working as a cowboy. He tells the story of his young life, weaving it together with love and grace and doubts and wisdom. It is beautifully written, and the reading will reveal a vision of the indomitable human spirit. Questions fall out of the story. You will not lack for ideas to talk about together. If your family likes fantasy, read Walter Wangerin Jr.'s *The Book of the Dun Cow*, which takes more mature readers into the lives of creatures in the barnyard, but you will recognize many people you know as you read. It is a story of conflict between good and evil.

An excellent non-fiction book, current and up-to-date, will add depth and discussion to your family life: *Know What You Believe* by Paul Little.

So many other books beckon, calling for you to share as families. I like the idea of reading aloud together, but that is not the only way to do this. You can read the same books and talk about them after you have read them.

## Understanding Worldviews

As teens put together their own worldviews, they need to be able to verbalize what they believe not only so they can share it with others, but also to see how their beliefs are shaping in their own lives. This is a significant step toward maturity. Good literature provides the help we need to do this. Books are about other people—their actions, their choices, their characters. Books not only help us verbalize; they help us evaluate. We can look at the character's worldview, what the author is advocating, and see if it measures up to what we know of Truth.

What are the elements that make up a worldview? By identifying some common worldviews, we begin to understand better where other people are coming from when they share ideas. (I have adapted the following information about worldviews from an excellent book, *The Universe Next Door* by James W. Sire.)

What do we believe? How do we find out what our worldview is? Our basic worldview should answer the following questions.

1. *What is the really real?* Is it God or the gods, or the material universe? What will always be there?
2. *What is the world around us like?* Is it created? Is the universe chaos or ordered? How do we relate to it?
3. *What is a human being?* A machine? A sleeping god? A person made in the image of God? A naked ape?
4. *What happens at death?* Extinction? Transformation to a higher state? Resurrection? Is there life after death?
5. *Why is it possible to know anything at all?* Is it possible because we are made in the image of an all-knowing God? Or is rationality developed in the process of evolution?
6. *How do we know what is right and wrong?* Tradition? Made in the image of God whose character is good? Human choice? Result of means of survival?
7. *What is the point of human history?* Where is it going? Is history taking us somewhere? Does it move in a line with an ending, or does it go around in cycles?

Some people may look at those questions and think, "Wow, how do you know the answers to questions like these?" The Westminster Catechism isn't a bad place to begin. It's a condensation of the biblical doctrines on which the civilization of the Western world is built. It summarizes what most would call the Christian worldview.

Let's look briefly at what this and some other popular worldviews believe:

A. *Christian theism.* God is beyond measurement (infinite) and yet personal. He is not a substance or a force, he is HE. God

*Right and wrong
is based on the
character of God.*

is also beyond us (transcendent) and yet everywhere present. He is the Creator, all-knowing, good, and human beings are made in his image. This God has communicated with us so that we can know him. Human beings were created good, but since the Fall the image of God has been marred (sinful) and is restored through the work of Christ, who redeems those who trust in him. Death is the gate to life with God or to eternal separation from God. Right and wrong is based on the character of God. History is linear; it is going someplace, to the fulfillment of God's purposes. Because of the Bible, this is the most clearly spelled out worldview.

B. *Deism.* God, like someone winding a clock, created the universe and then left it to run on its own. God is distant, foreign, and alien. Thus human beings are on their own. The universe is a closed system; everything can be explained. It operates according to the law of cause and effect. There are no miracles. Human beings are part of the clockwork—personal and yet unrelated to God. The Fall does not exist, so that what is wrong or right is God's responsibility. How things are is his fault.

Contemporary books that mention God (and many of them do) but have no sense of God's power to change anything reflect this worldview. God is there, but the characters are really "on their own."

C. *Naturalism.* God does not exist. Matter is all there is. Carl Sagan says, "The Cosmos is all that is or ever was or ever will be." Human beings are complex machines—with mind and personality as a function of the machine. There is but one substance with various modifications. Death is extinction. History is cause and effect but has no purpose. Values are man-made. Secular humanism (as opposed to Christian humanism) and Marxism both are forms of naturalism. Probably Leon Garfield, Philip Pullman, and Isaac Asimov reflect this worldview.

D. *Nihilism* (pronounced NEE-hill-ism). Nihilism is more a feeling than a philosophy. It is really not a philosophy at all, because it denies the possibility of knowing anything or that anything is valuable. Nihilism is negative about everything. Modern art galleries are full of its products and shout out "meaninglessness!" Samuel Beckett's play *Waiting for Godot* is a prime example of nihilism. The characters wait, but God never shows up. Beckett's *Breath* is a thirty-five-second play that has no human actors. The props are a pile of rubbish on stage. There are no words, only a recorded cry at the opening of the play, an inhaled breath, an exhaled breath, and a closing cry. That is Beckett's worldview. Nihilism is really unliveable; it leads to suicide. Robert Cormier has a nihilistic point of view in some of his stories, and many teens have written to him, asking for happier endings.

E. *Existentialism* (pronounced ex-i-STEN-shal-ism). Reality is subjective and objective. The world merely is. There is no God. Human beings define themselves and are totally free and determine their own destiny. The world does not have meaning unless people revolt and create meaning. Margaret Mahy, Cynthia Voigt, and Lois Lowry's books give evidence of this worldview. "Theistic existentialism" believes in an infinite God and is closer to theism except that people, not God, are center stage and responsible for the outcome of events. Karen Cushman's books reflect this worldview.

F. *Pantheism.* Eastern religions are pantheistic. Pantheism takes various forms. God is in everything. There are many gods. Each person is God. God is in all. Some things are more One than others, but many roads lead to the One. The goal is to become one with the cosmos and thus pass beyond good and evil. Death ends the individual, but his essence goes on into something else (reincarnation or back to the soil). Nothing of value perishes. History is cyclical; it goes round and round. Some of Gary Paulsen's books come close to this worldview.

G. *New Age.* New Age thinking borrows heavily from Eastern religion, from theism, and from naturalism. There is no Lord of the universe. Self is the kingpin. People use their senses to get in touch with the invisible universe through "doors of perception" like drugs, meditation, trance, biofeedback, acupuncture, ritualized dance, certain kinds of music, and so forth. Self can get in touch with Mind at Large, which does not obey the laws of the universe. The conscious self can travel across the earth and into time and space. Some New-agers are heavily into the occult; others are into shamanism. They believe that extraordinary power and energy can surge through a person and be transmitted to others. Shirley MacLaine is a proponent of this worldview. People have adopted it without even knowing what it is about, believing in a person's power to heal self, consulting channelers and the stars for guidance. It is a hodge-podge worldview in which humans are god.

Many good stories reflect one of these points of view—stories that offer insights, show us the consequences of choice, show us courage, and teach us good things—but are written out of a basic worldview. This is true even of newspaper stories, to say nothing of movies, television, and other forms of story telling. We know people who hold these views. That is why it is important to help young people see what lies underneath, so they can take the good, but recognize the false in any story.

Recently a group of adults were discussing Lois Lowry's Newbery Medal book, *The Giver,* a book aimed at young adults, but widely read by adults interested in literature. Several in the group were emotionally moved by the story and were praising it without questions, until one person in the group began asking worldview questions. *Who is in charge of the world in this story? What is the author's view of human beings, of eternal destiny?* The discussion suddenly became alive with meaning. Everyone in the group had new insights. The questions had taught them more than the author may have intended in the story.

Discussing worldviews has never been more critical. If you want to raise teens who know what they believe and can stand in the marketplace of ideas with firm convictions, then you have to engage your children in conversation about these things. We live in such a slippery time in history. All ideas cannot be true. Truth is not wishy-washy; it may be costly to take a stand for Truth, but that is how character is formed. Truth is not always what makes me feel good. Remember that whether it is defined or not, we are all constructing a belief system of some kind. When we talk about it we are helping to define it.

This may be more than you want to know about worldviews, but there it is. You *do* need to know something about this and so does your teen if you are to face the world squarely. You don't need either

## If You Want to Visit Latin America

*Heart of a Jaguar* by Marc Talbert
*The Power and the Glory* by Graham Greene
*Green Mansions* by William Hudson
*The Shadow of the Almighty* by Elisabeth Elliot
*Bridge of San Luis Rey* by Thorton Wilder
*Dragons in the Water* by Madeleine L'Engle

to memorize these worldviews or feel overwhelmed by them. It helps you simply to know that they exist. You can always refer to these pages as you read and ask questions of the novels you read. The most important observation to make in determining a worldview is to notice who acts as god in the story.

"I just sort of accept the world the way it is, and don't think much about it" is a common remark. Too many people go through life with a careless belief system—a little of this and a little of that—making themselves the final judge of whether it is a good system or not. And when you read books, you will find that the authors reveal their worldview. In discerning theirs, your own will become more clearly focused. Questions, questions. Always ask questions.

## Finding Time

This chapter may leave you feeling overwhelmed and asking, "Where would I find time to do all of this?" First of all, you probably are already doing more of this than you know. This chapter is a reservoir of ideas for parents; don't pour all of this over a child's head at one time. It is intended to stimulate you to think of ways to help young adults make sense out of the world and their place in it, and to give you some background for the task. Instead of feeling overwhelmed, be challenged to think what you will do with all of this.

Second, this encourages you to plan ahead, to be intentional about influencing young people. You will notice that many of my illustrations of reading books aloud involve vacations or time spent in travel. You don't even have to read aloud yourself what with the availability of so many wonderful books-on-tape, many read by professional actors, which you can listen to in the car. But you have to plan ahead and believe this is important enough to make a plan for available time and something specific.

Third, you have to decide what is important for your family. Is it important to read the Bible together? How often? When is a good time to read a book together? How could you do this so that it is fun and comfortable for both you and your family? Will someone have to make some sacrifice of time (and choice) to make this possible?

When Shireen Dodson lamented the lack of time she had to spend with her young daughter, she felt she had to come up with some idea that would encourage sharing on an emotional level. They were just not talking about ideas and values in helpful ways. She

*Questions,
questions. Always
ask questions.*

mentioned the idea of a book club to her daughter Morgan and got a response that surprised her. Morgan quickly produced a list of mother/daughter friends to invite. Ten busy mothers and daughters began reading books together and talking about them. It was so successful that Shireen Dodson wrote *The Mother-Daughter Book Club,* a book that recounts the method and the results. Many public libraries now have mother-daughter book clubs. It's an idea to investigate.

I mentioned earlier the idea of picking up "little bits of wisdom" along the way. That's what we want our children to do—and in the best way possible. Remember the fellow who was beating his donkey with a stick to get him moving, without much result, until a bystander suggested that he hold out a carrot just ahead of the donkey's nose. What I am suggesting is "more carrot" and "less stick" in the matter of raising our children. Books can be the stuff that gets us moving while providing at the same time a mighty tasty treat.

# Chapter 7

# Fantasy in a Real World

Creative imagination is more than mere invention. It is that power which creates, out of abstractions, life. It goes to the heart of the unseen, and puts that which is so mysteriously hidden from ordinary mortals into the clear light of their understanding. . . Writers of fantasy, more than any other writers except poets, are able to evoke ideas and clothe them in symbols, allegory, and dream.

LILLIAN H. SMITH

It does not do to leave a dragon out of your calculations if you live near him.

J. R. R. TOLKIEN

**O**nce upon a time there was a dragon, or *In a hole in the ground there lived a hobbit.* It is by such beautiful non-facts as these, wrote Ursula LeGuin, that we fantastic human beings may arrive at the truth.

Fantasy is reality in unreality. The question about fantasy is not whether the story has happened in our history but is there truth in what happened. In fact, the power of fantasy is that it knows nothing of the limitations of the modern world. In the real world that has "exiled gods and heroes" we need the help of fantasy to express all

*Fantasy can put our personal problems into perspective.*

the Truth of transcendent themes like deity, glory, heroism, courage, goodness, or beauty. Fantasy is always bigger than life and yet it must reveal life. It takes place in a world remote from ours, yet at the same time it is rooted in our world. Just because we live in time doesn't mean that we have to stay in time.

In a fine essay on myth, Thomas Howard writes that we don't want myths crowded or spoiled by the immediate world, but we do want them to ring bells that our ears can hear.

> A Christian, especially, living as he does in a huge universe all ringing with the footfalls of hurrying seraphim, cherubim, archangels, angels, men, and devils, will never be too quick to judge what creatures aren't in on the traffic. He can only demur and say, "Elves? I don't know much about them. I've never come across one (worse luck)."

Howard is essentially saying that Christians know they can't explain everything, that what is real is not necessarily seen. The question about fantasy is *How true does it ring?* Is there consistency in the world that has been created by the writer? Does it live by its own laws so that it hangs together? Does it show me reality in a way that I can understand?

The fantasies of writers like C. S. Lewis and J. R. R. Tolkien are not only first-class adventures but their visions of a golden-maned lion named Aslan and the courage of valiant hobbits have nourished the understanding of countless readers. Some have wondered if it is possible to describe the Christian experience effectively outside of fantasy. Katherine Paterson writes about Tolkien's trilogy:

> Those of us who have followed Frodo on his quest have had a vision of the true darkness. We know that we, like him, would have never gotten up the steep slope of Mount Doom had the faithful Sam not flung us on his back and carried us up, crawling at the last. We know, too, that we would never have parted with the baneful ring or power had not the piteous Gollum torn it from our bleeding finger and, in the effort, fallen screeching into the abyss, clutching his damned treasure and ours.

Our response to such a story is surely, "That's me." We recognize the awfulness of the way we clutch at the control over our own lives, our rebellion, our cowardice, our sin. Fantasy stands off from our experience but is about our experience. Howard insists that "excursions into that world are never a flight away from reality; they are, rather, a flight to reality."

Fantasy demands something extra of its readers; it asks them to pay close attention to the rich details of the story. Fantasy invites readers to read and reread it, like exploring a gold mine for nuggets. Our imaginations can soar. I, for one, do not want to watch movies of Tolkien's *The Lord of the Rings* because I don't want anyone to spoil my mental image of what a hobbit looks like. I felt the same way about the Narnia Chronicles in cartoon fashion, although the productions using real children have been well done and better than I expected.

## Why Teens Like Fantasy

Fantasy can put our personal problems into perspective. When we get carried away with a really large story, our own dark moments disappear. It's rather like Alice in Wonderland falling mile after mile down the rabbit's hole until she thinks she might be near the center of the earth. "Well," thought Alice to herself, "after a fall such as this, I shall think nothing of tumbling down the stairs."

A twenty-year-old student wrote to author Susan Cooper about her fantasy books, "You give all of us the chance to leave the mundane struggles we face and enter a slightly grander struggle for a while." Another wrote to her, "Your books are my escape from the world I live in. I often wish I were one of the Old Ones, fighting the Dark and protecting Mankind from harm."

Teens need adventure, and it is easier to handle through the pages of a good book than when it actually arrives. Afterward, if an adventure does happen to overtake us, somewhere in our subconscious mind we will be equipped to endure and handle it. Michele Landsberg in her book *Reading for the Love of It* tells a wonderful story about her son, Avi, who was a very bright, gifted child, reading at an early age. One day when she went into his room she found this six-year-old weeping over a book. She took him on her lap as he sobbed out, "I can't go on. Drem has failed his wolf slaying." She assured him that things would get better and read aloud from his story, Sutcliff's *Warrior Scarlet*, until Avi had composed himself. Three years later, Avi agreed to work on his lateral lisp with a speech therapist. In fewer than three weeks the childhood lisp had disappeared. His mother was amazed. How had he managed to deal so swiftly with this trial in his life? "I remembered Drem," Avi said. "He was handicapped like me." Drem had slain his wolf, and Avi had determined to slay his as well.

Susan Cooper, who writes fantasy largely based on Celtic myths, complains that Americans have increasingly taken all ritual out of their lives. That is why people instead join fraternities, sororities, the Elks, and even country clubs—which all thrive on rituals of membership. American football is the ritualization of rugby, in her mind. She fears that the newest and fastest growing new ritual imposed on our lives is that of the computer, whose complexities amount to a new language and a new way of thinking. She writes, "There are no longer any sacred festivals in the American calendar, religious or otherwise; there are only celebrations of commerce. We don't have heroes; we have celebrities." Cooper believes that young people long for rituals and that these are given them in the mysterious world of fantasy. She urges families to establish rituals, to find special ways of celebrating. And above all, she urges young people to read fantasies.

## What If My Teens Don't Like Fantasies?

So much in our culture borders on the fantastic today that fantasies seem more popular than ever, particularly with boys. Yet not everyone takes to fantasy. Some readers want only real-life, contemporary stories they can relate to without having to translate too many allegories or symbols. Often these readers are more drawn to nonfiction than to fiction in any form. Some people have difficulty believing anything they can't see.

You will notice that the bibliography has a sizable listing of fantasy books. All of them good reading for fantasy lovers. Many readers have read Madeleine L'Engle's *A Wrinkle in Time* and its sequels as younger children. John Bibee (and his Magic Bicycle series) have found good readership in ages ten through fourteen. Ursula LeGuin needs a thoughtful, mature reader to get all the nuances of her stories. John White *(Tower of Geburah)* began writing a series of five fantasies in response to his children's lament that they wished there were more Narnia Chronicles. His Gaal is a different Christ-figure from Aslan. Pat O'Shea takes the reader into the richness of Irish myths and celebrates the goodness of created life. Walter Wangerin Jr. writes a fantasy-fable that reveals the undeserved salvation of unworthy creatures. There are still more to discover. Teenage readers especially ought to try more than one of these.

Over the years, I have received a few letters from parents who have told me in one way or another that they only give their children books that contain true things. Animals don't talk, so they think it is misleading to give children books in which animals do. They believe that many of the books on my children's list, because they are not true, are not good for children. Such people may not value imagination, nor understand that they themselves have one as a natural gift. Imagination is one of the great gifts God has given to human beings. And children are the best imaginers whose gifts need to be encouraged.

I don't know any children who have read *Stuart Little* who wish he was a boy instead of a mouse. Readers love him for his integrity and fortitude. When someone says that Stuart is "just the best kind of mouse," we know they are not talking about how he looks but of what he is inside. And think of Winnie-the-Pooh! Who would want to miss out on his wisdom, merely because he is stuffed!

Jane Stephens, an English professor, tells how she used to talk with horses as a small girl. Driving along, her parents had to stop for any horse who came to the fence, so that she could talk to it. But when the television program *Mr. Ed* featured a talking horse, she was horrified. She knew that horses could talk, but they did not talk as loudly as Mr. Ed and never to a whole room full of people. And they did not say the kind of things that Mr. Ed said!

We must not make the world too small for growing up people. Life is largely understood through metaphors. We use metaphors when we say, "This is like that"; "Jack is a mad dog when he gets angry"; "The room was a beehive with people going in all directions"; "War is hell." None of these statements are literally true, but they convey a picture.

Think of the imaginative ways the Bible describes the joy of Creation: the trees clapping their hands and the morning stars singing together. Twenty-five percent of the Bible is poetry; and Job contains thirty-four verses about the glory of the crocodile and ten verses on

## If You want a Good Laugh

*Walking Across Egypt* by Clyde Edgerton

The Mitford series by Jan Karon

*A Dog Who Wouldn't Be* by Farley Mowat

*The Ghost Belonged to Me* by Richard Peck

*All Creatures Great and Small* by James Herriot

Harry Potter series by J. K. Rowling

*A Long Way from Chicago* by Richard Peck

*The Thurber Carnival* by James Thurber

*Birds, Beasts and Relatives* by Gerald Durrell

the hippopotamus. Why does God get so carried away with his own creation?

Imagination is one of the chief glories of being created human, in the image of God. No other created being can imagine things that can't be seen and then make connections between what is visible and what is invisible. For Christians, whose most important investment *is* in the invisible, the imagination is of greatest importance. No wonder *Timothy Twinge* exclaims, "This is cause for celebration! A human with imagination!" (a book by Florence Heide).

Czeslaw Milosz, the Nobel-prize-winning poet, said that the minds of Americans have been dangerously diluted by explanations. He is convinced that our educational process has left us with an inadequate view of the world. The universe has space and time and nothing else—no values, no God—and human beings end up being no different from bacteria. Our educational system is imagination-deficient, he says.

Imagination is important. C. S. Lewis calls it the organ of meaning. It is the way we sub-create, as those who are related to the Creator. We take the stuff of this world, including words, and put them together into new forms to say what is true. That is the basis of all art. Creativity is a way of noticing. Praise is also a way of noticing. Could it be that the two are connected? Grown-ups sometimes feel uncomfortable with questions, the kind of questions I have already noted that cause us to build our worldview. We want to give answers. We sometimes act as if all the answers are already in. That kills creativity.

## Why Are People Sometimes Afraid of the Imagination?

It may be because, as Eugene Peterson writes in *Reversed Thunder,*

> Explanation pins things down so we can handle and use them—obey and teach, help and guide. Imagination opens things up so that we can grow into maturity—worship and adore, exclaim and honor, follow and trust. Explanation restricts and defines and holds down; imagination expands and lets loose. Explanation keeps our feet on the ground; imagination lifts our heads into the clouds. Explanation puts us in harness; imagination catapults us into mystery. Explanation reduces life to what can be used; imagination enlarges life into what can be adored.

Surely imagination without explanation is a disaster. Imagination is only useful if it relates to reality. But maybe we need to think more about how flat explanations are without imagination. Both are needed.

When a teacher read to her class from one of C. S. Lewis's Narnia books, some parents went to the principal, complaining that they did not want their children reading about witches. One woman chastised me for encouraging people to read the Narnia Chronicles because, she said, they portrayed Jesus as an animal. I've known people to question *The Witch of Blackbird Pond* by Elizabeth George Speare, a novel about the witch-hunts in the 1600s, that won the Newbery Medal back in 1959. It would be better if parents had read *The Lion, the Witch and the Wardrobe* or *The Witch of Blackbird Pond* before making their complaints. The witch is the right symbol for the first novel, and the second novel is historically based. Certainly with the increase of satanism and interest in the occult, parents are rightly concerned about forces that might entice their children into occultic beliefs, but fear has to be balanced with knowledge. Don't judge books you haven't read yourself.

Which brings up the question of Harry Potter, the J. K. Rowling series of seven books about a boy attending a school for wizards—a series that has proven so attractive to children, teens, and even some parents that readers are undaunted by a 700-page book. Some parental response to these books made the front pages of magazines and newspapers, talk shows and conversations over dinner. Often the people most upset had one thing in common: They had not read the books. Their response was based on hearsay. Many of these people object on the basis of their faith. The fact that they haven't read them, and still speak so vociferously, has regrettably made them look foolish.

The problem with the Harry Potter books was exacerbated by an email sent out by *The Onion*, a satirical newspaper published on www.theonion.com. *The Onion* uses invented "information" and invented names in its outrageous stories (stories about obese people winning million dollar lawsuits against Hershey's, etc.), and this one was composed to make fun of the fears voiced by

## Mother/(Younger) Daughter Read Alouds

Austin Family or Times series by
    Madeleine L'Engle
*Anne of Green Gables* by L. M.
    Montgomery
*Sound of Chariots* by Mollie Hunter
*The Ark* by Margot Benary-Isbert
*The Root Cellar* by Janet Lunn
*Magic Circle* by Donna Jo Napoli
*A String in the Harp* by Nancy Bond

the Christian community over Harry Potter. When this got on the Internet, some well-meaning person, not realizing it was a hoax, sen it far and wide. Those receiving it added religious warnings and sent i to an even wider circle of people. For those who had read the books it was an obvious bit of tomfoolery; for those who had not read them it was a red flag. The email, full of inaccuracies, was far more offensiv to Christian truth than the books it was criticizing. It quoted fictiona children by name with such outrageous state ments as, "The Harry Potter books showed m that magic is real, something I can learn an use right now, and that the Bible is nothing bu boring lies." That Christians grabbed at it an spread it all over the country (I received th email from ten different people) says some thing about gullibility.

Having exposed the hoax, what abou Harry Potter? The books are great fun to read The author is imaginative; her characters ar well-developed; the plotline is the basic figh between good and evil. Her invention of Hog wart School for Wizards, whose motto is *Neve Tickle a Sleeping Dragon*, the game of Quidditch and the use of owls for mail-delivery service ar only a sampling of what has made the books s popular. It satisfies the love of mystery an magic in everyone. Bravery, courage, loyalt humility, goodness—these themes emerge i the books. Remember, Rowling created this as

## Father/(Younger) Son Read Alouds

*Walker's Crossing* by Phyllis Reynolds Naylor
*A Day No Pigs Would Die* by Robert Newton Peck
*Bud, Not Buddy* by Christopher Curtis
*Castaways of the Flying Dutchman* by Brian Jacques
*Redwall* by Brian Jacques
*Jim the Boy* by Tony Earley
*Where the Red Fern Grows* by Wilson Rawls
*Saint Ben* by John Fischer

parallel world (which is always part of fantasy); this one just happens t be a School for Wizards.

What about the witchcraft element? Will these books encour age the exploration of the occult? The best response to those wh question these books I found in the May/June 2000 issue of the *Hor Book Magazine*. Author Kimbra Wilder Gish, a librarian committe to Christian truth, reminds her readers that Christians believe th devil is real and take evil seriously. That alone needs to be talked abou within our families. We don't say, "Oh, demons are not real!" She cite Deuteronomy 18:9–12 where the use of divination and spirits or wiz ards is forbidden. She says these books open up an opportunity to tal about biblical truths as a family, without taking away the fun of read ing a good fantasy. She does not believe in censorship. She believes in talking about Truth and worldview. She also points out other books that have similar themes which, seen from a biblical point of view, may have implications the author did not intend—but these books have not come under such adverse scrutiny.

Gish's illustration is my favorite. She suggests we remember the story of Sleeping Beauty who is cursed to prick her finger on a spindle and die by her sixteenth birthday. The royal parents banish every spindle from the kingdom to protect their daughter. Yet on her sixteenth birthday she wanders into the castle tower and finds a dusty old spindle. Innocent and unknowingly she explores the spindle, pricks her finger and the curse comes true. Perhaps, says Gish, if Beauty has been told how dangerous spinning wheels would be for her, she might have turned back and averted the event (which of course would have eliminated the story of Sleeping Beauty!).

Although Harry Potter remains controversial, I have not yet found that the world Rowling created parallels either New Age or Eastern religion. The stories seem a clear depiction of good versus evil, but I have only read through book four. We come back to the issue of talking about what we read. One thing that is obvious in this series of seven is that Harry keeps getting older. He was eleven when the books began. With each book he is older and the story gets more complex. Should pre-teens be reading books about the older Harry? Rowling herself says that the plot darkens as the story continues. That may be a question worth asking.

For more discussion about the merits of these books, you may want to look for Connie Neal's *What's a Christian to Do With Harry Potter?* She evaluates the books much as I do. Richard Abanes' book *Harry Potter and the Bible* takes a more restrictive view. My own fears are that parents will hone in on the Harry Potter books because of their popularity and never question other books that may contain more dangerous ideas.

I am more concerned about Philip Pullman's trilogy of fantasies, *The Golden Compass, The Subtle Knife*, and *The Amber Spyglass*, which Pullman calls His Dark Materials series, if they are read uncritically. He prefers to call them stark realism, rather than fantasy. Pullman takes Milton's Paradise Lost story and turns it upside down. He takes a bold stand with the rebels against Authority. He makes no secret that he is anti-God, and in these stories he creates a universe prior to the Fall, a universe where the rules are different. The Fall, when it

*A good story always has a spiritual dimension and speaks about what is real and true.*

comes, brings freedom and maturity—as he believes is true in our world when people rebel against a tyrannical Authority (God). His well-written and engaging books are on the best-seller lists just behind the Harry Potter books. Be sure to read Barbara Hampton's excellent analysis of both Rowling and Pullman in the bibliography. These are books that reward discussion with the very kind of maturity that Pullman rejects.

## Fantasy and Spirituality

A few years ago a priest wrote an article in his diocesan newspaper in response to a question about developing a young person's spirituality. His short answer was flippant but true. "Give them A. A. Milne, the brothers Grimm, Kenneth Grahame, J. M. Barrie, C. S. Lewis, J. R. R. Tolkien, Shel Silverstein, and Ursula LeGuin . . . and get out of their way." All of these authors write imaginative fantasy. How did he dare say that? Because a good story always has a spiritual dimension and speaks about what is real and true.

The practice of questioning the story applies to fantasy as well as to other stories. If we ask questions about meaning, about truth, about intent of the fantasies we read, if we ask, "What is this story really saying?" we will know if the book has enough substance to qualify as good literature.

Good writers define reality; bad ones merely restate it. A good writer writes what he believes to be true; a bad writer puts down what he believes that his readers should believe to be true. Good writers write about the eternal questions; inferior writers deny the eternal.

## Chapter 8

# Getting Teens
# into the Bible

One of the gifts of knowing how to read is knowing what is best
to read.

ANONYMOUS

One of my professors during my freshman year in college asked class
members to prepare papers giving their personal worldview. What did
we perceive to be true and what was the basis for that perception? I
spelled mine out in detail and gave the Bible as the basis for my belief
system. My paper was returned with a note to make an appointment
to see him. Later, as he listened to my fervent assertions, he asked,
"About basing your beliefs on this book, have you read all of the
Bible?" He pointed out that it was pretty dumb to claim to believe
what a book says if you hadn't even read it.

Fortunately, for me, I had read the whole Bible—not on my
own—but because faithful parents read it daily aloud to us following
our evening meal. Still, I would have to confess that I had no clues as
to how it was put together or anything of its history.

The Bible is the most relevant and challenging book available.
By what strange misuse has it become a book to own, but not to read?
We could ask ourselves and teens, *If this is a book from God, why do
you let someone else tell you what it says?* It may be the best book

they've ever read! And its claim to be the very Word of God is awesome!

Think of how long the Bible has been around, still a bestseller to this very day. Think of its influence on our civilization. Rarely does one read a book that doesn't have a biblical allusion, and no one ever writes a letter or a check without indicating the date, which is simply the number of years since the time of Christ. Often we write dates with an AD attached; Anno Domini—the year of our Lord. No one can understand our history and even the prevailing culture without knowing the roots from which it has come.

In 1350 a college student at Oxford, named John Wycliffe, risked his life to translate the Bible from the Latin into English so that the common people could read it. Subsequently, many people died for the right to read and preserve the book. Today in third world countries those who have been denied access to this book snatch up copies as quickly as they are produced.

## The Bible As Literature

Only 10 percent of the Bible is written as the logical presentation of abstract ideas. Those are the epistles, or letters, included in the New Testament. These powerful letters explain not only what Christians believe but the lifestyle of those who are believers. The people who wrote these communications intended that they be read the way any letter is read—from beginning to end in one sitting. Taking a phrase or a sentence or two from a letter is hardly a way to understand its message.

Four books of the Bible—Matthew, Mark, Luke, John—give the story of Jesus' life and what he taught. What can you know about who Jesus was without the story from the gospel? Secular scholars continue to publish books on the search for the historical Jesus, but they end up having to refer to the gospels. Too many teens are in the third grade when it comes to understanding about God, Jesus, and the Holy Spirit, even though they may be seniors in high school.

The rest of the Bible contains love stories, drama, history, poetry, and parables, with humanity and truth presented as realistically as in any of the world's greatest literature. It is filled with stories, poems, visions, and letters. It contains more than most people realize.

To say that the Bible is literature, or that it is imaginative, is not to say that it is fictional rather than historical and factual. To say that it is literature is to say that it needs to be read. Too many people take bits and pieces from the Bible and never think of reading the books within it. We don't read anything else that way.

While it is more than literature, the Bible is certainly a model of the finest literature. In terms of the use of language, it is a masterpiece. On every level from word choice and sentence structure to larger units of composition, the Bible is a delight in literary craftsmanship. This alone could convince me that it is inspired by the Spirit. Is it possible that the artistic craftsmanship of the Bible tells us something important about God? Is it not significant that a book we regard as sacred is not a dull book but an interesting one?

Literature presents human experience. The Bible does this in profound ways. It tells stories. In terms of reality, it tells the truth. Philip Yancey remarks that a Jeremiah can end up in a pit; a saint named John can end up in a lonely exile on Patmos. How things worked out for Hosea are quite unclear: Why the Holy God told this man to marry a harlot raises all kinds of questions. The fact that Job had many good things at the end of his life hardly erases the excruciating loss of loved ones along the way.

And as for adventure, mystery, rescue, suspense, pageantry, celebration, heroes, and villains, the Bible has plenty of them. The story of Paul's journey to Rome aboard a ship in the storm (Acts 27–28) grips the imagination. In the Old Testament, one man's large family was given hospitality in Egypt and multiplied into a great nation. The story of their exodus into a promised land is one of the most significant stories of history.

One night, after we had finished reading about Joseph's being kidnapped by his brothers, sold into Egypt, and later saving his family from famine, our little boy sighed and said, "I like God. He likes adventure." Indeed, God is the greatest adventurer of all.

Some people do not like thinking of the Bible as literature, almost as if that would take away its sacredness. "Sacredness" sometimes

## If You're Facing Death and Grief

*Bridge to Terabithia* by Katherine Paterson
*Walk Two Moons* by Sharon Creech
*I Heard the Owl Call My Name* by Margaret Craven
*A String in the Harp* by Nancy Bond
*Sound of Chariots* by Mollie Hunter
*The Wanderer* by Sharon Creech
*After the Dancing Days* by Margaret Rostkowski
*Yesterday's Child* by Sonia Levitin
*Memory* by Margaret Mahy
*Death Be Not Proud* by John Gunther
*Missing May* by Cynthia Rylant

makes a thing untouchable. People use its sacredness as an excuse not to read it. The Bible is meant to be read and understood. It covers subjects that are basic and enduring in our human experience—God, nature, love, relationships, death, evil, guilt, salvation, family life, judgment, and forgiveness. Getting teens into it will help them understand themselves and the world better.

## How Can We Get Our Teens Into the Bible?

First, we can help them understand how the Bible is put together. It is a collection of books. It is a library of books, in a sense. The big picture of this "library" is the story of human beings and how God sets out to rescue them from the disaster of their disobedience in the Garden of Eden. In the course of time God chose one man, Abraham, to become the Father of what would become the Jewish nation. Abraham was really the first Jew. (These people were called Hebrews before the children of Judah were in captivity in Babylon. The word Jew is likely a shortened version of Judah—probably a derogatory name.) To Abraham God revealed truth about himself so that he could pass it on to the rest of mankind. The Old Testament is the history of Abraham's family, how it became a nation of people, how they responded to God in obedience or disobedience. It is a story of God's patience and love—until the time was right for God to send the Savior into the world.

I distinctly remember how helpful it was to me as a young person to have someone take the Table of Contents of the Bible and show me its structure. (Up until then I never thought of the Bible as even having a table of contents; I thought you could only find your way if you memorized the books of the Bible!) What I was shown was something like the chart on the next page.

That simple exercise gave me a useful handle on a book that seemed mysterious and holy to me. It opened the way for me to understand it and use it in my life. We think our teens know more

### There's Spiritual Strength in These

*Joni* by Joni Eareckson

*The Hobbit* and the sequels by J. R. R. Tolkien

*North to Freedom* by Ann Holm

*The Book of the Dun Cow* by Walter Wangerin Jr.

*Bud, Not Buddy* by Christopher Curtis

*Saint Ben* by John Fischer

Zion Chronicle and Covenant series by Bodie Thoene

*Roll of Thunder* and sequels by Mildred Taylor

*Journey through the Night* by Anne DeVries

*She Said Yes* by Misty Bernall

than they sometimes do. Some Sunday schools no longer teach the books of the Bible by rote to children. Teens may be taught to revere this book, but may wonder as one neighbor asked me, "Where does one begin in a book like this?"

The gospels in the New Testament are obviously the most relevant place to begin. They tell the reader who Jesus is and what he said about himself, about us, about religious people, about faith. Why did he die? Was that the end of the story? Then the story of how the Christian church began is told in Acts.

Increasingly, as our culture moves away from biblical mooring with God as the center, the book of Genesis becomes an important piece in understanding the good news about Jesus. When many gods are accepted, when the possibility that we are all gods is introduced, when evolutionary theories are everywhere from school rooms to

**The Books of the Old Testament**

*God Establishes a Nation:*
*(The Pentatuch)*
  Genesis
  Exodus
  Leviticus
  Numbers
  Deuteronomy
*The History Books of the Jews:*
  Joshua
  Judges
  Ruth
  I & II Samuel
  I & II Kings
  I & II Chronicles
  Ezra
  Nehemiah
  Esther
*Poetry:*
  Job
  Psalms
  Proverbs
  Ecclesiastes
  Song of Songs

*Major Prophets:*
  Isaiah
  Jeremiah
  Lamentations
  Ezekiel
  Daniel
*Minor Prophets:*
  Hosea
  Joel
  Amos
  Obadiah
  Jonah
  Micah
  Nahum
  Habakkuk
  Zephaniah
  Haggai
  Zechariah
  Malachi

**The Books of the New Testament**

*The Gospels:*
  Matthew
  Mark

  Luke
  John
*History:*
  Acts of the Apostles
*Paul's Letters:*
  Romans
  I & II Corinthians
  Galatians
  Ephesians
  Phillipians
  Colossians
  I & II Thessalonians
  I & II Timothy
  Titus
  Philemon
*General Letters:*
  Hebrews
  James
  I & II Peter
  I, II & III John
  Jude
*Apocalypse:*
  The Revelation

museums, it is necessary to go back to the revelation of the Beginning and see who God really is and why we need a savior. The Old Testament does reveal the God against whom we have sinned.

## How to Read the Bible with Teens

We read the Bible like we read any other book. We read it for what it says, and then we ask questions. You can ask questions about the literary style: Is this narrative, poetry, history, or teaching? That helps you understand how to read and what you are reading.

Three basic sets of questions will open up what the text is saying and make it relevant to life.

1. What does it say? Make observations about what you are reading. What are the facts? Ask, Who? When? Where? What?
2. What does it mean? Interpret the meaning or significance of what you have read. Ask, Why? How?
3. What does it mean to me? What can I learn from this? How does what I have read affect the way I think, act, or believe?

More than listening to other people telling them what the Bible says, teens need to read it themselves and discuss it. The best place to start this is in your home, maybe at your dinner or breakfast table. If you get teens (and yourself) in the habit of asking these questions of the Bible, the Scriptures will not only come alive, but become part of life. These questions are essentially the same questions a student should ask of any text, whether history or geography or whatever.

This works! Start early, when your children are still pliable. Make it something your family does. We called it "spiritual dessert." We began with the gospel of Mark, read a short passage. Everyone at the table had to ask a question of the person next to him, and answer one, too, as it became their turn. That means everyone has to listen. Someone might use your question before your turn came! Avoid questions that can be answered by yes or no because they are often too easy unless a *why?* is added.

Younger children will ask simple fact questions: Where was the blind man when he met Jesus? Soon the older children will begin with questions of interpretation: What does this mean? Why did Jesus do it that way? You will probably have to ask the application questions, especially in the beginning, since they are the hardest to ask and to answer. Don't make this a prolonged event that makes the family restless. Little by little, each time you do this, the children around your table are building a storehouse of biblical information and insight. Move on next to the book of Acts to see how the church began.

Children like rituals; they like things their family does together, even older teens. Make this a fun time in family life, not a "heavy" time. Have no agenda other than finding out what the text says. No preaching allowed. After all, whose book is this anyway? Can the Holy Spirit, our real teacher, use a simple family gathering like this to our good and God's glory?

You will be amazed at the truth you will be able to discuss as a family. Technically this is called the inductive method. Ask, don't tell. The answers are found in the text; that's the rule. The purpose is to find out what the passage is saying. Studies show that people forget about 90 percent of what they hear, but remember about 90 percent of what they discover for themselves. The goal is not to make quiz-club winners, but to have children who understand truth. When teens find they can understand the Bible, it is easier for them to read it on their own.

## If You're Intrigued by the Indian Subcontinent

*Shiva's Fire* by Suzanne Fisher Staples
*Shabanu* by Suzanne Fisher Staples
*Homeless Bird* by Gloria Whelan
*Kingfishers Catch Fire* by Rumer Godden
*Kim* by Rudyard Kipling
*River* by Rumer Godden

## It's Foundational Truth: The Basis of Everything Else

Even from a totally secular point of view, our children ought to know what is in the Bible, because it is foundational for our whole value system. It has always seemed strange to me that those who claim so passionately to believe it often know so little of its contents.

Let's not let our kids be like contestants on the *Jeopardy!* show who avoid the biblical category until all the other categories are finished. We want them to know who Abraham is and why we refer to Solomon's wisdom, or why Israel and Judah separated from each other, or why Daniel was in Babylon. And above all, not ignorant of the marvelous evangel the angels heralded to shepherds one night on a Judean hillside!

# Chapter 9

# Encourage
# the Best in Books

I was always told that I should read *The Odyssey*. It popped up in small doses in English and Latin textbooks as I was growing up. But somehow I never got around to the whole thing until I was forty-six years old. I gave myself the assignment to read *The Odyssey* (Rouse's translation) all the way through from the beginning to end. Do you know why *The Odyssey* has lasted for nearly three thousand years? Because it is a simply marvelous story. Why did people keep telling me that I ought to read it so that I could be an educated person? I can't imagine anyone who had ever really read it, telling someone else to read it because it was good for him. Read it because it's one of the best stories you'll ever read. Read it because it's one of the best stories I ever read.

KATHERINE PATERSON

## Reading the Tried and True

If you are like me, you probably feel like you didn't read enough while you were growing up—that you missed some good stuff. At least that is the way I react when I look at reading lists and book reviews. That's why being a parent is so wonderful. You get to catch up on the good things you missed. I had never read much of Charles Dickens, other than what I was assigned at school and in a university course. When we made a commitment to read aloud as a family, we included *David Copperfield*, *A Tale of Two Cities*, and *Oliver Twist*. Sharing those books as a family brought a dimension I hadn't counted on. We were all interested in the same people, and there is nothing "mere" about the characters in the tried-and-true books. We didn't sigh or groan or read against our will—not one of us. It was like entering another world every time we opened the book.

A really good book hypnotizes the reader so that he or she *wants* to read it. The writer gives us words and ideas that are like chocolates; you eat one and want to have some more. That's why I respond to the tried-and-true books (listed in the bibliography) for the same reason that Paterson encourages people to read *The Odyssey*. If a book lasts beyond a generation, it is guaranteed to be a good read.

For over a hundred and fifty years the exciting plot of *The Last of the Mohicans* has kept readers on the edges of their chairs. Suspense, pursuit, captivity, rescue, Indian lore—all masterfully woven into this tale by James Fenimore Cooper. Daphne Du Maurier's *Rebecca* still haunts the young women who read her story. Something about the mystery surrounding the death of Maxim de Winter's beautiful first wife tingles the spine while still allowing the reader to enjoy the magnificent estate of Manderley—a dream world as enchanting today as when it was first written.

My heart responds warmly to what Anna Quindlen writes about *A Tale of Two Cities,*

> Simply by words, words that would always be the same, only the reader different each time, so that today, or next year, or a hundred years from now, someone could pick up *A Tale of Two Cities*, turn to the last page and see that same final sentence, that coda that Dickens first offered readers in 1859: "It is a far, far better thing that I do, than I have ever done; it is a far, far better rest that I go to, than I have ever known."

Dickens' two sentences—his first "It was the best of times, it was the worst of times" and that one last sentence Quindlen quotes—evoke the rich memories of a moving story, beautifully told. The film version, however riveting it proves, cannot match the reading of the book. What memorable characters are Charles Darnay and Sydney Carton! Some characters we read about evaporate quickly from our memory. Others will stay with us all our lives.

Don't shy away from these classics in reading aloud with your family. After Dickens' account of the French Revolution in *A Tale of Two Cities*, read Victor Hugo's account of revolutionary France in *Les Miserables*. It's long, but enthralling. Jean Valjean is imprisoned for nineteen years for stealing a loaf of bread to feed his starving sister. This book is considered one of the best stories of all times.

Books like Lloyd C. Douglas's *Magnificent Obsession* and *The Robe* have a goodness to them that will stay in a teen's heart for years to come. For all the family you can't lose with Charles and Mary Lamb's *Tales from Shakespeare* written in 1807. It's a wonderful retelling of the stories that make up Shakespeare's plays and a very good way to let your children in on the bard's plotlines. It's good for any age.

There are many great writers: Rumer Godden, Elizabeth Goudge, Alan Paton, Harper Lee, and hundreds of others. Our list isn't complete—just enough to give a taste of lasting literature. Don't even think of them as classics (although they are that!), for that might intimidate some readers. If you found a chest full of buried gold, you wouldn't avoid it because it's old. Reading tried-and-true books gives us immediate rapport with a great host of other readers, who, on seeing you reading a certain book, might say, "Oh, you, too? I thought I was the only one!"

Most of the tried-and-true books listed in the bibliography are for mid- to late-teen readers, because they are essentially adult books. Reading them too soon can cheat readers from appreciating them. However, when these books were first written they were quickly purloined by young adult readers.

## Mother/(Older) Daughter Read Alouds

*Christy* by Catherine Marshall
*I Capture the Castle* by Dodie Smith
Mitford series by Jan Karon
*A Tree Grows in Brooklyn* by Betty Smith
*Till We Have Faces* by C. S. Lewis
*In This House of Brede* by Rumer Godden
Zion Chronicle and Covenant series by Bodie Thoene

## Why Not Go On an Adventure?

Where did I learn to love Alaska and dream of adventure whenever I picture it in my mind? Surely it began with meeting the marvelous dog Buck in *The Call of the Wild* in Jack London's story set in the gold rush days. Using a contemporary setting, Gary Paulsen also writes

## Father/(Older) Son Read Alouds

*Breaking of Ezra Riley* by John Moore

*Shane* by Jack Schaefer

*The Chosen* by Chaim Potok

*Northwest Passage* (and others) by
    Kenneth Roberts

*Riding for the Brand* (and others) by
    Louis L'Amour

*Tales of Tahitian Waters* (and others)
    by Zane Grey

*A Bell for Adano* by John Hersey

*Eric Liddell: Pure Gold* by David
    McCasland

Lord of the Rings trilogy by J. R. R.
    Tolkien

about Alaska in *Dogsong,* a Newbery Honor book. Ivan Southall writes stories set in contemporary Australia, another frontier country. His characters confront the challenges of an untamed land; his stories are wonderful tales of human endurance and enterprising action.

When a librarian friend sent me a copy of *The Outlaws of Sherwood* by Robin McKinley, I could hardly put it down—I think it is the best retelling of the popular Robin Hood legend I have ever read. And no teen should become an adult before first enjoying Robert Louis Stevenson's *Kidnapped* and *Treasure Island.* They are two of the most gripping tales ever written. So many books are worth reading more than once, and many require face tissues at some point of the story.

Others make you laugh. Our family read James Herriot's *All Creatures Great and Small* aloud together on a trip through England and sometimes feared we might be thrown out of our lodgings because we had laughed so loudly into the night. Look for others in this category. Robert Siegel's *Whalesong* seems to contain all the wonderful mystery of the sea as he writes from the point of view of the whale. These books are now a trilogy.

## Mystery Stories

Many younger teens get into reading mysteries through the Hardy Boys series or Nancy Drew's adventures. (For those who haven't met her yet, Nancy Drew has been brought up to date. She now has a luxuriant swing of blond hair, wears designer jeans, and has even discovered kissing. A cadre of writers have been churning out updated versions during the late 1980s. She is no longer Nancy Drew.) The predictability of the characters in these stories soon led mystery lovers to look for others.

The appeal of mysteries will last well into adulthood when a reader discovers such writers as Agatha Christie, Dorothy Sayers, Josephine Tey, and Ellis Peters (who writes the engaging Brother Cadfael mysteries), Tony Hillerman and Dick Francis. Sir Arthur Conan Doyle's *The Hound of the Baskervilles* is a classic mystery. Mysteries aren't usually the best read-aloud books, although you might try one on audio-tape and listen on a trip somewhere.

## Science Fiction

Escape to hair-raising tales and other worlds with Ray Bradbury, John Christopher, Ursula LeGuin, C. S. Lewis, Jules Verne, and H. G. Wells. Be sure to evaluate the "universes" created by these authors. For example, compare what C. S. Lewis creates in Perelandra with H. G. Wells' *The War of the Worlds.* Mysteries and science fiction keep you reading carefully, examining the clues, and asking questions. It is a good exercise, as well as enjoyment. Your teen may want to try Orson Scott Card's *Ender's Game* or Stephen Donaldson's *Thomas Covenant Unbeliever.*

## Western Stories

Some of these make gripping read-alouds, and are always good to recommend to a teen, especially males. Louis L'Amour, a prolific and fine writer, gives us some wonderful tales, with a variety of settings. Try his books on the Sackett family. *The Virginian* by Owen Wister is by now a classic. A. B. Guthrie's *The Big Sky* is the first book in a six-book series that has a Pulitzer prize, recommended for readers in late teens. Zane Grey also has some hair-raising winners. We read *Thirty Thousand on the Hoof* with our family while traveling in Arizona.

## Historical Fiction: The Real Stuff of Life

Historical fiction is often more real than "contemporary realism." That is, it isn't based on faddish interests or a tendency to make reality bizarre. It must be true on two levels: It must be true to its setting and time, and have true-to-life characters.

Historical fiction is anchored in the past but peopled with characters the reader can relate to even though continents and circumstances are vastly different. People are the same in every age, at least on the inside, with the same dreams and fears and hopes. The plots in historical fiction may sweep across time and events that are new to the reader, but the people and the circumstances will be familiar. The people are like us or like someone we know. This allows the writer to plot the story in the past and people it with characters that we can identify with. Teens who have read Joan Blos's *A Gathering of Days* or Elizabeth George Speare's *The Bronze Bow* or *The Witch of Blackbird Pond* will know exactly what I mean.

Good historical fiction gives a fascinating "read." Esther Forbes' *Johnny Tremain* may be the book that could best introduce readers to this category. Leon Garfield's books give a realistic picture of life in eighteenth-century London, and his characters are fascinating. Look for his *Shakespeare Stories*. I love Esther Hautzig's *The Endless Steppe*, about a Polish girl exiled to Siberia. More mature readers will enjoy John Hersey's *The Wall*. Irene Hunt's *Across Five Aprils* makes the struggles of the Civil War seem more personal and tragic. What a terrible thing to have members of the same family divided by loyalty to different sides of a war. It is interesting to compare this book with Bruce Catton's nonfiction about the Civil War, books very popular with teenage boys.

Kenneth Roberts' novels, set during the Revolutionary War, have been family read-alouds for us. Roberts' careful historical research and strong writing make you care about his characters. Most of his books are about the bravery and daring of the early colonists. But I had never thought about what it would be like to be a loyalist during the Revolutionary War until we read his *Oliver Wiswell*. It is a wonderfully compelling look at the rag-tag army of the colonists and the problems facing the nonrevolutionaries.

Some historical fiction picks up more recent events. Readers are sure to enjoy Sonia Levitin's *The Return*, a story of an Ethiopian Jewish girl airlifted during the 1984 Operation Moses rescue mission.

Historical fiction must be one of the most satisfying kinds of writing to do because there is so much of it. It certainly is satisfying to read. What we have listed for you in the bibliography will whet your appetite for more.

## Biography and Nonfiction

The lives of other people are not only intriguing but give us concrete examples of courage, heroism, sorrow, and success. Such books show us a broad sweep of human lives, and their appeal is ageless. Virginia Hamilton's *Anthony Burns: The Defeat and Triumph of a Fugitive Slave* is one such story. Philip Hallie's *Lest Innocent Blood Be Shed* is a true story of a miracle of goodness in a small French Heugonot village vhere two pastors save hundreds of Jews. Both stories have a similar heme, but are set in far different worlds.

Biographies are always enriching reading experiences; they do omething special for their readers—encourage, motivate, inspire. We iave chosen stories of people our typical reader would not normally neet. For one thing, reading these books will widen a reader's undertanding of people and ways of behaving. Their stories give us new riends, people whom we think we surely must know by the end of he book. Many leaders point to the reading of biographies as their nost influential exposure to books—reading that gives inspiration, ncouragement, and motivation.

Several of the biographies (or autobiographies) in our bibliograhy center on events surrounding World War II, the Holocaust, and he Nazi prison camps. Corrie ten Boom's *The Hiding Place* has been one of the most inspirng of these. Elie Wiesel's *Night* is a must read or adults—young and old. Other biographies enter on the African-American experience. *Black Like Me* by John Howard Griffin tells a eal story about prejudice; Haley's *The Autoiography of Malcolm X* is a "shocker," but it rticulates the rage prejudice produces.

Your family will howl with laughter over ome other nonfiction works, like the fun of *The Thurber Carnival.* You'll love meeting Gerald Durrell's zany family in *Birds, Beasts ind Relatives,* and you'll discover courage and aith by living through Joni Eareckson's recovry after a diving accident that left her paralyzed in *Joni.*

Nonfiction exposes us to people and to acts. Everything that is not fiction (except oetry) falls in this category. We have not made lengthy nonfiction istings in our bibliography inasmuch as these books are perhaps the asiest kind of good reading to find and to evaluate.

## The War in the Pacific Theater

*Eric Liddell: Pure Gold* by David McCasland
*Under the Blood-Red Sun* by Graham Salisbury
*Farewell to Manzanar* by Houston and Houston
*Eternal Spring of Mr. Ito* by Sheila Garrigue
*A Town Like Alice* by Nevil Shute
*Friends and Enemies* by Louanne Gaeddert

## ;ing a Word-Song

'oetry is verbal music. It is more than doggerel that rhymes. It gives is the feel and shape of words. We understand the purpose and feel of metaphors and see things we never saw before. When giving gifts to your children, remember to include poetry books.

Many people first met poetry in nursery rhymes, most of which seem nonsensical, but when they were first written, many nursery rhymes had political implications.

> Sing a song of sixpence,
> A pocketful of rye,
> Four and twenty blackbirds
> Baked in a pie.

It doesn't make much sense, but its singing-ness and rhyme make it fun to say. Dr. Seuss has written books full of outrageous rhymes and adventures that have probably delighted your children as they grew up. His book *Oh, the Places You'll Go* is a great book for a graduating senior who will find he has not outgrown Seuss after all.

Poems are meant to be read aloud because of the way that words rise and fall and flow and pause and echo. My husband's father liked poetry and often read it aloud to the family at the dinner table. It is no wonder, then, that when Keith went off to study engineering at the university he chose poetry for his one elective. And then he later read poetry at our family dinner table. It's contagious.

It is fun to read aloud the story poems by Henry Wadsworth Longfellow about Hiawatha and Paul Revere.

> *Listen my children, and you shall hear*
> *Of the midnight ride of Paul Revere,*
> *On the eighteenth of April, in Seventy-five;*
> *Hardly a man is now alive*
> *That remembers that famous day and year.*

Later, perhaps in an English class, some student will encounter Edna St. Vincent Millay's descriptive poetry and begin to see the world differently. Some teens are prompted to write poetry themselves after reading this:

> *O world, I cannot hold thee close enough!*
> *Thy winds, thy wide gray skies!*
> *Thy mists that roll and rise!*
> *Thy woods, this autumn day, that ache and sag*
> *And all but cry with color!*

Robert Frost is almost everyone's favorite. A book of his poems for your own family library is a good investment.

> *Whose woods are these I think I know*
> *His house is in the village, though;*
> *He will not see me stopping here*
> *To watch his woods fill up with snow.*

Sometimes teachers spoil poetry by making students go on a deep search for hidden meanings. We had a woods exactly like the one Robert Frost describes above in his poem, "Stopping by Woods on a Snowy Evening." When we drove from our farm into the village on snowy evenings, we would chant "Whose woods are these I think I know . . ." Then our son studied the poem in a literature class and was told there were all sorts of hidden meanings. It reminds me of a poem Jean Little wrote called "After English Class":

> *I used to like "Stopping by Woods on a Snowy Evening."*
> *I liked the coming darkness,*
> *The jingle of harness bells, breaking—and adding to—the stillness,*
> *The gentle drift of snow . . .*
> *But today, the teacher told us what everything stood for.*
> *The woods, the horse, the miles to go, the sleep—*
> *They all have "hidden meanings."*
> *It's grown so complicated now that,*
> *Next time I drive by,*
> *I don't think I'll bother to stop.*

On Easter morning try reading John Updike's "Seven Stanzas at Easter" to your older teens—or better still, have one of them read it. Here are some of the stanzas from the poem:

> *Make no mistake if he rose at all*
> *it was as his body;*
> *if the cells' dissolution did not reverse, the molecules reknit,*
> *the amino acids rekindle,*
> *the church will fall . . .*
> *Let us not mock God with metaphor*
> *analogy, sidestepping transcendence;*
> *making of the event a parable, a sign painted in the faded*
> *credulity of earlier ages:*
> *let us walk through the door.*

*The stone is rolled back, not papier-mâché,*
*not a stone in a story,*
*but the vast rock of materiality that in the slow grinding*
*of time will eclipse for each of us*
*the wide light of day.*

It is unlikely that a family will check poetry out of the library to read. Poetry is better left just sitting around the room waiting for someone to pick it up. Don't be too macho or too sophisticated to do it—and listen to your own voice reading it.

If you are considering putting books of poetry in your personal library or on birthday lists, here some suggestions:

*The Best Loved Poems of the American People,* selected by Hazel Felleman, is a thick book, full of favorites of all kinds—serious, humorous, and classic.

*The Oxford Book of Children's Verse,* edited by Peter Opie and Iona Opie, is still one of my favorites. It is really a book for all ages, as is *The Oxford Book of Children's Verse in America,* edited by Donald Hall.

Add to your personal collection *Polishing the Petoskey Stone,* a collection of contemporary Christian poetry by Luci Shaw and *Otherwise: New & Selected Poems* by Jane Kenyon.

Words, words, words—wonderful words. May your family's heart be fed with the richness of "a word fitly spoken."

## Chapter 10

# A Word for the College-Bound

I am the very model
   of a modern Major-General,
I've information vegetable,
   animal and mineral,
I know the kings of England,
   and I quote the fights historical,
From Marathon to Waterloo,
   in order categorical;
I'm very well acquainted
   too with matters mathematical,
I understand equations,
   both the simple and quadratical,
About binomial theorem
   I'm teeming with a lot o' news—
With many cheerful facts about
   the square of the hypotenuse.

Thus sings the Major-General in Gilbert and Sullivan's comic opera *The Pirates of Penzance* about the excessive information he has collected. He later finds "these cheerful facts" are void of military strategy for the battle. Military strategy may well depend, however, on the cheerful facts he knows.

Today's university students seem to want the details of military strategy. They want to learn quickly all they need to know to get a good job and earn a good salary. Once upon a time students went to college to get an education instead of a job. The result of this change in purpose makes for some amusing and amazing stories coming from universities.

One professor said that he had not found a single student in the Los Angeles area, whether in college or high school, who could tell him when World War II was fought. Few knew how many senators Nevada or Oregon have in Congress. A college junior thought Toronto must be in Italy; and another junior at the University of California thought that Washington, D.C., must be in Washington state. Only two could identify the place in history held by people like Thomas Jefferson or Ben Franklin. On and on it goes. Stories like these may make your teens feel pretty smart!

In general students know a great deal; they share a lot of information among themselves. The problem is that what they know doesn't seem to relate to history or literature or any kind of intergenerational information.

Sooner or later as we go on to school we find that there is a body of information that every person in the land ought to know because it is good and because other people know it. That is called *cultural literacy*. It is a body of information that allows people to communicate with each other. The information is assumed. Newspapers and books are written on the basis of this body of information. For instance, a casual reference may be made to the meeting of Ulysses S. Grant and Robert E. Lee in Appomattox Courthouse, Virginia, in 1865. Who these men are and why they are meeting should be part of a teen's store of information. Everything doesn't always have to be explained when people have this common body of information.

Professor E. D. Hirsch has tried to organize what should be included in "that body of knowledge." At the back of his book *Cultural Literacy: What Every American Needs to Know*, Hirsch has a list of 5000 essential names, phrases, dates, and concepts. This, he claims, is background information that writers and speakers assume their

## Surviving High School Life

*The Veritas Project: Hangman's Curse* by Frank Peretti
*She Said Yes* by Misty Bernall
*Body of Christopher Creed* by Carol Plum-Ucci
*Diary of a Teenage Girl* by Melody Carlson
*Nothing but the Truth* by Avi

audience already has. Even if a student has good reading skills, he or she has little chance of entering the American mainstream, says Hirsch, without knowing what a silicon chip is, or when the Civil War was fought.

Test your teen's cultural literacy. How much do they know about the following?

The Alamo
1492
Billy the Kid
carpetbagger
El Greco
lame duck
gamma rays
nom de plume

There are 5000 more items in Hirsch's list, enough to intimidate those who assume that they are literate. Why do I mention this? Because cultural literacy is related to *reading*, and that is why parents should make certain their children are readers. Not so that your children can spout off a list of information like egocentric prigs but so that they can understand and communicate with the larger world in which they live.

Cultural literacy is especially important for college-bound teens (to whom this chapter specifically applies). Hopefully, it is important for everyone. The crux of the matter is not whether people go to college but whether they read. Many college graduates are essentially culturally illiterate by Hirsch's definition; others who read but have never entered the door of a college are not. People who read put into their lives more understanding than they realize. Serious teens need to make picking up a book and reading for pleasure (and for information) a regular habit—even when school assignments seem to weigh them down.

## What Should Be in a Teen's "Reservoir"?

No two people include exactly the same titles when listing books that all young people should know. Many colleges and universities have their own lists made up for incoming freshmen. The National Council of Teachers of English publishes an enormous book called *The College and Adult Reading List*, covering 700 titles or more, an overwhelming volume to encounter. The American Library Association prints a short pamphlet of books for college-bound students. Don't take some of these long lists too seriously. It could be that even the people who put them together have not read everything on the list.

Here, culled from the lists, are those most often mentioned. These books make up a good place to start some catch-up reading. Reading them aloud as a family, or getting an audio-tape from the library when you are going to be driving long distances may be a good way to begin. Parents, too, get a chance to play "catch-up" this way.

1.  *The Mother Goose Rhymes.* Don't laugh. Today's teens do not know basic nursery rhymes. One night on the televison program *Who Wants To Be a Millionaire*, a university student contestant had to use two of his lifelines to get help to answer this question:

    > Little Jack Horner sat in a corner, eating his Christmas pie,
    > He stuck in his thumb and pulled out what...?

    Four choices were given him. He simply didn't know. I was recounting this as a humorous happening the next day at lunch for college students, and none of them knew the answer either. They couldn't see why I was so surprised. I thought it was part of a child's heritage—at least it used to be.

2.  *The basic fairy tales.* "Cinderella," "Little Red Riding Hood," "Sleeping Beauty," "Puss in Boots," "Jack and the Beanstalk," "The Three Bears," "Chicken Little," and more.

3.  *Aesop's Fables.* These animal fables are almost universally known in Western culture. Remember "The Boy Who Cried Wolf"?

4.  *The Bible.* Certainly you should know the more familiar stories—Abraham, Moses, David, Isaac, Ruth, Esther, the parables, etc. Robert Carlsen of the University of Iowa writes "These stories are all inextricably woven through Western literature and philosophy. Furthermore, the rhythm of biblical language has had a significant impact on the rhythm of our language as a whole."

---

[3] I have been most influenced by the list composed by G. Robert Carlsen, Professor and Head of English at the University of Iowa and author of *Books and the Teen-Age Reader.*

5. *The Greek myths.* These are terribly confusing—all these gods and goddesses and their relationships. As a quick introduction to what mythology is about, I recommend an old book that is still in print: *The Golden Fleece and the Heroes Who Lived Before Achilles* by Padraic Colum. Have it on your shelf for reference.

6. *The Iliad* and *The Odyssey.* These are stories of the Trojan War and Ulysses and of his long voyage home. Look for some simplified translations in your library. These two stories are good read-alouds, and teens should know at least the plotline, but remember the Katherine Paterson quote in Chapter 9. We listened to these on audio tapes from the library when we took a trip to another city.

7. *Oedipus Rex* by Sophocles is one of the best-remembered Greek tragedies. Most of the lists have Greek tragedies on them. Watch for this play on stage or on television. Or read a synopsis of this play so that teens will know what someone means when they talk about an oedipal complex.

8. *Alice in Wonderland* by Lewis Carroll. It's one of the foundational books and a mighty good read too. Try reading it aloud together as a family. It was intended as a children's book, but many say it is not meant to be read until you are at least a senior in high school.

9. *Robinson Crusoe* by Daniel Defoe. This is the most enduring of the survival stories. Boys will like this story. In the unabridged edition Crusoe finds an old trunk washed ashore, and in it finds a Bible. His outlook on life is grim; his hope is depleted, and then he reads Romans 3–5 and learns how a person can become right with God. It is a wonderfully written conversion story. Suddenly the island looks very different. He is eager to share the good news with his man Friday. Although this incident is left out in the abridged editions, the advantage of the abridged book is the deletion of pages and pages of descriptions before getting to the heart of the story.

10. *Little Women* by Louisa May Alcott. An enduring family story for over a hundred years, the story of spirited Jo March and her family is a wonderful read-aloud book, especially with daughters in your family. It portrays loving, warm family relationships.

11. *Pilgrim's Progress* by John Bunyan. This book will surprise you with its pleasure. So many wonderful abridged editions exist now that can be shared as a family. Your children will probably not read this unless you make a family adventure of it. The descriptions of places along the way to the Heavenly City will become part of your family vernacular: the Slough of Despond, Vanity Fair, the Straight Road, or the Narrow Gate. John Bunyan wrote this while in Bedford prison in 1675.

12. *Don Quixote de la Mancha* by Cervantes. An abridged version of this will do. This erratic knight has become so firmly embedded in Western culture that he has even given the word *quixotic* to the English language. Besides, it is a humorous book. Don Quixote sets out to put right all the wrongs in the world. Much of the humor in the book comes from the interchanges between Don Quixote and Sancho Panza, his simple rustic squire.

13. *Gulliver's Travels* by Jonathan Swift. The two most important of Gulliver's four voyages are *Voyage to the Land of the Lilliputians* and *The Voyage to the Land of the Brobdingnags*. Literary references to this book are frequent. There's a wonderful simplified children's edition that I have given to many young teens.

14. *Shakespeare.* By the time teens becomes high school seniors, they are probably familiar with *A Midsummer Night's Dream, Romeo and Juliet,* and *The Merchant of Venice.* The tragedies you will want to read are *Julius Caesar, Macbeth, Hamlet,* and *King Lear.* If Shakespeare scares you off, get Charles and Mary Lamb's book, *Tales from Shakespeare* and read the simplified plots so that you know where the plays are going when you later read the original. Many good videos of Shakespeare's plays are also available.

15. *Uncle Tom's Cabin* by Harriet Beecher Stowe. This book was the match that ignited the Civil War and is still widely read. It makes good family reading. It's rather sentimental, but important to our history.

16. Nineteenth-century British novels. Read *David Copperfield* or *A Tale of Two Cities, Wuthering Heights, Jane Eyre,* or *Pride and Prejudice.* All of these are available on wonderful videos. Our family enjoyed reading Dickens aloud—wonderful characters that we will never forget.

17. Selected works by Mark Twain. At least *Tom Sawyer, Huckleberry Finn,* and *The Prince and the Pauper.*
18. Nineteenth-century American novels like *The Scarlet Letter, Moby Dick, The Red Badge of Courage,* and *Ethan Frome.*
19. Some European and Russian goodies like *Les Miserables* or *The Brothers Karamazov.*
20. Twentieth-century novels like the ones we have talked about in this book.

Students may be chanting "Hey, hey, ho, ho; Western Civ has got to go" at Standford University, but familiarity with these titles, even in a superficial way, is the mark of having an education.

Teens may surprise themselves by noting how many of these are already familiar, and that's to their credit. Lists like these should not bully anyone; they are simply a guide composed by mortal men and women. You do with it what you want. Sprinkled in among reading like this, teens should read some light books, just for sheer fun and relaxation.

## Reading Is Cool, Man

The biggest asset for the college-bound is the right mental attitude: Learning is fun. Studying may not be, but learning is.

While fostering that attitude, keep a dictionary handy in your house. Be quick to look up words and ideas. "Look it up" ought to be your first response when either you or your teen meets something new. We keep a dictionary near the table where we eat our meals. It is amazing how often something comes up that needs to be checked out.

### Romance, Take Two

Any book by Janette Oke
Any book by Bodie Thoene
Any book by Eugenia Price
Any book by George MacDonald
Any book by T. Davis Bunn

The most important asset for teens involves their convictions about their own value. "*You* are special because you are *you;* no one else can be who you are." Sharing books with teens, listening to their ideas, expecting them to think—all of these tell a teen that he or she has a contribution to make to the world.

In urging teens to read books, it is not that *books* are so important that they must read them. It is rather because *they* are so important that they *must* read them, because we want to make their lives as rich as possible.

# Part 2

# Book Lists to Help You Choose

## Chapter 11

# How to Use the Book Annotations

**W**e have tried to make the book evaluations user-friendly. Each review is followed by symbols that indicate the age for which the book is intended.

**ET**—Early Teens (middle school)
**MT**—Mid Teens (early high school)
**LT**—Late Teens (senior high to college)
**AA**—All Ages (good family read-alouds)

Remember, however, that many young teens read books beyond what "experts" think is their ability, and many older teens continue to reread old favorites, bringing greater maturity and insight to what they are reading.

If an asterisk (*) follows a book annotation, it means that we feel that this book should belong in a basic collection for any school library, whether it is a private, parochial, or public school library.

We didn't put recommendations with the Tried and True titles or the Nonfiction titles. The Tried and True have already stood the test of time in ways that the books in the remaining categories have not and, you will notice, we don't predict that all of them will. If you can't find the book or author you are looking for, use the index.

Happy reading! Or should we say, *Happy questioning?*

## Asking Questions

Throughout the chapters of this book, we have suggested that you learn how to ask questions. Ask, don't tell. It has been the theme song of the book because questions can open up discussion about values, about truth, about worldviews. In addition to the many questions in the text of this book, you will notice that we have added questions in the annotations to help you engage your teenage reader in conversations about specific books.

You will find questions pouring out of some books. Your family members will add their own questions to the discussion. In these books it is as if the questions ignite from the spark of the reader's mind meeting the author's words, and it makes reading together great fun.

In contrast, the issues raised in other books are so complex and overwhelming that questions don't come easily. We experience the impact of the story but feel stymied in critiquing it. You may be wondering how to develop questions of your own in these instances. Trust your instincts and intuition. Together work on the meaning of the story.

It never hurts to look at the question forming process, however. Remember the three inductive questions suggested earlier in the text: *What does it say? What does it mean? What does it mean to me?* These are the basic questions from which all the others arise.

### What Does It Say?

Sometimes this level that seems the most simple is the hardest part of questioning. We can follow the plotline but wonder if it is saying something we are missing. Stick with it. What is it saying? It is good to have the book in front of you to solve the contradictions family members may raise. Ask *What? Where? How? When? Who?* to get your facts straight. After all, you want to be fair to the author. None of us likes to be accused of saying something we haven't.

### What Does It Mean?

This second question often illumines the story. Ask *Why?* or *What is the significance of this?* If anything surprises, pleases, puzzles, or angers you, you can create a question about it. *What did the author mean by this? Why did this character act that way? Why did I dislike this character,* or *why did I admire that one?* These are the best kinds of questions for discussion of values. Remember the Pied Piper. "Is he good, bad, or both?" the Hunts wondered, and much rich conversation followed. Questions of interpretation often have multiple and sometimes contradictory answers, but your answers can be supported by what the book says. Worldview questions can add much to these discussions of meaning.

### What Does This Mean to Me?

This final question is one that makes us reach within ourselves so that we can personally evaluate the reading experience and the book. *What does this mean to me? How has it affected me? Has it changed my thinking in any way? How would I act in a similar situation?* Sometimes we will reject an author's thesis. We look at it and say, "Interesting reading, and now I understand more about a particular cultural current that is tugging on me, or now I see better why a friend's choice has saddened me. But it is not Truth."

Use our questions if they are helpful, but trust your own judgment in asking your own questions. Listen to each other. You are sure to enrich each other's lives as you do this.

And so, we invite you again to happy reading and happy questioning!

## A Note About Longer Author Reviews

Sprinkled throughout the annotations are longer examinations of several authors. Just because we have written more about them does not mean we are recommending them more highly than others. Several important writers on our list are familiar—or even famous—and so we do not give them extensive reviews. These others may be less familiar or may be more complex but nevertheless are significant for at least two reasons: The children and adolescent literature experts regard them as the very best, and they skillfully reveal their worldviews in their fiction. Therefore, it is worth our while to understand them in particular even if we treasure other books and writers more highly.

# Chapter 12

# Adventure and Suspense

AUTHOR: **Richard Adams**

TITLE: ***Watership Down* (1972)**

DESCRIPTION: Warned by a farsighted rabbit that their warren is going to be destroyed by an encroaching housing development, a group of rabbits flees into the unknown. After confronting both danger and temptation to an easy life, they find a new home but then must find female rabbits to join them. A nearby overcrowded warren might be glad to let some does go, but its dictatorial leader prevents it. The rabbits must succeed in this conflict or die out even though they have been sustained thus far by faith in their mythical god, have developed the necessary leadership qualities, and even have evolved to adapt to their dire circumstances.

RECOMMENDATION: This terrific story reads like a suspenseful epic. The rabbits are not thinly disguised humans although each has his or her own vividly drawn personality as well as a shared myth-based religion, a government, and a history. You can also read *Watership Down* as an allegory for our civilization threatened by decay, and, if you do, you will find many parallels to familiar items from Western culture to discuss, from Brer Rabbit, to the Creation story, to totalitarian dictators. **MT, LT**\*

AUTHOR: **James BeauSeigneur**

TITLE: ***In His Image* (1997)**

DESCRIPTION: First in the Christ Clone trilogy. A skeptic scientist on the expedition to examine the Shroud of Turin in 1978 makes a startling discovery—living cells! His subsequent cloning experiments using these cells result in Christopher Goodman, "the Christ Clone," whose advent sets in motion the events that bring the end of the world.

RECOMMENDATION: You should try the book if you liked the Left Behind series. While the end-times events may not toe a premillenialist's ideological line, BeauSeigneur has meticulously researched and carefully crafted a believable end of the world scenario with many surprising plot turns. However, the drama gets bogged down in BeauSeigneur's peripheral technical descriptions and analysis, especially in the subsequent volumes. Also try the Gilbert Morris's The Omega Trilogy (first title, *The Beginning of Sorrows*) if this kind of theological adventure makes you eager to read more. Comparing them can lead to some fascinating discussions. **LT**

**ET**—Early Teens
**MT**—Mid Teens
**LT**—Late Teens
**AA**—All Ages

AUTHOR: **T. Davis Bunn**
TITLE:   ***The Great Divide* (2000)**

DESCRIPTION: Marcus Glenwood, a lawyer broken by personal tragedy, makes a humble new beginning in a small North Carolina town. There he is caught up in a case of international intrigue, fueled by the human rights abuses of a Chinese *lao gai* prison factory that has suspicious ties to a multinational clothing factory in his backyard. Gloria Hall, the daughter of Marcus's new friends, has disappeared in China while investigating those abuses.

RECOMMENDATION: This book will grab you by the throat in the first paragraph and never let go. Most of the action takes place in the courtroom, yet the issues of human rights and truth, commitment and suffering, guilt and redemption have consequences far beyond those walls. Bunn explores them without being preachy. You may wonder what the title *The Great Divide* has to do with the story. Read carefully, find the references, and see if you can't come up with an answer. **LT**

AUTHOR: **Frances Hodgson Burnett**
TITLE:   ***The Lost Prince* (1915)**

DESCRIPTION: Marco Loristan and his desperately poor but proud and self-educated father crisscross Europe, working always for the redemption of their beautiful but savage country, Samavia, kept in the grip of wicked rulers for 500 years. During those 500 years a legend has circulated about Samavia's Lost Prince. Would he ever be found? With Samavia embroiled in yet another civil war, he is needed more than ever. Marco and his London street-beggar friend, the crippled Rat, are entrusted to be Bearers of the Sign of the Prince's return to the Forgers of the Sword, hidden all through Europe.

RECOMMENDATION: When Rat and his gang of street urchins first heard the story of the Lost Prince from Marco, "it made them think they saw things; it fired their blood; it set them wanting to fight for ideals they knew nothing about—adventurous things, for instance, and high and noble young princes who were full of the possibility of great and good deeds." *The Lost Prince* is that kind of book. You may find it having that same effect on you! **ET***

AUTHOR: **Sharon Creech**

TITLE: *The Wanderer* (2000)

DESCRIPTION: Thirteen-year-old Sophie prepares a sailboat with her cousins, Cody and Brian, and her three uncles for its journey across the Atlantic. As they venture off into perilous northern waters, she recalls incidents from her grandfather's life to give them all courage. Cody, always considered a cynical do-nothing, wonders what he can give them during their journey as well.

RECOMMENDATION: The journals of Sophie and Cody, which form alternate chapters, reveal that all six wanderers have much to give to and much to learn from each other. What did they discover about the ties that truly make up a family? Do you agree? **ET**

AUTHOR: **Michael Crichton**

TITLE: *The Great Train Robbery* (1975)

DESCRIPTION: Crichton, the author of *The Andromeda Strain*, reconstructs in minute detail the preparations Edward Pierce made to rob the invulnerable safe containing the gold to pay Her Majesty's soldiers fighting bravely in the Crimea.

RECOMMENDATION: *The Great Train Robbery*, as it became known to the proper Victorians hungry for scandal, provided Crichton not only an opportunity to look into an intriguing criminal's mind and methods but also a chance to examine the society in which Pierce and his accomplices worked. (Interestingly, some people in Africa today believe what some Victorians did—that having sex with a virgin would protect them from sexually transmitted diseases.) **LT**

AUTHOR: **Colin Dann**

TITLE: *The Animals of Farthing Wood* (1979)

DESCRIPTION: When their home in Farthing Wood is threatened by a new housing development, the animals (some of whom are natural enemies and some of whom move so slowly they would endanger the community) take the Oath of Common Safety so they can travel together to a wildlife refuge Toad has heard about. Toad is their guide, but Fox and Badger provide the leadership; and Owl and Kestral, the protection by scouting. They face natural dangers such as a forest fire, and man-made dangers such as highways and fox hunts, paying the high-but-necessary price to achieve their goal.

RECOMMENDATION: This is a wonderful and heartwarming story you will enjoy sharing aloud with your family. Its sequel is *In the Grip of Winter.* ET, MT, AA*

AUTHOR: **Will Hobbs**

TITLE:     ***Jason's Gold*** (1999)

DESCRIPTION: ALA Best Book. Fifteen-year-old Jason risks the little he has to strike it rich in the Yukon gold rush of 1897. What he gains is far more than gold.

RECOMMENDATION: Filled with come-to-life historical detail, this book is a fine coming-of-age adventure. Look for the sequel, *Down the Yukon.* ET

AUTHOR: **Ann Holm**

TITLE:     ***North to Freedom*** (1974)

DESCRIPTION: Twelve-year-old David cannot figure out why the guard at the prison camp where he has lived his whole life has engineered his escape. Now he is free and must make his way from there to Italy, then north to Denmark, with only a water bottle, a piece of soap, a loaf of bread, a compass, matches, and his unchildlike wariness. His fierce honesty and desire for freedom are softened by tasting the sweetness of beauty, faith, and even love. They leave this splendid boy more human but more vulnerable when his freedom is threatened again.

RECOMMENDATION: Though Holm carefully expands David's thoughts only as his vocabulary expands on his learning journey, many significant ideas crowd the pages of David's wonderful story. Among them are the importance of individual freedom of conscience and self-determination; the necessity of having a childhood if one is to grow up healthy; the foundational significance of both faith and the acceptance of God's unconditional love. But more than these themes, David himself—the courageous boy with the eyes of an old man searching for his mother, whose "eyes look as if she'd known a great deal, and yet she's still smiling"—will capture you and haunt you and encourage you and give you hope. This is a wonderful book to read aloud as a family or class. ET, MT, AA*

ET—Early Teens
MT—Mid Teens
LT—Late Teens
AA—All Ages

AUTHOR: **Tim LaHaye and Jerry Jenkins**

TITLE:    ***Left Behind*** (1995)

DESCRIPTION: This is the first in a still continuing series of novels about the fate of the earth and its inhabitants after the Rapture takes believers out of the world when those left behind must face the Antichrist and the Armageddon. Pilot Rayford Steele, his daughter Chloe, and journalist Buck Williams are the primary protagonists.

RECOMMENDATION: These novels, based on a premillenialist, pretribulation interpretation of Revelation, have taken the evangelical world by storm and have even prompted secular media attention. They combine the fast-moving intrigue of the spy thriller format with earnest sermons explaining political and spiritual history. A cursory glance at the amazon.com customer reviews will reveal that many people, including non-Christians, have examined their faith more closely after reading these books. Others, in contrast, criticize their poor quality of writing, their shallow interpretation of world events and, more disturbingly, their treatment of people as objects, not of God's love but wrath. (Even if God's wrath is real, are people just objects?) It is worth the effort to make up your own mind by reading critically. **MT**, **LT**

There are many other end-times books, some written in response to the Left Behind publishing phenomenon. See our reviews of The Christ Clone Trilogy by James BeauSeigneur, and *Father Elijah* by Michael O'Brien. If you have checked out the amazon.com reviews, you will have noticed favorable mention of a book called *We All Fall Down* by Brian Caldwell. While the book does explore the nature of hatred, forgiveness, belief versus faith, and redemption, it doesn't do so from a discernable Christian perspective, and it contains explicit language and many scenes of a sexual and violent nature. Hence, we warn that Caldwell's book is not suitable for teen readers.

AUTHOR: **Louis L'Amour**

TITLE:    ***Last of the Breed*** (1986)

DESCRIPTION: Air Force Major General Joe Mack is shot down over Siberia during the Cold War and escapes from a prison camp. To survive in this remote wilderness, he must remember and practice all the skills of his Sioux heritage. Other people rise out of the harsh Siberian landscape to help or to pursue him.

RECOMMENDATION: L'Amour is the master of adventure, though Siberia is a new backdrop for his heroes. Many families enjoy reading L'Amour aloud together. Try his Sackett family saga, which tells the story of America through its frontier life, and collections of his short stories, full of "old-time fights, rustling cattle, round-ups, camp cooks and drifting cowhands." **LT, AA**

AUTHOR: **Jack London**

TITLE:    ***The Call of the Wild*** (1903)

DESCRIPTION: Long a favorite of young men, *The Call of the Wild* is the story of Buck, a domesticated dog transported to Alaska during the territory's gold rush days, where he learned to adapt to the harsh environment, harsh treatment, and arduous work of pulling sleds. He makes a human friend but finally, after Thornton is killed, succumbs to the "call of the wild," to run with a wolf pack.

RECOMMENDATION: London's love of animals and nature is apparent on these pages. **MT***

AUTHOR: **John Marsden**

TITLE:    ***Tomorrow, When the War Began*** (1993)

DESCRIPTION: Seven Australian teens go camping in the remote bush country called Hell during Christmas vacation. When they return, they discover that their country has been invaded, their parents are missing, and their animals destroyed. Their most pressing problem is how to survive undetected.

RECOMMENDATION: Their extreme circumstances cause some of these teens, particularly the narrator Ellie, to find hidden reserves of courage, strength, wisdom, and passion (some of it physical). During these days, they struggle with the question of whether Hell is a place—in their case, a literal place of refuge—or is within people, even themselves. What do you think? Only Robyn has a biblical touchstone, but none of them is like the children in *Lord of the Flies*. **MT, LT**

AUTHOR: **Robin McKinley**

TITLE:    ***The Outlaws of Sherwood*** (1988)

DESCRIPTION: In this splendid retelling of the Robin Hood legend, McKinley brings the famous merry outlaws and their not-so-famous companions to life with all their strengths and weaknesses, joys and discontents. From the beginning when you first meet the forester, Robin, on his way to the fair at Nottingham, musing that his friend Marian is a better archer than he, to the ending, which King Richard the Lionheart himself engineers to the surprise of them all, you'll be entranced by the adventures of these twelve outlaws.

RECOMMENDATION: Don't miss the afterword in which McKinley discusses her search for the historical Robin Hood. She quotes one source who says that the Robin Hood stories "have always reflected what the teller and the audience needed him to be *at the time of the telling.*" Then you might ask what need of yours McKinley's flesh-and-blood Robin meets as you encounter him on these pages. Look also for McKinley's retelling of the Beauty and the Beast fairytale, *Beauty,* or of Sleeping Beauty in *Spindle's End,* and for her fantasy *The Hero and the Crown.* **ET, MT***

AUTHOR: **John L. Moore**

TITLE:    ***The Breaking of Ezra Riley* (1990)**

DESCRIPTION: The prairies of eastern Montana are an unforgiving environment, but for Ezra their harshness is compounded by an aloof, unforgiving rancher-father and cowboy uncles who do not comprehend what is happening to him. He runs away, but when his father dies and someone must take over the ranch, he returns with his wife and baby. There he must face what caused him to flee in the first place as he tries to make the ranch profitable.

RECOMMENDATION: The biblical messages of freedom and forgiveness are woven so carefully and subtly and truly into this splendid western that they will surprise you with their inevitable rightness as they did Ezra Riley. This is a book that boys especially will not want to miss. Be sure to hunt this title down in used bookstores if you can't find it in the library. Check for the sequel, *Leaving the Land.* **LT***

AUTHOR: **Michael O'Brien**

TITLE:    ***Father Elijah: An Apocalypse* (1996)**

DESCRIPTION: Father Elijah is a Holocaust survivor turned Catholic convert and Carmelite priest plucked from his obscure monastery in order to undertake a challenging secret mission. He is to preach the Gospel to the person whom the authorities in the Vatican believe is the Antichrist. If that person is converted, they hope that the Tribulation can be delayed so that more people across the world can come to salvation.

RECOMMENDATION: O'Brien has created an apocalypse in the grand literary tradition. Not only does he explore end-times issues, but also theological and philosophical issues such as truth and the unity of the church, the problem of evil and suffering, and especially God's desire for the redemption of the world. There is a lot of external action and intrigue in *Father Elijah,* but there is even more internal examination of ideas. It is obviously a much deeper, more intellectual book than the Left Behind series, and so it rewards careful reading and family discussion. It is destined to become a classic, so if it is too much to chew on now, wait a few years. You can come back to it later. **LT**

AUTHOR: **Baroness Orczy**

TITLE: *The Scarlet Pimpernel* (1884)

DESCRIPTION: In Paris during the month of September, 1792, aristocratic Frenchmen were losing their lives on the guillotine unless the mysterious British Scarlet Pimpernel managed to contrive dangerous escapes for them right under the eyes of the authorities.

RECOMMENDATION: The story of one such escape full of "turmoil, passion and intrigues" is told in this book from a decidedly aristocratic and anti-republican point of view. **MT, LT**

AUTHOR: **Gary Paulsen**

TITLE: *Tracker* (1984)

DESCRIPTION: John must hunt the deer alone this year because he and his grandparents depend on the meat, but his grandfather is dying of cancer. The doe captivates John with her beauty, and John feels deep in his sensitive soul that if only he can touch her, he can cheat death. For two days he tracks her, alone in the frozen swamp.

RECOMMENDATION: In this lyrical, extended short story, Gary Paulsen takes you into the mind and heart of a young boy who longs to prevent the changes he knows are coming to both his beloved grandfather and the splendid deer. There is nothing beyond the physical for either of them even though their lives have been beautiful, joyful, and meaningful. But can a mere boy halt that inevitable change? What are the consequences of this belief? See also *Alida's Song* about a boy and his relationship with his grandmother. **ET**

AUTHOR: **Gary Paulsen**

TITLE: *Dogsong* (1985)

DESCRIPTION: Newbery Honor, 1986. Russel is disturbed by the destruction that accompanies modern inroads into Eskimo culture. He leaves his father (who at least gave up drinking because he loved the Jesus that Russel can't understand) to live with the oldest man in the winter settlement. In a trance, he passes on to Russel some of the old wisdom the villagers had lost. He sends the boy out alone on a dogsled run to survive in the Arctic winter, to find his song by merging into his dogs, the snow, a prehistoric man and in the process, also finding a very modern girl who, in the end, needs civilization's help.

RECOMMENDATION: Gary Paulsen understands the almost animistic Eskimo mindset and can take you deep inside Russel's experience until you, too, feel that you are part of the dogs, part of the past, and part of the wild Arctic environment. You'll find yourself wondering if Russel is right to reject modern ways. And are the missionaries right to make the Eskimos give up their songs? **MT**

AUTHOR: **Gary Paulsen**

TITLE: ***The Crossing* (1987)**

DESCRIPTION: Fourteen-year-old Manny, a street kid existing by his wits in Juarez, Mexico, wants nothing more than to cross into the United States, the land of milk and honey. Sgt. Robert Locke, the perfect Army officer, wants nothing more than to kill the voices of his dead Vietnam buddies with the most powerful liquor he can find. They chance to meet behind a Juarez bar, there learning something about truth and companionship.

RECOMMENDATION: Paulsen sustains his lyric style even in this book, which is not about oneness with nature but about a boy and a man out of joint with themselves and their environment. Your heart will ache for Manny and Robert both, and you will puzzle for a long time about whether Paulsen means you to think that Locke's death was necessary for his crossing into the kind of humanity that helps the dying. Or, having offered help to Manny, does his death show that any such acts are as meaningless as the ones in the bullring? **ET**, **MT**

**Gary Paulsen**, the person, is found in all of his writing for young people. Teens are the right audience for him, he believes, because adults "have created the mess we are struggling to outlive." He has hunted, trapped, driven dogsleds, soldiered, worked as a migrant farmhand, thirsted after knowledge, meditated, and—perhaps most importantly for his stories—experienced that piercingly beautiful oneness with an animal and its natural environment, which he tries to recapture again and again. It is probably not quite accurate to call him a pantheist, for he never indicates that nature is to be worshiped, but it does seem to be Everything for him. (He never, for example, refers to a possible Creator for it.) Also, his writing is a seamless whole; he believes that all his ideas are interrelated. No wonder, then, that he also is a vigorous campaigner for nuclear disarmament (apparent in *The Sentries*, another of his books)—nothing would be unaffected if a nuclear weapon were to explode! Paulsen writes with a songlike, deceptively simple beauty and has earned the right for young people to examine his ideas seriously.

AUTHOR: **Gary Paulsen**

TITLE: *Hatchet* (1987)

DESCRIPTION: Newbery Honor, 1988. Brian's parents have recently divorced, and he is flying up to spend his first summer with his father on a Canadian oil field. After the pilot of the private plane dies of a heart attack, Brian crashes the plane into a lake. With only the hatchet his mother gave him, he must survive in the isolated wilderness alone.

RECOMMENDATION: The Canadian wilderness, though not friendly, is not hostile to Brian if only he can learn to be a part of it and so discover its secrets of food, work, and patience. It is nature he must get along with, not people. The city boy toughens and so gains the hope he needs to continue. When rescue comes, it is almost anticlimactic. Paulsen continues to explore the meaning of survival in *Brian's Return*. How would you define it? **ET, MT**

AUTHOR: **Anton Quintana**

TITLE: *The Baboon King* (1996)

DESCRIPTION: Despised by the Masai—his father's people—and banished by the Kikuyu—his mother's tribe—Morengaru, a superb hunter, walks across the vast Kenyan plain away from all society. After he kills a baboon and is severely injured in the process, he slowly earns his place as the king of the baboons.

RECOMMENDATION: Although there are several highly charged scenes of fights to the death, most of the action in this unusual novel is internal. Morengaru struggles to survive by reflecting on the meaning of society, both human and ape, and on the meaning of loneliness and dignity. How do you think the author distinguishes between primates and humans? How do you? **MT, LT**

AUTHOR: **Jack Schaefer**

TITLE: *Shane* (1949)

DESCRIPTION: This old-fashioned western has many of the ingredients of that genre, including the beleaguered farmers vs. the land-hungry cattlemen and a climactic shootout. But in *Shane*, the good guy wears black and has a mysterious past though he does come riding unannounced into young Bob's life at a crucial moment. How Shane physically helps Bob and his father and other farmers wrest a new living from the raw prairie and how he more significantly helps Bob "stay clean inside through the muddled, dirtied years of growing up" make up the taut pages of this exciting book.

RECOMMENDATION: If you never read any other westerns, you will be glad to have read this one. How do you evaluate the role of violence in the book? Do the ends—or circumstances—justify the means? Bob comments, "The man and the tool, a good man and a good tool, doing what had to be done." **MT, LT***

AUTHOR: **Ivan Southall**

TITLE: ***Ash Road*** (1965)

DESCRIPTION: Three teenage boys camping in the Australian bush accidently start a fire that ravages a whole district. They and the residents left on Ash Road—youngsters and two old men—must discover in themselves reserves of strength, courage, and forgiveness to help each other stay alive.

RECOMMENDATION: Peter finds his manhood; Lorna, love for her dour father; Graham, the ability to admit his guilt; Pippa, the strength to do what must be done; Gramps, compassion for a neighbor; and Grandpa Tanner, the humility not to shake his fist at God in fury but to forget about himself and pray for little children. This fine novel pits ordinary people against an extraordinary fire before which they can only humbly acknowledge their finiteness. Most of Southall's books are no longer in print in the United States, so check your library or used bookshop to give yourselves the treat of reading them. **ET, MT***

**Ivan Southall** is one of Australia's most respected novelists, one who deserves to be read more in North America. (See other titles listed under Contemporary Fiction.) He puts his characters in extreme situations, and so his stories are thrilling adventures of human endurance. More important, he explores how young people respond, react, and grow in those situations. He exults in people—varied, fascinating people. Almost all of his characters believe rather matter-of-factly in God, though rarely is he a personal friend to them. In fact, Gerald, who had to fly the Egret after Jim's heart attack, remembered that his father sometimes said, "Praying's all right for parsons, [but] speaking for myself I'd rather roll up my sleeves and rely on my own sweat." Gerald thought, "That was all right to a point, but it didn't seem to cover situations like this. Perhaps his father had never been in a situation like this." And so for some of Southall's characters—not all—their growth is a growth toward a first kind of foxhole faith as well as maturity.

AUTHOR: **Ivan Southall**

TITLE:   ***To the Wild Sky*** (1969)

DESCRIPTION: The pilot flying six children to Gerald's birthday party on a ranch in Australia dies of a heart attack. Gerald takes over the plane, but a dust storm and strong headwinds prevent him from crashlanding it near his home. Crash, they do—on the shore of a deserted island. The children must bury the pilot and figure out how to stay alive until help arrives, if indeed it will.

RECOMMENDATION: As always, Southall puts his children in an extreme situation to explore how they respond, and as always, his children grow closer to maturity, finding reserves of courage, resourcefulness, strength—and even faith. (This is in contrast to how the children act in *Lord of the Flies*, to which the book is often compared.) In *To the Wild Sky*, it is left to the reader to complete the novel. After all they have been through, after all they have learned, will Colin and Mark, Bruce and Jan, Gerald and Carol be rescued or will they, as Jan has a premonition, die one by one? **MT**, **LT**

AUTHOR: **Ivan Southall**

TITLE:   ***What About Tomorrow*** (1977)

DESCRIPTION: Sam's family desperately needs his paper route money during the Depression in Melbourne, Australia, but on the day he was 14 years, 4 months, and 8 days, he crashes his brakeless bike into a tram and scatters his 64 papers to the wind. Rather than face the consequences, he runs away, and from that day his life is profoundly different, as we see during flash-forwards to one of his missions as a fighter pilot during World War II.

RECOMMENDATION: If you have ever marveled at the unique circumstances that make up *you*, you will thrill to Sam's discovery that God has worked overtime to engineer the days just after his accident so that he could manage a job big enough for a man—growing up. **MT**, **LT***

AUTHOR: **Robert Louis Stevenson**

TITLE:   ***Kidnapped*** (1886)

DESCRIPTION: David Balfour receives a letter of introduction to his Uncle Ebenezer of the great Scottish family, the Shaws, as an inheritance from his father. But Uncle Ebenezer tries to have David killed and then later tricks him into going on a ship that is headed with its prisoners to slavery in the New World. Find out how David escapes this condition; helps a new friend, Alan Stewart, who is part of a scheme to overthrow King George; and regains his rightful inheritance.

RECOMMENDATION: If you are looking for an exciting adventure, *Kidnapped* may be your book. Reading this book will reaffirm your values of perseverance and loyalty. Look for the edition with the wonderful N. C. Wyeth illustrations. **AA***

AUTHOR: **Robert Louis Stevenson**
TITLE:    ***Treasure Island*** (1883)

DESCRIPTION: If you don't have to read *Treasure Island* for school, you may want to try it on your own. Jim Hawkins is the boy hero of this fast-paced story about a mysterious treasure map, a mutinous crew, battles between adventurers and pirates—the most infamous being Long John Silver—and, at last, rewards for all who survive, even the pirate.

RECOMMENDATION: This Stevenson novel is also illustrated by N. C. Wyeth, making it an edition worth owning. **AA***

AUTHOR: **Megan Whalen Turner**
TITLE:    ***The Thief*** (1996)

DESCRIPTION: Newbery Honor. Gen had bragged about his thieving abilities a little too loudly and so found himself in prison. The king's magus needs a thief—not just any thief, but the best one—to find an ancient Gift, hidden by the gods, to secure his country's political advantage. He releases Gen from prison and forces him into the dangerous job.

RECOMMENDATION: Set in mythical lands that strongly resemble ancient Greece, this story is about how one proud young man encounters the gods. He tells their tales and wonders "what it meant to be the focus of the gods' attention, to be their instrument, used to change the shape of the world." Since that is a meaning worth exploring, you should ask how Gen's experiences are similar and/or unlike your own. **ET, MT**

# Chapter 13

# Contemporary

AUTHOR: **David Almond**

TITLE: ***Kit's Wilderness* (1999)**

DESCRIPTION: Kit Watson and his parents move to his grandfather's decrepit old mining town after his grandmother's death. Among his new friends at school are the troubled John Askew and the restless Alison Keenan. Askew compels Kit into his game of Death in an abandoned mining pit even as Kit's grandpa pulls him into his memories of mining days and a teacher and Allie coax him into learning about the Ice Age. All the worlds mingle on winter solstice as Kit struggles for Askew's future—even soul—deep beneath the earth.

RECOMMENDATION: Life and death, good and evil, love and cruelty, creativity and destruction are all competing for supremacy in this disturbing yet hopeful novel. One of the questions its characters ask is how good and evil can co-exist inside a single person. Should anyone ever be written off as Evil? You will want to ask how death can be conquered in Kit's world where there are loving and protective adults but no religious faith. MT

AUTHOR: **Avi**

TITLE: ***Nothing but the Truth: A Documentary Novel* (1991)**

DESCRIPTION: Newbery Honor. Philip Malloy, a ninth grader who hates his English class and is looking forward to running track, hums the "Star

Spangled Banner" during homeroom instead of remaining respectfull
silent. His English/homeroom teacher sends him to the principal's offic
When a neighbor who is running for the school board hears about it, th
incident takes on a life of its own, rippling across the entire country.

RECOMMENDATION: We learn about Philip's actions and his teacher's reac
tions from their own perspectives. Multiple viewpoints—from schoc
memos to talk radio dialogue—highlight the complexity of the primar
issue of the book: "What is the truth?" How can you know anything fo
certain? When are you tempted to shade the meaning of somethin
just a little bit and why? Or doesn't it matter? Do you believe as th
school superintendent says, ". . .you know as well as I, it doesn't mat
ter if it's true or not. It's what people are saying that's important"
Given the context of an average American high school, perhaps lik
yours, you can chew on these issues for a long time. **MT**

AUTHOR: **Bruce Brooks**
TITLE: *Midnight Hour Encores* (1986)

DESCRIPTION: Sibilance T. Spooner was born sixteen years ago as Esale
Starness Blue, child of two Berkeley hippies. Her mother wanted he
freedom, so, when Sib was twenty hours old, her father took his daugh
ter away to the East. There she becomes a musical prodigy—a cellis
who wins every world-class competition going. Because she wants t
meet her mother (or so she says—this brash egotist has ulterio
motives), her father takes her cross-country in an old VW bus, giving he
"lessons" on the Age of Aquarius as they go. After they arrive in Sa
Francisco, Sib has to make a critical choice.

RECOMMENDATION: At one level the vivid descriptions in *Midnight Hou
Encores* are tinged with nostalgia for the hang-loose days of the '60s, bu
at a deeper level the story is a biting satire about people who sang c
freedom and love but refused responsibility and commitment. You ma
be startled by Sib's sassy irreverence at times, but you will also find mos
satisfying just how she discovers that she has only developed her incred
ible talent because of her father's commited love. **MT**

AUTHOR: **Melody Carlson**
TITLE: *Diary of a Teenage Girl* (2000)

DESCRIPTION: From New Year's Day until summer, sixteen-year-old Caitli
O'Connor records all the complexities of her teenage world in he
diary—her uncertainties about school, about what it means to be a rea
friend, about how she looks, about her troubled family life and inne
conflicts over being herself or one of the crowd at school. She become

interested in God through the pain of her love life and uncertainty over how to handle strong sexual emotions. Now she must discover how to remain true to God as well as herself and her friends.

**ET**—Early Teens
**MT**—Mid Teens
**LT**—Late Teens
**AA**—All Ages

RECOMMENDATION: The diary is a page-turner, genuinely exploring values, personhood, choices, and maturity. By the time she makes her last entry, Caitlin has worked her way to maturity. Strong on high school realities and Christian themes. See the sequel, *It's My Life.* **MT**, **LT**

AUTHOR: **Barbara Cohen**

TITLE: ***Unicorns in the Rain*** (1981)

DESCRIPTION: Nikki, a lonely, angry teen, meets the magnetically attractive Sam on a train and, against her better judgment, goes home with him to his family's animal farm. There she realizes she is caught up in a cataclysmic event that will force her to make life and death choices.

RECOMMENDATION: The intriguing front piece of this novel reads: "Imagine a world not in which God is dead, but to which he has not yet been born." This modern day Noah's Ark story is disturbingly honest about the kinds of evils—including sexual—that caused God to give up on his world, even in "Noah," his family, and Nikki herself. It is a book worth talking about with your family. You might want to compare this book to L'Engle's *Many Waters* and of course to Genesis. **LT**

AUTHOR: **Carolyn Coman**

TITLE: ***Many Stones*** (2000)

DESCRIPTION: Berry is dead inside, figuratively buried under the stones she actually places on her chest before going to sleep each night. She may have felt this way anyhow, but the death of her vivacious, activist sister Laura at the hands of South African thugs has sealed her reality. When her divorced father forces her to travel with him to South Africa for a memorial service, she slowly and painfully realizes that she can only experience life fully again if she faces the truth about herself and her family.

RECOMMENDATION: Berry says at one point, "I'm not dumb; I know this whole trip is metaphor city—everyone everywhere trying to forgive each other and get on with it: South Africans, us about Laura, Dad and me. I get it, I just don't get how." Has she caught on to the "how" enough at the end of the trip—no remorse and no forgiveness necessary—to justify the hope with which her story ends? **LT**

AUTHOR: **Robert Cormier**

TITLE:     ***After the First Death*** (1979)

DESCRIPTION: Three teens—Miro, the terrorist-kidnapper who must kill his first victim; Kate, the substitute driver of the bus full of day-camp children; and Ben, the son of the general in charge of the secret rescue unit—must all face death one summer day on a bridge in New England.

RECOMMENDATION: Like all of Cormier's books, this one too has an ending of shattering despair, but the context surrounding the terrorist incident in which he explores the notion that innocence can cause evil seems better to justify the inevitable end. Cormier says that though he would love to write happy endings, realism must deny them. Do you agree? **MT, LT**

AUTHOR: **Robert Cormier**

TITLE:     ***The Chocolate War*** (1974)

DESCRIPTION: Though he just wants to fit in, play football, and forget his mother's death, Jerry Renault nevertheless refuses to sell chocolates to raise money for Trinity, his Catholic prep school, defying the cruel clique that controls the place. In so doing he has disturbed the universe as the poster in his locker had dared him to. Ultimately, though, he pays a staggering price to confirm the Vigils' creed: that everyone is cruel and greedy; that everyone is either a victim or a victimizer.

**Robert Cormier**, though he is very controversial in the young-adult literature field, is thought by many critics to be its finest writer. Many high school teachers assign his novels. If nothing else, he certainly succeeds in getting you to care about his characters. He has said that teens write to him with two messages: (1) Please change your endings to happy ones since writers have the power to do that, and (2) You have created characters like us.

What would you ask or tell Cormier if you had the chance? Do you wonder if his unremitting nihilism (there is no meaning or purpose to life, even in the noblest resistance to the evil around us) is truly realistic, truly the way the world is? Does good never triumph? Is suffering never redemptive or worthwhile for a good cause? Is every person like Archie or Obie or Jerry or Kate? You don't have to like Cormier to gain insights through him into some of the darker realities of our culture.

RECOMMENDATION: Everyone at Trinity is evil to the core, including the Brother-teachers. Everyone is either a delighted victimizer or frightened victim whose very status contributes to the victory of evil. This book that vaulted Cormier to fame can be described as "nihilistic," because there is no meaning even to the seemingly "good" acts of Jerry and Brother Jacques and Goober. Cormier says students tell him all the time that what he writes is mild in comparison to what goes on in their schools. How does Jerry's experience at Trinity compare to your school? (The sequel is *Beyond the Chocolate War*.) **MT, LT**

AUTHOR: **Margaret Craven**

TITLE: *I Heard the Owl Call My Name* (1973)

DESCRIPTION: When the bishop learns that his young priest, Mark Brian, only has two years to live, he sends Mark, who is ignorant of his condition, to live and work in his most difficult parish, among a vanishing tribe of Kwakiutl Indians in the wilds of British Columbia. There "where death waited behind every tree," his faith has to construct a wall to support him as he "made friends with loneliness, death and deprivation"—and with many of the Indians. There, the bishop's desire for Mark to learn so much about life that he not fear death is also realized.

RECOMMENDATION: You will want to share this deeply sensitive yet not sentimental book with your family. **MT, LT***

AUTHOR: **Sharon Creech**

TITLE: *Walk Two Moons* (1994)

DESCRIPTION: Newbery Medal, 1995. On their long car trip west to Idaho, Salamanca Tree Hiddle tells her gramps and gram the story of how her new friend Phoebe lost and found her mother. What she discovers along the way is that she is telling her own story of losing and finding.

RECOMMENDATION: These many-layered stories are tender and rich in the telling, framed as they are in the certain—yet human—love of her grandparents and parents for Sal and in the myths and tales of both Greece and American Indians. How much richer it could have been with the even more certain love of God! Look for other Creech titles, including *Chasing Redbird*. **ET, MT**

AUTHOR: **Berlie Doherty**

TITLE: *Granny Was a Buffer Girl* (1986)

DESCRIPTION: As Jess gets ready to leave for a college year abroad, her family gathers to celebrate and to share their own coming-of-age stories.

RECOMMENDATION: Though by no means perfect, either externally or internally, Jess's three-generation family has conveyed to her values worth living by. Jess's own choices are enriched by the choices made before her even though her family's religious convictions become less certain. Is Jess living on the borrowed cultural and religious capital of the past? What do you think she will pass along to her children? **MT, LT**

AUTHOR: **Clyde Edgerton**

TITLE: *Walking Across Egypt* (1987)

DESCRIPTION: Mattie Rigsbee is slowing down a bit at age seventy-eight, but she doesn't want to burden her unmarried son and daughter—in fact, her sense of humor is as good as ever, thank you. What she really wants is to follow her Lord's commandment to "do unto the least of these," including a stray dog and the dogcatcher. Then there is the "very least," the dogcatcher's nephew, Wesley, who might just respond to some good, southern home cooking and a taste of Sunday school.

RECOMMENDATION: Even teens who don't particularly enjoy reading have loved *Walking Across Egypt* with its natural story-telling style and humor and its deep commitment to homespun, even biblical, values. Be prepared for the characters' language to fit them, from proper Baptist to juvenile delinquent. **MT, LT***

AUTHOR: **Nancy Farmer**

TITLE: *A Girl Named Disaster* (1998)

DESCRIPTION: Newbery Honor. Nhamo is only a girl of eleven when she flees her village in Mozambique to avoid being married to a cruel old man. Stealing a canoe with the blessing of her beloved grandmother, she heads towards Zimbabwe to find the father she has never known. The treacherous lake currents drive her instead to an island where she must scavenge for her physical survival and communicate with baboons for companionship.

RECOMMENDATION: This book is a compelling adventure story. However, it is much more than that. It allows you the rare privilege of entering into the heart and soul of another culture with all its beauties and horrors. Nhamo is your guide into a still pre-modern though contemporary southern African society, and you will come to respect and even love her. **ET, MT***

AUTHOR: **Paula Fox**

TITLE: *The Moonlight Man* (1986)

DESCRIPTION: Catherine, fifteen, has long anticipated a vacation with her divorced father, an unreliable alcoholic and witty though failing writer.

During their month together in an isolated Nova Scotia cottage, her daydreams about "dear Papa," the moonlight man, are shattered with the reality of his dreadful binges, yet she must learn to temper her disillusionment with love and hope for happiness.

RECOMMENDATION: As in several of Fox's books, there is a religionless minister who plays a secondary role—this time helping Catherine when her father has passed out in the middle of the night from a drinking binge. Reverend Ross does not speak of his faith to Catherine but does put Christ's love into action for her though her father had thought him superficial and hypocritical. Fox seems to need a religious figure of some sort when she expresses her ideas of guilt and forgiveness and love, but is she just saying here that the only victory people can have is their honest facing up to their own deaths? **MT**

AUTHOR: **Paula Fox**

TITLE: ***One-Eyed Cat*** (1984)

DESCRIPTION: Newbery Honor. Ned Wallis, the only child of a village minister and an invalid mother, receives a blowgun for his eleventh birthday from his uncle but is forbidden to use it. He disobeys, however, and believes that he shot out the eye of a wild cat. Ned must be freed from the guilt that consumes him and his loving-though-isolated family.

**Paula Fox** is considered one of America's best writers for young people. Her books are not particularly fast-paced, so reading them rewards patience. Her themes of separation, communication, guilt, and love are all important ones, and her careful, controlled words convey them with power. You will not find her sympathetic to God-given solutions; rather, her characters must work out their own painful choices and thus find their humanity—if it is findable.

RECOMMENDATION: Paula Fox's recurring themes of isolation, guilt, and love are apparent in this award-winning book. There is not much action, and so it may be hard to get into, but reading it carefully will give you much to think about. It's interesting that Ned can only connect with people when he has confessed his guilt. What do you think about Ned's minister-father's goodness? Does it smother his family or does it help Ned and his mother confess and be welcomed home? **ET**

AUTHOR: **Sheila Garrigue**

TITLE: ***The Eternal Spring of Mr. Ito*** (1985)

DESCRIPTION: Sara had been evacuated from London to Vancouver, British Columbia, to escape the World War II bombings. She is anticipating her cousin's wedding and learning how to care for bonsai plants from the Japanese gardener when Pearl Harbor is attacked. With death and alienation surrounding her, Sara tends her plants in secret and finds a daring way to help Mr. Ito and his now-interned family.

ET—Early Teens
MT—Mid Teens
LT—Late Teens
AA—All Ages

RECOMMENDATION: The quiet and effective message of this book is that "All over the world people were weeping because of the war—Russian mothers and Italian wives and Japanese children" (p. 95). Buddhist Mr. Ito goes on to tell Christian Sara that essentially all religions are the same as well, just different roads to the same God. Does he provide persuasive evidence for this significant claim? **ET**

AUTHOR: **Karen Hesse**

TITLE: *The Music of Dolphins* (1996)

DESCRIPTION: Mila was raised as a dolphin within a dolphin colony. After the girl is rescued, scientists are eager to discover everything they can about humans, dolphins, and communication from her. Mila is fascinated by language, music, and human affection, but she is also alarmed by human restrictions, which have no counterpart in the dolphin's world.

RECOMMENDATION: The central issue of this multiple-perspective book is the meaning of being human. You will rejoice with Mila as she masters so many skills yet share her longing as she is haunted by the question, "Am I human enough?" What do you think? **ET**

AUTHOR: **Janet Hickman**

TITLE: *Jericho* (1994)

DESCRIPTION: Angela is on the verge of becoming a teenager when she must spend her vacation helping her parents and grandparents take care of her garrulous great-grandmother.

RECOMMENDATION: Although she is a typical girl with typical growing pains that cause her to think primarily of herself, Angela takes the opportunity she has been given to grow in empathy for her great-grandmother, whose story we also learn. How do you compare Angela's challenges in growing up to those her great-grandmother faced? **ET**

AUTHOR: **Felice Holman**

TITLE: *Slake's Limbo* (1974)

DESCRIPTION: Aremis Slake was a castaway kid who made a home for himself in a hole in the side of a New York subway station, managing to live there for 121 days until an accident caused him to lose his "nest" and to desire a "resurrection" above ground. Or was it he who caused the events that led to the new Slake?

RECOMMENDATION: This book explores the notions of personhood and chance or determination in a very simple yet layered and powerful story about a haunting boy. Even reluctant readers have been known to value *Slake's Limbo*. **ET**, **MT**

AUTHOR: **Irene Hunt**

TITLE:    *Up a Road Slowly* (1966)

DESCRIPTION: Newbery Medal, 1967. At age seven, Julie went to live with her spinster schoolteacher aunt and her ne'er-do-well alcoholic uncle because her mother had died. With them and the other country school-children, she begins to walk "up a road slowly" toward life in all its joys and sorrows, choosing its wisdom and love.

RECOMMENDATION: Many consider this to be a classic coming-of-age love story. Especially if you are introspective, you may find Julie's growing awareness of her values paralleling your own. **ET, MT***

AUTHOR: **Daniel Keyes**

TITLE:    *Flowers for Algernon* (1966)

DESCRIPTION: Keyes expanded into this full-length book his moving short story about a young retarded man who is operated on to increase his intelligence but, like the experimental mouse before him, all too soon loses what he has so longed for. The book also explores Charlie's previously suppressed memories of his difficult childhood and his desires for a normal emotional and sexual life as well.

RECOMMENDATION: What you will find so powerful about Charlie's story is that it is all written by him, from his first stumbling attempts at English to his masterful insights that surpass even his experimenters' and then poignantly back again—for Charlie, unlike Algernon, realizes what he is losing. You may prefer the short story if you can find it in a collection. **LT**

AUTHOR: **Madeleine L'Engle** (See author overview on page 207.)

TITLE:    *Meet the Austins* (1960)

DESCRIPTION: First in the Austin Family series (which, like the Times Quartet, grows increasingly complex). A country doctor, his wife, and four children must accept the death of a family friend and the intrusion of a disturbed orphan into their happy family. In the second book, *Moon by Night*, the Austins, minus orphan Maggy, take a cross-country camping trip. Fourteen-year-old Vicky meets two boys, Zachary and Andy. Zachary leads her into physical danger during an earthquake. They question the goodness of God to allow such a natural disaster and they compare it to the man-made one that engulfed Anne Frank. **ET***

AUTHOR: **Madeleine L'Engle**

TITLE:    *The Young Unicorns* (1968)

DESCRIPTION: Third in the Austin series. The Austins have moved to New York for their father to do research on medical uses of the laser. There they meet a piano prodigy (blinded by a laser), a bitter former gang member, and various characters associated with the great cathedral of St. John the Divine. Has the evil so pervaded the city, as the Bishop seems to have decided, that people need help choosing good? Free choice and the redeeming qualities of music overcome the threat to the Austins and New York. **ET, MT***

AUTHOR: **Madeleine L'Engle**

TITLE:    ***A Ring of Endless Light*** (1980)

DESCRIPTION: Fourth in the Austin series. Newbery Honor. Vicky's story continues the following summer. Her minister grandfather is dying; thoughtless, suicidal Zachary reappears, causing the death of a family friend who rescued him; she meets Adam who needs her to help in his experiment with dolphins and who grieves over the serious accident of his boss. Death is everywhere, and Vicky must decide if eternity is, indeed—as her grandfather's favorite poet declared—"a great ring of pure and endless light," or if God is just a "deep and dazzling darkness." In typical L'Engle style she receives the help she needs from literature and nature as well as people. *Troubling a Star* is the final Austin book, set in Antarctica. **ET, MT***

AUTHOR: **Madeleine L'Engle**

TITLE:    ***Arm of a Starfish*** (1965)

DESCRIPTION: First in a quartet about Meg Murry and Calvin O'Keefe's daughter, Polyhymnia. Twelve-year-old Poly is kidnapped while under the care of marine biology student, Adam Eddington, by people who want the results of her father's experiments in regeneration of starfish. Adam must decide between beautiful Kali and the kidnappers or the O'Keefes and their Embassy friend, Joshua, just who has the best interests of America at heart. His choice does not come in time to save Joshua but does come in time to understand that even enemies are under the care of a loving Father. *Dragons in the Water* is the sequel. **MT***

AUTHOR: **Madeleine L'Engle**

TITLE:    ***A House Like a Lotus*** (1984)

DESCRIPTION: Third in the O'Keefe series. The title is from the Hindu scriptures, the Upanishads. Poly is now sixteen, a brilliant misfit in her regional high school, who blossoms under the tutelage of dying lesbian Maximiliana Horne. Max has arranged for Poly to be a gofer at a conference on Crete, but just before she is to leave, Max makes a drunken pass at her. Destroyed by her fallen idol, Poly assuages her pain in the arms of her boyfriend. However, healing and forgiveness are not hers until after she encounters troubled Zachary *(Moon* and *Ring)* in Athens, and the innocent friendship of a married Polynesian delegate in Crete, and finds refuge in the monastery and music of the conference.

RECOMMENDATION: Though many of the themes and eclectic philosophical conversations resemble L'Engle's other books, Poly's insistence that her sexual encounter with her shamed boyfriend was wonderful betrays a wavering from biblical truth. Even by secular standards, how her boyfriend took advantage of Poly would be called date rape or sexual abuse. This particular L'Engle novel has disturbed many of her fans because of the way it legitimizes hurtful and immoral relationships and even courts New Age thinking. Perhaps L'Engle's warning not to idolize others can be applied to herself in this instance! (L'Engle's "realistic" Poly O'Keefe stories and her "fantasy" Murry ones merge in this sequel to both series. See annotation of *An Acceptable Time* with her fantasy titles, page 209.) **MT, LT**

AUTHOR: **Sonia Levitin**

TITLE: *Yesterday's Child* **(1997)**

DESCRIPTION: The sudden death of Laura's mother prompts the teenager to try to fill in the many holes in her knowledge about her often moody parent. What she discovers while on a class trip to Washington, D.C. causes her to question her understanding of human nature, her own included. She begins to wonder if evil can be inherited.

RECOMMENDATION: Don't let the superficiality of this book's opening chapters deceive you because soon you will—with Laura—plunge into the depths of the human heart. No one mentions the concept of original sin in this novel (though Laura quotes a Holocaust survivor). What difference would accepting that concept have made for the data that confounds Laura? You may want to compare this book with Coman's *Many Stones.* Another book by Levitin worth reading is *The Singing Mountain* that explores how young secular Jews can rediscover their spiritual heritage. **MT, LT**

AUTHOR: **Robert Lipsite**

TITLE: *The Contender* **(1967)**

DESCRIPTION: A dropout on the edge of involvement in ghetto drugs and despair, Alfred impulsively joins a boxing gym and discovers the inner discipline that he needs to choose what is best for his future.

RECOMMENDATION: Though realistic in its dialogue and the violence it depicts, this book is hopeful at the same time. The physical action parallels the moral crises of the book well. **ET, MT**

AUTHOR: **Margaret Mahy**

TITLE:  ***Memory* (1988)**

DESCRIPTION:  Nineteen-year-old Jonny Dart, plagued by guilt and his vivid memory of his sister Janine's death five years before, searches for the only other witness to the accident—Bonny, her best friend. Instead, he finds Sophie, a senile, dirty, memoryless old woman. In helping her, Jonny discovers some truth about the death, friendship, and himself.

RECOMMENDATION:  To become part of Jonny's story is to get inside the skin of a sensitive existentialist who, in the surrealistic setting of a senile woman's filthy home, must come to grips with life, love, death, and guilt. The story itself is compelling, as are the array of characters. Jonny makes brave and good choices at almost every turn, yet his journey toward goodness and forgiveness stops tantalizingly short of its destination. **MT, LT**

AUTHOR: **Walter Dean Myers**

TITLE:  ***Fallen Angels* (1988)**

DESCRIPTION:  Richie Perry is only seventeen when he leaves Harlem for the army and is sent to Vietnam. He and the other soldiers have a lot of learning and growing and figuring out to do: Why are they in Vietnam? Are they ready to die? Will they become such different people by their devastating experiences that they won't know themselves when they get back to America? Are the Vietnamese human like themselves? In fact, to the Army, are the black soldiers fully human?

RECOMMENDATION:  Myers wrote this book in memory of his brother who died in Vietnam in 1968. You may be shocked by the raw, Army vocabulary, but it probably was impossible for Myers to write this account accurately with cleaned-up language. Through it all you will feel compassion for young—very young—men struggling to maintain their dignity and integrity, and, for one of the bunkmates at least, his faith, in the complex circumstances of a war that they had not been prepared to understand. **MT, LT**

AUTHOR: **Walter Dean Myers**

TITLE:  ***Monster* (1999)**

DESCRIPTION:  National Book Award Finalist. Steve, sixteen and awaiting his trial as an accomplice to murder, creates a movie script in his head of the events surrounding that fateful day in a Harlem drugstore and its aftermath. His journal, in contrast, reveals his panic and remorse at becoming what the prosecutor calls him—a Monster. Is that who Steve is? Is he guilty of the crime? Of what is the prison system guilty?

RECOMMENDATION: Whether you're reading Steve's "objective" movie or his painfully subjective journal, you will be moved to compassion for a boy who is—rightly or wrongly—caught in an often abusive criminal justice system. You will long for him to learn from this experience what he needs to live outside again if he isn't destroyed in the process. You will have evidence to be able to judge Steve's guilt or innocence, but a family member or friend reading the same evidence may come to a different conclusion, giving you much to talk about. Another, simpler book in the same genre which leaves you wondering about a young criminal's motive is *Making Up Megaboy* by Virginia Walter. **MT**

ET—Early Teens
MT—Mid Teens
LT—Late Teens
AA—All Ages

AUTHOR: **An Na**

TITLE: *A Step from Heaven* (2001)

DESCRIPTION: Young Ju mistakenly thinks that she has arrived in heaven when in reality the truck-in-the-air has taken the four-year-old Korean girl only to America. There her family works hard to get ahead but also experiences personal failures and the violence that comes, for some, from defeated hopes and dreams.

RECOMMENDATION: An Na's first novel is an astonishingly rich record of one family's immigrant experience told from the expanding perspective of the oldest daughter, from the time she sets out from Korea at age four until she leaves for college. Although her circumstances are grim and even bleak at times, hope and courage frame Young's days. You'll feel both the family's despair and hope and wonder if God, to whom they sometimes pray, has indeed answered their prayers. **LT**

AUTHOR: **Phyllis Reynolds Naylor**

TITLE: *Walker's Crossing* (1999)

DESCRIPTION: Out on the wide Wyoming ranch where he lives, twelve-year-old Ryan may not have fit his ever-growing body, but he knows that he fits the land and its cowboy lifestyle. In contrast, his older brother, Gil, and best friend, Matt, think that nothing fits in American culture any more. They turn to a local militia group for explanations and solutions. Ryan is caught in the middle of the community's arguments until they explode into tragedy.

RECOMMENDATION: Naylor skillfully gets inside the heart and mind of a boy who must become a man by deciding what he believes and how hard he will work to continue to nurture his beloved land and its cattle and traditions. **ET**

AUTHOR: **Katherine Paterson**

TITLE:   ***Angels and Other Strangers*** (1979)

DESCRIPTION:  Decide today that your family will include reading a story or two aloud from this wonderful collection as part of your Christmas rituals. You will find your own understanding of the Christ-event enriched as "Woodrow Kennington Works Practically a Miracle" to coax his bratty sister back into the circle of his family's love; or as lonely Japanese Pastor Nagai, considered a traitor to his country during World War II for worshiping the Westerners' God, holds a Christmas Eve service for two "guests," one a beggar girl and the other a spying policeman; or as black Jacob looms out of a snowstorm to become a fearsome angel to Julia and her tiny children, stranded on an errand she feared would ruin the perfect Christmas she had planned.

RECOMMENDATION:  Paterson wrote these nine stories to be read aloud during the Christmas Eve service of the Presbyterian church her husband pastored. With little Elizabeth, finally assured that she hadn't killed her three-day-old brother and that Jesus did love her, you'll find yourself saying, "Happy Birthday, Jesus, and many happy returns of the day." **AA\***

AUTHOR: **Katherine Paterson**

TITLE:   ***Bridge to Terabithia*** (1978)

DESCRIPTION:  Newbery Medal, 1978. Jesse was, in his own words, "a stupid, weird little kid who drew funny pictures and chased around a cowfield

**Katherine Paterson** is a prolific and much-honored writer of both historical fiction and "realistic" novels for preteens and their older brothers and sisters. Brought up on the mission field in China and having returned to Japan to work in Christian education as an adult, Paterson brings a Christian vision to bear on her fiction, from novels about gospel singers to members of a nineteenth-century political-religious sect. But that does not mean that everything works out "happily ever after" for her characters, nor that her most overtly religious characters are especially attractive. In fact, she tells about a professor who once told her that he doubted that a writer could describe the Christian experience effectively except by fantasy or science fiction (*Gates of Excellence*, 60). Family relationships for Paterson remain the most problematic; it is in the family scene that redemption can be found but also where separation and lack of communication bring the most pain. Nevertheless, she always holds out lifelines of hope to her readers, declaring that she will "not write a book that closes in despair" (*Gates*, 38). See titles under Historical Fiction as well.

trying to act big" when Leslie Burke arrived in his country school. Together these improbable friends create a secret kingdom, Terabithia, with which Leslie tries "to push back the walls of his mind and make him see beyond to the shining world—huge and terrible and beautiful and very fragile." A tragedy precipitates Jesse's and Leslie's premature "moving out" from their Terabithia.

RECOMMENDATION: If you enter into Jesse's experience, as Paterson allows you to do, the walls of your mind will be pushed back as well to see the shining world both terrible and beautiful. You will rejoice and you will mourn and you too will move out beyond. Be glad, however, that Paterson doesn't ask you to make an either/or choice about her story, which she seems to be suggesting that Jesse and Leslie have to make about the Easter story: a hated truth or a beautiful myth. **ET***

AUTHOR: **Katherine Paterson**

TITLE: *The Great Gilly Hopkins* (1978)

DESCRIPTION: "God help the children of the flower children," Gilly Hopkins' social worker sighed when gutsy Gilly had gotten herself into her biggest fix yet. Abandoned by her mother years before, shuttled from one foster home to the next, she has now landed with hippo-sized Maime Trotter, scared William Ernest, and their blind and black neighbor, Mr. Randolph. Determined to outwit both them and cool Ms. Harris, her new school teacher, Gilly finds herself being made soft by their unconditional love, when toughness was what she needed for survival. However, when her "softness" is strong enough to withstand a broken heart, she sets forth once more to be "Galadriel Hopkins, come into her own."

RECOMMENDATION: There isn't a caricature among this odd mix of characters, and you will come to love them all as you share in their pain and triumphs. **ET***

AUTHOR: **Katherine Paterson**

TITLE: *Jacob Have I Loved* (1981)

DESCRIPTION: Newbery Medal, 1981. Louise is the elder and less favored twin of fragile, musically gifted Caroline. Isolated on a small island in the Chesapeake Bay, where the villagers wrestle a living from crab and oyster fishing and where educational opportunities are limited and a wrathful Methodism seems to dominate, Louise watches her sister gain favors from everyone she cares about—the only good teacher, the mysterious Captain Wallace who returned to Rass after a thirty-year absence, and steady Call who has crabbed with her until World War II takes him away.

How Louise slowly decides to root out her own bitter spirit and choose a good life for herself—off the island—is the climax to this story.

RECOMMENDATION: "Jacob have I loved, but Esau have I hated," bitter, Bible-spouting Grandma whispers to Louise, and Louise believes she is the God-hated elder Esau. Whether her own hardened heart has prevented her from hearing it or whether it was never emphasized, teenaged Louise cannot seem to respond to the grace of God that Caroline sang about in the folk-carol, "I Wonder as I Wander." Ultimately that grace triumphs as Louise chooses not to become what her vindictive (crazy?) grandmother is, but in so doing she must slough off the shell of self and of Rass Island. You will rejoice in her final choice but be saddened that she earlier missed so many opportunities for redemption. **MT**

AUTHOR: **Katherine Paterson**

TITLE: *Park's Quest* (1988)

DESCRIPTION: Though eleven-year-old Park lives in a fantasy world of knights in shining armor, questing for the Holy Grail, a real-life quest overwhelms his dreams: He wants to find out about his father who died in the Vietnam war, but his mother is not talking. Reading his father's books, sneaking away to the Memorial in Washington, D.C., and finally spending two weeks at his father's boyhood farm where he meets his grandfather (who cannot speak due to a stroke), his Uncle Frank, and a Vietnamese girl named Thanh, are all paths he must travel to successfully complete the quest and drink from the cup of Holy Grail.

RECOMMENDATION: Even if Park's acceptance of the circumstances of his father's death and his mother's sorrow seems a little too easy, you will nonetheless acknowledge with him that truth has begun to make him free. The blending of the Arthurian legend with the realities of a boy in a single-parent home is especially meaningful. See also Paterson's retelling of the Arthurian legend, *Parsival*. Other titles of interest are *Flip-Flop Girl* and *Preacher's Boy*. **ET**

AUTHOR: **Gary Paulsen** (See author overview on page 145.)

TITLE: *The Island* (1988)

DESCRIPTION: Wil's parents move him abruptly from Madison, Wisconsin, to a tiny town far north. At first he is disgruntled, but soon, out exploring, he comes on an island, where he begins to feel a harmony with the herons and frogs he observes. He also feels an obsessive thirst to know about the creatures of the island and himself, so he camps out there. His parents, the shrink they send after him, the town bully, its nicest girl, and finally the media all succeed in varying degrees to figure out Wil as he tries to figure out his world.

RECOMMENDATION: Paulsen explores his theme about oneness with the natural world once again in this beautiful story about a boy's self-imposed exile that is really a journey for understanding. However, the flaws in Wil's pantheism (surely it is also Paulsen's) are most apparent here, as well as its great emotional appeal to those who are sensitive to the natural world. How can Wil, who becomes the predator turtle as he attacks Ray, know that somehow he is wrong? What basis does he have for saying that everything in nature just is, and that nature has no moral code? Wil, as a moral boy, has appealed to a standard outside of nature, outside of the All. If you have felt a great thirst to learn, you will also be fascinated by Paulsen's ideas about how we learn, how we can know (in several ways), and how the various arts help us know. **ET, MT**

**ET**—Early Teens
**MT**—Mid Teens
**LT**—Late Teens
**AA**—All Ages

AUTHOR: **Gudrun Pausewang**

TITLE: ***Fall-Out* (1987)**

DESCRIPTION: Janna is in school when the nuclear power plant accident is announced. The only other person in their village that day is her little brother, Uli. Together they make their way through the chaos, and Janna must make life and death decisions for both of them. The radiation leak was far worse than at Chernobyl. How is a civilization to survive such technology?

RECOMMENDATION: This book, which won a prize in Germany for Children and Young Adult Literature, is a powerful statement against any use of nuclear power. Does the message overwhelm the human story for you so that it is reduced to propaganda? Or do you find in Janna's—and others'—reactions to the tragedy an enlightening, sympathetic look at the range of human resourcefulness? Is the Almighty trying to tell the Germans something, as an old man rails at Janna, or is that assertion an arrogance of his own? **MT, LT**

AUTHOR: **Carol Plum-Ucci**

TITLE: ***The Body of Christopher Creed* (2000)**

DESCRIPTION: Torey Adams is a nicer-than-normal, popular high school junior at the center of the in-crowd and, like them, disdainful of the class freak and the "boons" from the wrong side of the track. When that freak, Chris Creed, disappears, leaving an enigmatic note on the school library's computer, the veneer of the school's normality is blown away. As the community tries to pin the blame for Creed's murder (or is it a suicide? an abduction?) on the obvious suspects, Torey learns that guilt and responsibility must be accepted by everyone—including himself.

RECOMMENDATION: Be warned that this book is filled with much gutter language, many casual references to sex, and an uncertain worldview.

However, if you can stomach that, you can walk in the shoes of a young man who—for no apparent reason—begins to allow his conscience to convict him of his sins of prejudice, lack of compassion, hypocrisy, and even violent self-centeredness. His friends—one a Pentecostal proud of her viginity but with a vile, gossiping mouth—are even worse. In light of Columbine, it is important to see ourselves in such a searching light. It reveals more than many a sermon. Yet for poor Torey, despite all his religious insights, there is no grace or forgiveness, just therapy and a fresh start at a new school. Examine the fatalistic explanation of events that claims all people are dealt fifty-two cards from which to make up their lives. Into which of the worldview categories (see pages 84–88) would you put this philosophy of life? **LT**

AUTHOR: **Robert Newton Peck**

TITLE: *A Day No Pigs Would Die* (1972)

DESCRIPTION: Rob was a twelve-year-old boy in April when he cut school, helped his neighbor's distressed cow give birth, and got mauled in the process. He was a man a year later, the day no pigs would die. In the intervening year, he raised the newborn pig he had received as a thank-you from the neighbor, absorbed from his taciturn pig-butchering Shaker father not only the bone-deep values of hard work but also hard faith, had a joyous day at the Rutland Fair, and made the sacrifice necessary for manhood, "just doing what's got to be done."

RECOMMENDATION: This book may stir you like no other father-son book has. Rob's father, who cannot read or write and has difficulty expressing his profound love for his son, nevertheless has built so much of his deep faith in God and in his Vermont land into Rob that you will be richer for having met them both. **ET**

AUTHOR: **Chaim Potok**

TITLE: *The Chosen* (1960)

DESCRIPTION: Reuven and Danny's friendship began with a play-for-blood softball game between their two yeshiva high schools, though Jewish boys in Brooklyn during World War II were known more for their scholarship than their athletic prowess. Brilliant Danny is being groomed to take his Hasidic rabbi father's place but is compelled to master forbidden "secular" ideas as well. Reuven's father secretly helps him find the books he desires. This most wonderful of stories is about father-son relationships and about faith-knowledge relationships.

RECOMMENDATION: If you have grown up in any kind of subculture (religious or ethnic, or, as with Hasidic Judaism, both), you will feel this book and most others by Chaim Potok echoing marvelously in your heart and mind. If you haven't, you will feel like a member of one before you reach the last page. *The Promise* continues Danny and Reuven's story into their post-college days. **LT***

AUTHOR: **Chaim Potok**

TITLE:   *My Name is Asher Lev* (1972)

DESCRIPTION: Asher Lev is a young Hasidic Jew with a gift, the ability to paint, who, in his compelling need to exercise that gift, breaks the commandment of his faith, "Thou shalt make no graven image." Not only that, he paints crucifixes, the symbol of the people who have attempted to destroy the Jews. And so Asher grows up with a tension that finally must explode, learning that his gifted hands hold power both demonic and divine, able both to destroy and to create.

RECOMMENDATION: Like all of Potok's books, this one is about family and faith and their roles in the meaning of the life young people must construct for themselves. Eighteen years later, Potok published a sequel about Asher as an adult, *The Gift of Asher Lev*, in which he comes home to Brooklyn from his European exile when his uncle dies and finds the ties just as binding and just as demanding of choice and sacrifice. **LT***

AUTHOR: **Chaim Potok**

TITLE:   *Zebra and Other Stories* (2000)

DESCRIPTION: A reader can only sigh after finishing any one of the six short stories in this book. Each is a beautifully crafted and poignant experience of ordinary young people involved in situations of trust, grief, divorce, self-absorption, and family dynamics. Potok clearly respects the intelligence and intuitions of his characters and his readers, allowing them to handle their own truths and conclusions.

RECOMMENDATION: Potok's use of language—his simplicity and clarity— makes these stories linger in memory and seem such ordinary accounts that they leave the reader asking questions of meaning and significance. This is a masterful collection from a great writer. **LT**

AUTHOR: **Heather Quarles**

TITLE:   *A Door Near Here* (2000)

DESCRIPTION: Fifteen-year-old Katherine finds herself the head of a household with three younger siblings, physically abandoned by their father and emotionally abandoned by their mother. The resourceful children band together in an attempt to maintain some stability and to ward off the dreaded Department of Social Services. However, Alicia, the

ET—Early Teens
MT—Mid Teens
LT—Late Teens
AA—All Ages

youngest, makes their situation more vulnerable as she begins to lose touch with reality, retreating into her search for the door to Narnia and Aslan.

RECOMMENDATION: Readers easily take sides with these four bright and courageous children and get a look at what happens when two adults abandon children to their own devices. Some of their habits (lying, bad language, smoking) are survival tactics, but Quarles allows mature teen readers to enter into the pain of some of their peers who live on the edge of their in-crowd. Good book for discussion. **LT**

AUTHOR: **Wilson Rawls**

TITLE: ***Where the Red Fern Grows*** (1961)

DESCRIPTION: Billy, a ten-year-old boy who lives far back in the Ozark hills, is pining away for a hunting dog. How he makes his wishes—indeed, his prayers—come true and how Little Ann and Old Dan change his life, bringing deep joy, button-popping pride, and great sorrow, is the never-to-be-forgotten story *Where the Red Fern Grows*. It resonates with the author's deepfelt love for family, for nature, and for God.

RECOMMENDATION: Many classroom teachers read this book to their upper elementary students, and even "reluctant readers" have often gotten caught up in Billy's bittersweet pleasures. Families shouldn't miss the read-aloud experience. Rawls has written another Ozark boy-loves-animal book, *The Summer of the Monkeys*. **ET, MT***

AUTHOR: **Cynthia Rylant**

TITLE: ***The Islander*** (1998)

DESCRIPTION: This lyrical story is about Daniel's tenth year in which his loneliness abates because of the gifts of a mermaid.

RECOMMENDATION: Whether you believe Daniel met a mermaid on the edge of his island or not, you will be glad that he received its gifts of connection to the land, its animals, and the other islanders. Although religion often figures in Rylant's stories for older children, it is not by any means an orthodox religion as you can discern in another of her stories, *Missing May* (Newbery Medal, 1993). **ET**

AUTHOR: **Louis Sachar**

TITLE: ***Holes*** (1998)

DESCRIPTION: Newbery Medal, 1999. Stanley is sent to a surrealistic, sadistic boot camp for a crime he didn't commit where he is forced to dig a five-foot by five-foot hole every day in an old, dry lake bed in order to "build his character."

RECOMMENDATION: On the surface, it seems like this could be a bitter, "problem" novel, but dig deep like Stanley and his new friend Zero did, and you will discover truths about relationships, family histories, hope—and yes, character—that are worth the effort. A story that is as touching as it is important. **ET, MT***

AUTHOR: **J. D. Salinger**

TITLE: ***The Catcher in the Rye*** (1945)

DESCRIPTION: This book has the dubious honor of launching the movement toward "socially realistic" young-adult literature even though it was published for adults. For years it was on "forbidden" lists, though today its first-person narrator, flat "real" vocabulary laced with swear words, and an urban-rich-troubled-misunderstood protagonist are standard fare.

RECOMMENDATION: Do you feel sorry for Holden Caufield, kicked out of yet another prep school where all things phoney get on his nerves, victim perhaps of his parents' indifference? Or do you feel a good swift kick in the pants might do him some good? Or do you have yet another, more complex, response to him? Why do you think this book is so famous? More importantly, does his experience enrich your own? **LT**

AUTHOR: **Rafik Schami**

TITLE: ***A Hand Full of Stars*** (1987)

DESCRIPTION: In journal entry format, a Damascus teenager shares the struggles of three years. Some are universal to teens, like teachers who are obnoxious, parents who just don't get it, a girlfriend who is so desirable yet so distant, and others are specific to his situation in a repressive Middle Eastern society wracked by poverty and political corruption.

RECOMMENDATION: This nameless teen allows us to walk in his shoes as he becomes more adept at his chosen (yet forbidden) career of journalism. He is a Christian in a Muslim society. How central is his faith—or, for that matter, is the Muslim faith of his friends—to the very real political dangers and moral dilemmas he faces? How do you evaluate the maxims of his beloved Uncle Salim, such as "But falsehood is the twin sister of truth," and "Whoever forgives injustice, gets more injustice"? **MT, LT**

AUTHOR: **Ivan Southall**

TITLE: ***Let the Balloon Go*** (1968)

DESCRIPTION: A fiercely independent boy is trapped inside John's body, though he is plagued by cerebral palsy and by an overprotective mother. The first day that he is left alone he decides that he must climb a tree.

RECOMMENDATION: The saying, "A balloon that would never be a balloon until someone cut it free," provides the context to John's struggle to become an ordinary but free boy. (But then, John could be any child seeking to cut the restraints of childhood and so grow up.) Southall has a real knack for putting you right inside the skin of his heroes. Oh, how you want John to succeed and to "say 'Hi-ya' to God!" Afterward, his chastened parents have a word of wisdom about the true nature and price of freedom. ET*

AUTHOR: **Suzanne Fisher Staples**

TITLE: ***Dangerous Skies* (1996)**

DESCRIPTION: Buck and Tunes share a last name—Smith—that is a legacy of slavery. Tunes's family has worked on Buck's family's Chesapeake Bay farm for generations. They also share a love for the land and water where they have had the freedom to explore, work, and grow together. Everything changes the day Buck hauls the body of a neighbor's fore-man out of the water. Tunes is accused of the murder rather than community leader Jumbo Rawlins, whom the children have good reason to suspect. Buck tries to get Tunes to defend herself because the still real racism of his community threatens her.

RECOMMENDATION: This book comes close to Mildred Taylor's Roll of Thunder series in its powerful portrayal of courage and friendship in the face of contemporary racism. Whether justice is even possible in Tunes's situation becomes a heartbreaking question for Buck and his friend. What do you think? ET, MT*

AUTHOR: **Suzanne Fisher Staples**

TITLE: ***Shabanu: Daughter of the Wind* (1989)**

DESCRIPTION: At eleven, Shabanu, the younger daughter of a nomadic Muslim camel herder in the Pakistani desert of Cholistan, is old enough to know that her childhood freedoms are ending. Her sister, Phulan, will soon marry Hamir, and that means her own wedding will surely follow. Hamir is shot due to Shabanu's unthinking disregard of Islamic cultural customs, and this tragedy precipitates a critical choice for Shabanu. Should she accept her family's choice of a husband for her and so protect their precarious existence, or should she follow the dictates of her heart and so put them in jeopardy?

RECOMMENDATION: This wonderful Newbery Honor book reveals the heart of a young member of a culture distant from your own on two accounts—it is both Muslim and Pakistani—and compels you to share Shabanu's way of life and dilemma. See also *Shiva's Fire*, set in India. ET, MT*

AUTHOR: **Terry Trueman**

TITLE:    ***Stuck in Neutral*** (2000)

DESCRIPTION: Fourteen-year-old Shawn McDaniel, unable to communicate his brilliant thoughts because of profoundly handicapping cerebral palsy, believes that his father is planning to do away with him in a mercy killing.

RECOMMENDATION: Anyone who loves someone who is physically or mentally handicapped will have a hard time reading this book. While it raises interesting and important questions about euthanasia and about the problem of suffering, its premises seem so implausible that they undercut the author's intention to get us thinking about the ultimate value of every individual life. How could Shawn read and have cheery thoughts about his family, sex, and school when doctors believe he has no mental functioning at all? Are debilitating seizures really the equivalent of a happy '60s acid trip? Trueman admits he is projecting what he thinks *might possibly be* the case for his own profoundly handicapped C.P. son. As for the questions it raises, perhaps the most important thing for you to ask is whether giving and receiving love make us human. Should that love be the basis for deciding if someone should live or die? **MT**

AUTHOR: **Cynthia Voigt**

TITLE:    ***Homecoming*** (1981)

DESCRIPTION: Thirteen-year-old Dicey and her three younger siblings are abandoned in a shopping mall by their emotionally ill mother and must make their way on foot to their great-aunt Cilla's home in Bridgeport, Connecticut. When it becomes apparent that they will not be able to stay there, Dicey, James, Maybeth, and Sammy begin the trek again, this time to Maryland and their unknown grandmother Tillerman, who might well be crazy.

RECOMMENDATION: *Homecoming* is the first of Cynthia Voigt's splendid companion books about the young teens who live around Crisfield, Maryland. Dicey is the determined character who holds all the others together, quite literally in this first book. Like the hero in the ageless Greek epic tale *The Odyssey*, *Homecoming's* children face dangers and hardships but meet people who help them on their way until at last their hearts' longing is fulfilled. You may be intrigued to discover the parallels to *The Odyssey* as you read as well as be stimulated by Dicey and James' discussions about the ultimate questions of life and death and eternity. Where is their true home? What kind of people should they be as they search? Is personal integrity the highest good? Is Someone looking out for them or are they truly on their own? **ET, MT***

AUTHOR: **Cynthia Voigt**

TITLE: ***Dicey's Song* (1982)**

DESCRIPTION: Newbery Medal, 1983. Having gained her family a home with their grandmother *(Homecoming)*, Dicey must now get on with the business of growing up on the farm, at her part-time job, and in school. This she does by learning—sometimes painfully—to juggle the sometimes contradictory tasks of holding on to her family, reaching out for new friends, and letting go of her dying momma.

RECOMMENDATION: Those who admire the plucky Dicey will be glad to know how her new life develops. Though in the larger context, her gram cannot provide her with any certitudes ("Was that the right thing to do?" Dicey asks and Gram's reply is, "How should I know? It feels right and that's about all I have to go by."), she does provide love and much practical wisdom. For Dicey, life becomes a song well worth singing. **ET, MT***

AUTHOR: **Cynthia Voigt**

TITLE: ***Come a Stranger* (1986)**

DESCRIPTION: Mina Smiths is such an exceptional dancer that, although black, she wins a scholarship to a New England summer dance camp, where she learns about the world of music and ideas outside her own isolated Crisfield, Maryland. Coming home, she doesn't fit in again, but more devastating, she does not fit in again at the camp the next summer. After two weeks, she is sent home. Is it because she is black or because her maturing body can no longer dance? With Tamer Shipp, her minister-father's summer replacement, she first begins to sort out her feelings of rejection. Over the years to come, Mina learns the many meanings of love, courage, faith, and truth.

RECOMMENDATION: If you want to set the Tillermans' brave existentialism in the context of Christianity, it is Mina's story that will allow you to do so. Even so, Cynthia Voigt's most overtly religious characters either don't seem to think about their faith (as Mina's father does not) or are in the throes of doubt (as are Brother Thomas or Tamer Shipp). There is nothing much of God's love in Voigt's portrayal, either, unless it is through Mina's momma. On another level, *Come a Stranger* is also a touching story of a young teen's crush on an unavailable older—good—man, and here it resolves as truly and satisfactorily as it could possibly do. If you want to read more about Tamer and Bullet, Dicey's uncle, you may wish to find *The Runner.* **MT**

AUTHOR:  **Cynthia Voigt**

TITLE:    ***Seventeen Against the Dealer*** (1989)

DESCRIPTION:  This story completes the Tillerman saga with Dicey, now twenty-one, again the Odysseus figure, venturing out on uncharted waters, determined to make a go of her dream, to make a living as an independent boat builder. However, burying herself in the work, Dicey makes several mistakes not only about the business but about people—her grandmother, whose illness she underestimates; Jeff Greene, whose love she takes for granted; and an itinerant talker named Cisco whom she trusts. Having seemingly lost everything, Dicey learns—again—what it is that matters most in a world where there are no guarantees.

RECOMMENDATION:  Dicey is a doer like Sammy, not a thinker, so *Seventeen* is not as rich in ideas as is *Sons from Afar* (see below). Yet her story, and Jeff's, deserves this completion as she too chooses a moral and honest and loving life even though she does not believe that these attributes are built into the universe. **MT**, **LT**

**Cynthia Voigt** writes most frequently about the Tillermans, one of the most interesting families in fiction. The doers do fiercely and the thinkers think loudly, so there is much to involve most any kind of reader—those who like physical action and those who like mental puzzles. All of her characters are, in one way or another, with or without religious dress, existentialists. This means that they believe that each person's short existence on earth is meaningless in the long span of earth's history, but despite this reality, each person can create meaning for him or herself by choosing to live with integrity and to relate with love to other people, particularly family members. When you stop to think that most of her Crisfield characters had horrid things happen to them—usually abandonment of some kind—you may be astonished that they have the inner moral resources to make the choices you so often want to applaud. In each book there is at least one love-giver who enables the good in Voigt's characters to grow and function, though only in *Come a Stranger* can you see how that good may be grounded in an absolute moral standard. You will be glad that Cynthia Voigt has seen writing as a way that young people can look into her mind to see her "essential ideas, which in fact govern choices and action" as she commented in her Newbery Award acceptance speech. If you have loved the Tillerman books, go looking for other Voigt titles, especially *Jackaroo* and others set in the Middle Ages (*On Fortune's Wheel*, *The Wings of a Falcon*, and *Elske*).

**ET**—Early Teens
**MT**—Mid Teens
**LT**—Late Teens
**AA**—All Ages

AUTHOR: **Cynthia Voigt**

TITLE: *A Solitary Blue* (1983)

DESCRIPTION: Newbery Honor, 1984. Abandoned by his beautiful mothe Melody, when he was seven and living with his ineffectual professo father, Jeff grows up silent and withdrawn, coming totally alive onl when he spends a summer with Melody. Melody soon enough make clear that she loves Jeff only selfishly, and he withdraws completely. Th Professor is alarmed into action and together, with the help of hi father's friend, Brother Thomas, and a healing move to the blue-hero marshes of Crisfield, Maryland, they reach out to each other in love an forgiveness.

RECOMMENDATION: Jeff and his father stumble through their days sayin "I'm sorry. It doesn't make any difference, really." But the theme of *Solitary Blue*—and probably all of Voigt's writings—is that love—or a least what you do with love when it strikes you—makes all the differ ence in the world. Father and son learn that they don't have to be soli tary, that they make a difference to each other, and that they don't hav to apologize for who they are. They are people you will be most grate ful to make your friends. **MT**

AUTHOR: **Cynthia Voigt**

TITLE: *Sons from Afar* (1987)

DESCRIPTION: James Tillerman is a thinker and Sammy Tillerman a doer, a different as two brothers could be. But Sammy helps James search fo the father who had abandoned them twelve years ago. They sought th truth about the man but discover some truths about themselves, truth strong enough to live by.

RECOMMENDATION: If *The Odyssey* and "Hansel and Gretel" are the storie that haunt *The Homecoming*, then the Greek myth of a father and sor "Daedalus and Icarus," and the essay by the French existentialist, Camu "The Myth of Sisyphus," undergird *Sons from Afar*. James decides, i defiance of the evidence, that each individual, brief life is essentiall meaningless. He can create meaning for his own life primarily by hi commitment to be himself and by his strong bonds of love to his fam ily whose meaning and significance he knows, even if Truth cannot b known. If you are intrigued by ideas and have already been captured b the Tillermans, then you will cheer James' and Sammy's choices whil longing for them to discover that life really is meaningful. **MT**

AUTHOR: **Gloria Whelan**

TITLE:    *Homeless Bird* (2000)

DESCRIPTION: Thirteen-year-old Koly is given as a wife to a sickly boy in an arranged marriage in this moving novel about life in India. Even Koly's parents are helpless against the deceit of the boy's parents, who want Koly's dowry money to take their son to the River Ganges to be healed. Koly must survive her husband's death and his family's enslavement.

RECOMMENDATION: The engaging story chronicles the courage, the skill, and the goodness of this simple girl and gives wonderful insights into life in India. **MT**, **LT**

AUTHOR: **Virginia Euwer Wolff**

TITLE:    *Make Lemonade* (1993)

DESCRIPTION: Fourteen-year-old Verna answers an ad for a babysitter so that she can earn her way out of the projects by saving money to go to college. She meets seventeen-year-old mom Jolly and her two babies, Jeremy and Jilly, who change her life.

RECOMMENDATION: The moving prose poem pierces under the very skin of poverty—to its dirt and chaos and ignorance—an instructive place for us all to be from time to time. It also gets to the very heart of hope and responsibility, which can be poverty's antidotes. Verna is a very rich teenager. What do you think motivates her? Why is she so different from our social stereotypes of poor people? **MT**, **LT**

# Chapter 14

# Fantasy

AUTHOR: **David Almond**

TITLE: *Skellig* (1998)

DESCRIPTION: Michael is worried sick about his prematurely born infant sister's precarious health. His family's dilapidated "new" home reinforces his gloom. When he disobeys his dad to explore the dangerous garage, he discovers a creature—is it a man? a bird? an angel?—which also needs his help. He and his unusual new home-schooled neighbor, Mina, set out to restore Skellig's life and in the process are restored by the power of shared love.

RECOMMENDATION: The poetry of William Blake threads through this beautiful little book about the interpenetrating of the fantastical world and the ordinary burdens of human beings. Do Michael and Mina experience the fantastical as "God-breathed"? **ET**, **MT**

AUTHOR: **Natalie Babbitt**

TITLE: *Tuck Everlasting* (1975)

DESCRIPTION: When Winnie meets the wonderful Tucks, who had unintentionally drunk from a certain spring and are suspended forever in time, she is tempted to accept what each believes about life: Ma, that things just *are* and must be lived with; Pa, that life is a never-ending cycle of which death is a natural and good part; Jesse, that life is meant to be enjoyed; and Miles, that people must do something useful to be alive.

RECOMMENDATION: There are bits of Christian truth mixed in all that the Tucks say, though some of it, like Pa's Eastern mystical view of life, is not at all biblical. Like Winnie, you will probably be intrigued by these kindly people's dilemma as well as the choice she must make. Even college students enjoy discussing this book, which can be read by quite young children. Your family will find reading it together a rich experience. **ET**\*

**ET**—Early Teens
**MT**—Mid Teens
**LT**—Late Teens
**AA**—All Ages

AUTHOR: **John Bibee**

TITLE: *The Magic Bicycle* (1983)

DESCRIPTION: *The Toy Campaign* and *The Only Game in Town* are the next two titles in an eight-volume series published by InterVarsity Press. John is an orphan who lives with his uncle, the sheriff of Centerville, his aunt, and three cousins. He wants to win the bicycle race being promoted in town by the strange Horace Grinsby of Goliath Toys, but his bike had been run over in the driveway where he had carelessly left it. He uncovers an old-fashioned battered Spirit Flyer in the town dump and, in fixing it up for the race, discovers its magical powers. Grinsby knows them too and will stop at nothing to destroy the bike.

RECOMMENDATION: If you are familiar with Christian doctrine, you will enjoy finding the parallels between the exciting circumstances of this story and biblical truths. If you aren't, the story itself will easily capture your interest. The last line delightfully promises sequels, for while his family was learning about the magic that had captured him, "John was flying on the Spirit Flyer on a new adventure known only to the kings." **ET**\*

AUTHOR: **Nancy Bond**

TITLE: *A String in the Harp* (1976)

DESCRIPTION: Newbery Honor. Soon after their mother's unexpected death, Peter, Becky, and Jen's father takes them off to a bleak corner of Wales so that he can teach at the university in Aberystwyth. Each is isolated in his or her own grief until Peter—perhaps the most miserable of them all—discovers an ancient harp tuning key that slowly draws him into the sixth-century world of the bard, Taliesin. His sisters slowly get involved in the everyday worlds of their Welsh neighbors: a lonely bird-loving boy, Gwilym; and a down-to-earth farm girl, Rhian. Together all of them explore the surrounding land and their newly discovered feelings about life and the ancient magic.

RECOMMENDATION: You may find this to be one of the most satisfying books of fantasy you have read, as the events in Taliesin's life converge to heal the Morgans of their grief at the same time that Peter emerges from his grief-shell to save Taliesin for the land. Two themes are subtly woven throughout, one spoken by the Welsh language scholar, Dr. Rhys: "If we think a thing is impossible, does that truly make it so? Who are we, after all? Why should there not be forces that we do not understand?" Peter fumbles to the other: "The pattern was right, it was working itself out. People spent their lives weaving patterns, borrowing bits from one another. . ." This would make an excellent family read-aloud. **ET***

AUTHOR: **Dia Calhoun**

TITLE:    *Firegold* (1999)

DESCRIPTION: Jonathon knows that the Valley folk are suspicious of his blue eyes because only their arch enemies, the barbarian Dalriadas, have blue eyes. When the apple crop they depend on fails, the Valley folk blame him, so he escapes to the Dalriadas in order to discover his identity and destiny. His beloved mother has died at the Dalriadas's hands, however, and so he doesn't have much faith that life will be better on the wild mountainous side of the river.

RECOMMENDATION: An interesting book set in a timeless land that explores notions of tolerance and self-respect. Ask yourself, however, if all sources of healing and understanding come from within as Jonathon seems to discover. **MT**

AUTHOR: **Susan Cooper**

TITLE:    *Over Seas, Under Stone* (1965)

DESCRIPTION: Barney, Jane, and Simon Drew are caught up into the timeless battle between good and evil when they find an ancient map in their rented holiday house in Cornwall. Following its clues, they search "over sea and under stone" for King Arthur's grail, but so do sinister forces disguised as innocent villagers and tourists.

RECOMMENDATION: Susan Cooper thinks with Great-Uncle Merry that all "once upon a time" stories are, "underneath all the bits people have added, . . . about one thing—good against evil." *Over Seas, Under Stone* is the first in her marvelous contemporary Once Upon a Time series, and the bits she has added all echo the oldest stories of England and Wales, especially the King Arthur legends. **ET, MT***

AUTHOR: **Susan Cooper**

TITLE:    *The Dark is Rising* (1973)

DESCRIPTION: Newbery Honor. On his eleventh birthday, Will Stanton discovers his role in the cosmic battle of Light and Dark, as the last of the immortal Old Ones. His quest is to find the six signs of a cross inside a circle. They are made of wood, bronze, iron, water, fire, and stone. He must join them together because "the dark is rising," threatening to quench the power of light.

RECOMMENDATION:  In this second novel from which her Dark is Rising series takes its name, Susan Cooper deepens the layers of her story. Will Stanton is no ordinary child like the Drews, who are drawn to the good. He is an immortal, chosen like Merriman Lyon (the Drews' Great-Uncle Merry and also Merlin), from before time to fulfill a destiny that the Law demands, to serve the Light in its gripping battle with the Dark. One of the intriguing questions in this book concerns the relationship between Christian beliefs and practices and the older, more elemental beliefs of the Old Ones. Do you think that Cooper is presenting them as alternative, or even complementary, worldviews, or do you believe that she is promoting the ancient pagan ways as inherently more attractive than Christianity? **ET, MT\***

AUTHOR:  **Susan Cooper**
TITLE:    ***The Grey King*** (1975)

DESCRIPTION:  Newbery Medal, 1976. To recover from a serious illness, Will is sent to his aunt's farm in Wales where he meets a lonely albino boy, Bran, and his dog, Cafall, who also have dual identities. In the shadow

**Susan Cooper** has been compared to C. S. Lewis and J. R. R. Tolkein, both of whom she studied under at Oxford. Her fantasy series has high seriousness and terrific command of images and language, great for reading aloud. You can't help but long for good to defeat evil when you read her stories. Yet they are not an allegory for the Christian story of Jesus' defeating Satan even though they contain many allusions to the Bible as well as to myth. It is difficult to label her, but we can assert that the pagan Celtic myths seem more attractive to Cooper than the Christian story.

In the Dark is Rising sequence, good and evil have equal powers and exist independently of the older natural world—a belief often labeled "dualism." (In the Christian story, God created everything good, and evil is a corruption of the good. However, Christ proved that good is stronger and will ultimately triumph.) Even though Cooper thinks that all of human history shows the eternal struggle between good and evil, it is those equal forces in our human hearts that are more real than the spiritual world we cannot see. And because she didn't write about the Eternal battle, all the children in her stories have to hang on to is their "fierce caring [which] can fan [hope] into a fire to warm the world" and their promise to try their best to fight for good.

of the mountain controlled by the Dark's Grey King, Will and Bran continue the battle against the Dark, rescuing the gold harp and awakening the sleepers, who are necessary for the Light to gain the strength it needs for the final coming conflict.

RECOMMENDATION: Again, Cooper twists the strong threads of her story into more complex patterns. Bran is particularly compelling as he comes to terms with his human and his legendary identity. The particular issues that are highlighted against the larger pattern of Light vs. Dark are the free will of human beings and the sacrifices that must be made when we serve absolute principles. *(Greenwitch* precedes *The Grey King.)* **ET, MT***

AUTHOR: **Susan Cooper**
TITLE: ***Silver on the Tree* (1977)**

DESCRIPTION: The final confrontation of Light and Dark is at hand, drawing all five of the children and their protector, Merriman Lyon, into the conflict. To find the one last weapon, the crystal sword that alone can defeat the Dark, Will and Bran journey into the Lost Land, a visionary country that echoes of all the myths of Britain as well as the Apocalypse of the Bible. But for all their high adventure, in the end, the simple human bonds of love prove to be most crucial against the annihilating evil of the Dark.

RECOMMENDATION: The brilliant kaleidoscope turns again as Cooper's young heroes shift in and out of time and space. This fifth and final volume of the Dark Is Rising series has at the same time the strangest visual images and the most direct message: "We have delivered you from evil, but the evil that is inside of men is at the last a matter for men to control." There are several questions to puzzle out. For example, is it better for the children to forget all their otherworldly adventures? Does Uncle Merry's ascension promise the second coming that he said would never happen? **ET, MT***

AUTHOR: **Susan Cooper**
TITLE: ***King of Shadows* (1999)**

DESCRIPTION: Nat Field, an aspiring teen actor, is rehearsing his part of Puck in Shakespeare's *A Midsummer Night's Dream* at the newly restored Globe Theater in London when he falls seriously ill and awakens as Nat Field in 1599 to play Puck with Shakespeare himself in Shakespeare's own Globe Theater.

RECOMMENDATION: Because this book is written by Susan Cooper, you are right to expect that much more is going on in it than a simple, enjoyable time-slip adventure. On a deeper level, the story is about love and loss and grief and life with Shakespeare's own words providing the healing insights. **MT**

**ET**—Early Teens
**MT**—Mid Teens
**LT**—Late Teens
**AA**—All Ages

AUTHOR: **Stephen Donaldson**

TITLE:    *Lord Foul's Bane* (1984)

DESCRIPTION: First book in the Chronicles of Thomas Covenant, Unbeliever series. Thomas Covenant has leprosy, and his identity lies entrenched in the fact that, because of his disease, he is considered unclean, outcast from society and alienated from his family. Because of his isolation and self-loathing, when he suddenly finds himself in a magic and beautiful world, called The Land, he refuses to believe, not only in The Land ("It's all a dream," he tells himself), and in the central role he must play in the quest to save it from Lord Foul, but also in The Land's power to heal him of his physical and emotional wounds.

RECOMMENDATION: The strength of the Thomas Covenant, Unbeliever series lies in the fantastic mythical world Donaldson has created in The Land, which stands on its own next to the worlds of Tolkien and Lewis. Discussion surely will center on Donaldson's flawed anti-hero, Thomas Covenant. Is this world just his dream, or is it real? Will he believe? If he does, what will that do to his identity as the Unbeliever? **LT**

AUTHOR: **Pauline Fisk**

TITLE:    *Midnight Blue* (1990)

DESCRIPTION: Bonnie has just moved into a flat with her mother, Maybelle, near Highholly Hill after living with her vindictive grandmother who is still bent on destroying their emerging happiness. Running from Grandbag through the holly hedge, Bonnie glimpses a man, a shadowy boy, a hot air balloon, and a chance to escape to another world. Though it mirrors her own world, families are happy there, and her family—Mum, Dad, Arabella, and the baby—accept her with no questions asked. But even here a mirror of Grandbag pursues her. Will the ancient gods of Highholly Hill help her? Will Shadowboy? Or is the evil within, her own feelings of hatred? In making a quiet, ordinary sacrifice of herself, Bonnie learns that it is possible to run from hate and that things can change.

RECOMMENDATION: The writing of this complex fantasy is excellent (it may remind you of Susan Cooper), with characters drawn so surely that they will seem as real to you as the grubby girl in your class or the intense boy watching your soccer game. The moral dilemma of the story is resolved in a convincing way, yet the biblical truth that underlies it is not preachy. Lion published Fisk's book. **ET, MT**\*

AUTHOR: **Alan Garner**

TITLE: *The Weirdstone of Brisingamen* (1960)

DESCRIPTION: Susan discovers that her heirloom bracelet is really the lost weirdstone of Brisingamen, and many are the powers—both good and evil—who want it. She and her brother, Colin, lose and then find it and must, with the help of dwarves and the Lady of the Lake, set out on a quest to restore it to the good wizard Cadellin.

RECOMMENDATION: Garner has dug deeply into Celtic mythology to tell this contemporary good and evil story. It will remind you of Susan Cooper's and Lloyd Alexander's. Even some of the names are the same. If you ever feel as though you are in a battle with principalities and powers, the good dwarf Durathror's description of courage in such circumstances may give you heart. (*Moon of Gomrath* is the sequel.) **ET, MT**

AUTHOR: **Alan Garner**

TITLE: *Elidor* (1965)

DESCRIPTION: As with other of Garner's novels, contemporary British children are caught up in ancient stories of good and evil. This one echoes "Childe Rowland" as Roland and his brothers and sister are drawn into the wasteland kingdom of Elidor through a church being razed in a Manchester slum. Its evil follows them back home to destroy the gifts the king has given them and so prevent the prophesies of restoration from being fulfilled.

**Alan Garner** is a difficult—or challenging—author, depending on which critic you read. Some say he is the best young adults' author living, while others see fatal flaws in what could be masterpieces. He himself says that "there are no original stories," meaning that from prehistory, people have explored the same inexhaustible themes of love and courage, betrayal and death, time and eternity, justice and truth. Most of his novels take their shape from old Celtic and Norse myths because he believes that "fantasy is the intensification of reality." *Red Shift* ends on a totally negative note—"not really not now any more"—which is softened in his later, more warmly human *Stone Quartet* (which you will find under Historical Fiction on page 237). Even if you cannot stay in Garner's ever-expanding, god-abandoned yet god-haunted universe for very long, you will be rewarded by the effort you put into understanding his books.

RECOMMENDATION: Roland's family believes that there has to be a rational explanation for everything, but he keeps faith with what he knows to be true and real even though it means that the unicorn Findhorn must die and that Roland be left standing in a slum with only his memories. **ET, MT**

AUTHOR: **Alan Garner**

TITLE:    ***The Owl Service* (1967)**

DESCRIPTION: Carnegie Medal. Alison's mother and Roger's father have just married. The new family vacations at the Welsh cottage that had been Alison's dead father's. Gwyn and his mother come from Aberystwyth to do the housework. There the three teenagers discover old dishes with an owl pattern and are drawn into a triangle of love and jealousy that reenacts the ancient Welsh legend of Lleu, Gronw, and Blodeuwedd, of flowers and owls, and passion and death, which had its roots in their very valley.

RECOMMENDATION: This splendid modern story uses a timeless myth to probe the notions of the intertwining of love and jealousy, as well as possessive parental control and human freedom. Alison, Gwyn, and Roger "together are destroying each other" and must discover within themselves the key to break the ancient pattern of destruction. The words, the images, the characters, and the powerful brooding valley will all reverberate in your expanded understanding long after you finish the book. **MT**

AUTHOR: **Alan Garner**

TITLE:    ***The Red Shift* (1973)**

DESCRIPTION: The hills of Cheshire, a prehistoric stone axe, and the girls who love and protect them unite three boys otherwise separated by 2000 years. Garner's difficult-to-penetrate novel shifts from brilliant-but-bitter Tom in the twentieth century, lost without his girlfriend, Jan, who must study in London; to sentry, Thomas, in the senventeenth century, who must put aside fear to protect the village from the King's marauders; and to deserter, Macey, in the second century, who tries to "go native" but stumbles onto a local priestess. By the end these three profoundly sad stories merge into one.

RECOMMENDATION: A red shift is a paradoxical astronomical phenomenon associated with a retreating light source that implies that the passage of time is an illusion and that the galaxies are drifting apart. Are Macey and Thomas then inside the head of Tom? Can individuals ever really connect? If you are able to get into Tom's life—not an easy task in this difficult book—you will mourn with him his loss of love and trust. **LT**

ET—Early Teens
MT—Mid Teens
LT—Late Teens
AA—All Ages

AUTHOR: **Brian Jacques**

TITLE:   *Redwall* **(1986)**

DESCRIPTION: Redwall is a peaceful Abbey where the brother mice dedicate their lives (not to God—no worship here, just the cultural reverberations of a true monastic community) to preserving their pastoral environment and to healing any who need it. However, the evil rat, Cluny, and his hordes want to destroy the Abbey and its way of life. How will the nonviolent mice fight back? It is a young novice, Matthias, who—in outgrowing his bumbling habits—leads the way, first, to preparedness and, finally, to a full scale defense. But even Matthias needs a symbol of the righteousness of Redwall's cause, and with the help of the ancient recorder Methuselah, the love of a fieldmouse named Cornflower, and the tactical skills of other woodland folk—Constance, the Badger, in particular—he sets off on a quest to recover the lost sword of the Abbey's long-dead hero, Martin. Besides, the sword could come in handy for a final confrontation with Cluny.

RECOMMENDATION: A delightful story, one of a continuing series that also includes *Mossflower, Mattimeo, Mariel of Redwall, Pearls of Lutra*, and *The Legend of Luke*, all about different characters in the Redwall world. *Taggerung* is the newest volume. The books are a combination talking-animal story, tale of medieval courtly love and adventure, and exciting struggle between good and evil. You can enjoy this book on several levels, even reading into it, if you wish, how we as a society ought to confront the evil that threatens us. This series has legions of fans, young and old alike. **ET, MT, AA\***

AUTHOR: **Robin Jarvis**

TITLE:   *The Dark Portal* **(1989)**

DESCRIPTION: The first of the Deptford Mice trilogy, followed by *The Crystal Prison* and *The Final Reckoning*. A community of mice finds itself doing battle with the evil rat, Lord Jupiter, and his minions who live beneath the Grill in their cellar, after Albert, a loving husband and father, rashly slips through into rat territory. His children go in search of him.

RECOMMENDATION: The classic lines between good and evil are wonderfully drawn in this book in which the Good, under the Green Mouse's protection, longs to encompass all and the Evil turns on itself in wrangling factions. That doesn't mean that good is sugary sweet, not at all, or that evil is overdrawn. The appealing characters have depth and complexity. You'll love the tender, stubborn, brave and inventive mice. This series is sure to captivate Redwall fans. **ET, MT\***

AUTHOR: **Robert Jordan**

TITLE:   ***The Eye of the World*** (1990)

DESCRIPTION: First of the Wheel of Times series. Rand al 'Thor, an ordinary shepherd near Emond's Fields, is caught up in an epic battle against the very forces of the Evil One, who has gained strength in the ages since Time was broken. Two friends, the girl he loves and the village's Wisdom Woman, join him. Is he the savior the world needs in this critical hour?

RECOMMENDATION: Part of the fascination of this overly-long fantasy is figuring out how the individual warriors' freedom of choice fits with the turning of the wheel of time and the weaving of the web of destiny. A glossary of terms helps you discern the cosmology, derivative of Christianity, that Jordan is developing. **LT**

AUTHOR: **Madeleine L'Engle**

TITLE:   ***A Wrinkle in Time*** (1962)

DESCRIPTION: First in the Times Quartet, Newbery Award, 1963. Meg Murry tesseracts to another planet to battle the IT for control of her little brother Charles Wallace's mind, her only weapon powerful enough being love. In the second of the Times Quartet, *A Wind in the Door*, Meg and Charles Wallace are a year older. Meg, with the help of a cherub, must travel into the mitochondria of Charles's ill body to name a farandola. Thereby she not only saves his life but adds to the underlying harmonies of the universe and defeats the evil Echthroi. In *A Swiftly Tilting Planet*, a teenaged Charles Wallace, with the help of his grown sister and a unicorn named Gaudior, travels through both time and space to several critical "might-have beens" of history where small choices for good may prevent a nuclear holocaust in his own time.

RECOMMENDATION: These first three books of the series are worth coming back to again and again. **ET, MT***

AUTHOR: **Madeleine L'Engle**

TITLE:   ***Many Waters*** (1986)

DESCRIPTION: Fourth in the Times Quartet. The fifteen-year-old Murry twins, Sandy and Dennys, finally get their chance at time travel when they ask their father's computer to take them to a warm, dry place. They land in Noah's oasis before the Flood. Like Charles Wallace and Meg, they must discern good from evil, gain help from celestial creatures, make choices that will affect the history of their planet, and believe that El (God) has a pattern—not chaos—that will work out "in beauty in the end."

RECOMMENDATION: You may have to suspend your disbelief to enter a story you know so well from Sunday school through the medium of fantasy. Do you think that using a Bible story as a springboard to fiction has inherent dangers that an author must work extra hard to avoid? **ET, MT, LT**

AUTHOR: **Madeleine L'Engle**

TITLE: ***An Acceptable Time*** (1989)

DESCRIPTION: L'Engle's "realistic" Poly O'Keefe stories and her "fantasy" Murry ones merge in this sequel to both series. Poly, visiting her Murry grandparents, is pulled into a 3,000-year-old American Indian/British Druid society, along with her neighbor, Bishop Columbra, and the heartless Zachary *(A Moon by Night* and *House Like a Lotus).* There she discovers that two warring tribes consider her a goddess with magical powers. One of them decides to sacrifice her to bring the much-needed rain. Poly must determine whether she is willing to die for the people—and for the selfish Zachary who also believes that her death would heal his diseased heart.

RECOMMENDATION: All of L'Engle's themes are repeated here—the meaning of time, the crucial importance of love, and the necessity of sacrifice and forgiveness. She intersperses orthodox Christian doctrine with Druid and animistic beliefs and practices. Perhaps you will find that one

**Madeleine L'Engle** is a rare author, one who is both openly Christian and fully accepted in the secular publishing world. Not only does she weave biblical references into her books but at a deeper level alludes to mystics, theologians, writings from other faiths that echo Christianity, and to scientists who share her concerns: faith, hope, and love; the singular importance of the individual; and how his or her choices affect the whole of creation. The universe is the setting for a battle between good and evil; all characters in L'Engle's books, whether they are "fantasy" or "real," must throw in their lot with one side or the other—usually at a personal cost. Nor is right or wrong easy to discern from the externals of intelligence, beauty, wealth, or even religious trappings. L'Engle affirms created life and the ultimate, if not immediate, triumph of good. Her books are richly layered, surprisingly and challengingly eclectic, and, with one exception *(House Like a Lotus),* uncompromisingly true. They reward careful reading and rereading. (You'll find L'Engle's books listed under both categories, and—although they're not—some of her contemporary books could also be listed as mysteries.) Countless families and classrooms have shared these books by reading them aloud together.

of the most telling theological exchanges comes at the climax of the crisis when Poly refuses to take credit for doing what only God can do but does not give him the credit for it either, saying, "It just happened." How does this fit the L'Engle pattern and a coherent worldview? If she is implying that all belief systems are equally valid, has she betrayed her loyal readers? **MT**, **LT**

AUTHOR: **Ursula LeGuin**

TITLE: ***A Wizard of Earthsea*** (1968)

DESCRIPTION: Series continued in *The Tombs of Atuan* and *The Farthest Shore*. On an adult level, the series concludes with *Tehanu*. Because he saved his village from marauders, it is discovered that Sparrowhawk has magical powers. Sent to study with the sorcerers, he learns quickly, particularly the true name of things, but he uses his newly discovered power against a jealous fellow student. As a result, Ged—for that is Sparrowhawk's true name—disturbs the balance of the world by releasing a fearsome evil shadow. It takes three confrontations before Ged can be freed of his terrible quest to undo the harm he has begun. By the last volume, Ged is the Archmage, but the wells of magic are running dry and with it the Earthsea peoples' joy in living. With the young prince of Erlad, Arren, he seeks out the source of this wasting and despair but not without great cost to himself and the prince.

RECOMMENDATION: This lyrical fantasy series explores the ageless themes of good and evil, being and nonbeing, humility and arrogance. It affirms the good we all desire without denying the evil that resides in the hearts of all humans. Its stirring phrases and uncompromising integrity will etch Ged into your heart; it may disturb the balance of your own universe, but only for the good. Even though *A Wizard* is kept with the children's collection in most libraries, don't be in a hurry to read these books as their themes are ones that demand maturity to understand. If you grew up with Ged's stories, you may, as older teens and adults, want to see a new collection of short stories about Earthsea, called *Tales from Earthsea* (2001). Each has a simple theme expressed in beautiful language. LeGuin promises that the last story in her collection, "Dragonfly," is a bridge to a new Earthsea novel, *The Other Wind*. **MT**, **LT***

AUTHOR: **Gail Carson Levine**

TITLE: ***Ella Enchanted*** (1997)

DESCRIPTION: Newbery Honor, 1998. Ella is cursed at birth with the "gift" of absolute obedience by a confused fairy. After her mother dies and her father remarries, her new stepsisters take advantage of this fact to make life miserable for her. She can't even receive the gift of Prince Char's love for her lest she be forced to betray his kingdom.

RECOMMENDATION: Though Robin McKinley is the master—or should we say mistress?—of this burgeoning sub-genre of fantasy, the retold fairy tale, special pride of place must be given to this clever and tender retelling of the Cinderella story. **ET**

AUTHOR: **Janet Lunn**

TITLE: ***The Root Cellar*** (1981)

DESCRIPTION: A lonely orphan, Rose, is sent to her aunt's home in Canada where she finds she has more in common with the family who lived there during the Civil War era, more than a hundred years before. Rose and Susan set off to find Will after he hadn't returned with his New York regiment from the American war.

RECOMMENDATION: Through ways sorrowful and joyful, Rose, Susan, and Will change into the people they were meant to be in the times God put them into because they grow in the realization that "being a person is very hard" but oh, so right. What does it mean to "be a person"? You will also enjoy Lunn's *Shadow at Hawthorne Bay*. **ET**

AUTHOR: **William Mayne**

TITLE: ***Earthfasts*** (1967)

DESCRIPTION: Two fellows encounter a soldier about their age—but from an army garrisoned at their town's decrepit castle 200 years previously. It is the first of several unexplainable events that compel David and Kevin into great danger.

RECOMMENDATION: The strength of this well-written classic fantasy is in how we can see the boys' minds working to explain what they have experienced. Their encounters with the supernatural push at the boundaries of their scientific and moral explanations, but they are humble enough before the evidence to acknowledge their inadequacies. How would you explain what happened to them? Another Mayne title you may want to check out is *Antar and the Eagles*. **MT**

AUTHOR: **Donna Jo Napoli**

TITLE: ***The Magic Circle*** (1993)

DESCRIPTION: In a truly magical re-telling of the Hansel and Gretel story from the witch's perspective, Napoli compels us to experience as did the Ugly One the power of pride to deceive our hearts and the power of love and beauty and service to redeem us. Or does beauty deceive as well?

RECOMMENDATION: This short book deserves to be read aloud and shared with loved ones because it explores profound themes of sin and redemption in a way that touches both our hearts and minds deeply. It does so against the backdrop of late medieval beliefs about witches as well as a familiar fairy tale. **ET, AA**

**ET**—Early Teens
**MT**—Mid Teens
**LT**—Late Teens
**AA**—All Ages

AUTHOR: **Pat O'Shea**

TITLE: ***The Hounds of the Morrigan*** (1985)

DESCRIPTION: Pidge and Bridget are just ordinary Irish children, but they have been chosen by the creator-god, The Dagda, to thwart the Morrigan, the three-in-one goddess of death and destruction, by preventing her from regaining her ancient power from a bloody pebble and a hideous snake. On their quest they are pursued by the Morrigan's hounds and helped by the oddest, most enchanting assortment of creatures ever to take a life of their own on paper. Even Pidge and Bridget's smallest, seemingly insignificant actions in the "real" world become freighted with significance in the fairy world that hovers just out of sight of those who refuse to see that even natural apples coming from pink blossoms is miraculous.

RECOMMENDATION: More than in most good-versus-evil fantasies, you can catch glimpses of the parallels between Christianity and the old myths in this imaginative weaving of Irish myth into contemporary reality. Another wonderful distinctive is its celebration of the goodness of created life. Though he is beginning to be aware of the dangers that he and Bridget face, Pidge thinks, "In my heart I'm glad that I'm mixed up with [these supernatural events]. Not everyone gets this kind of chance." **ET, MT***

AUTHOR: **Kenneth Oppel**

TITLE: ***Silverwing*** (1997)

DESCRIPTION: Shade, a runty bat who makes up what he lacks in size with curiosity and daring, learns the traditions of his clan and the promise of Nocturna before he is separated from the other bats on their annual migration. Blown off course, he meets Marina, a banded bat from another clan, and together they seek the Silverwings' Hibernaculum, overcoming a multitude of dangers and learning to discern wisdom from folly.

RECOMMENDATION: Underneath the exciting adventure of Shade and Marina is an allegory of Faith that emerges only to those who—like the bats—have ears to hear it. The sequel is called *Sunwing.* **ET, MT**

AUTHOR: **Richard Peck**

TITLE: *The Ghost Belonged To Me* (1975)

DESCRIPTION: ALA Notable book. There are more laughs than shivers in this first farce, à la Mark Twain, about the ghosts that haunt Bluff City in 1913, Alexander Armsworth and Blossom Culp in particular. The pretentious get their comeuppance, and swindlers their just desserts thanks to them, saucy great-uncle Miles, and a ghost that just wants to be laid to rest properly.

RECOMMENDATION: Alexander comments that ghosts were falling out of fashion in the twentieth century as much as Victorian gingerbread architecture and his sister's ample figure. Peck is also a twentieth-century unbeliever who uses these vaudeville characters and slapstick comedy to poke fun at human frailties. Among its sequels are *Ghosts I Have Been* and *The Dreadful Future of Blossom Culp*. **ET**

AUTHOR: **Philip Pullman**

TITLE: *The Golden Compass* (1995)

DESCRIPTION: Carnegie Medal, ALA Notable Children's book. A ragtag girl, Lyra, and her daemon alter ego, Patalaimon, plays in the streets of Oxford (but is it the Oxford of our world?) with her pal Roger, but she begins to be disturbed by rumors of missing gyptian children. Her uncle, Lord Asriel, arrives, talking mysteriously about Dust and showing the severed head of an explorer. Lyra joins battle on the side of the gyptians, witches, and armored bears to find the threatened children in the far North, little dreaming that the stakes involve the past and futures of vast universes.

RECOMMENDATION: Be prepared to expand your theological knowledge as you read—and surely discuss—this book which is a *naturalistic* retelling of Milton's *Paradise Lost* and hence the Genesis account of the Fall. **MT, LT**

AUTHOR: **Philip Pullman**

TITLE: *The Subtle Knife* (1997)

DESCRIPTION: Second of the His Dark Materials trilogy. After Roger's death, when Lyra breaks through to another universe, she meets Will, a twelve-year-old who has murdered an intruder as he had set off from his Oxford home to find his long-lost father. Each is on a quest of eternal significance. Together they avoid the Spectors, who kill people a little older than they are. As Lyra had been destined to read the alethiometer, so Will was destined to use the subtle knife—fates that would send them to the heart of the battle between good and evil.

RECOMMENDATION: The questions that you will continue to ask yourselves (these books can only be talked about with family and friends) are what is good in Pullman's created universe and what is evil? What is Dust? Original sin, knowledge, experience? Is it to be sought or destroyed? **MT, LT**

AUTHOR: **Philip Pullman**

TITLE:    ***The Amber Spyglass*** **(2000)**

DESCRIPTION: The third and most critical of the His Dark Materials trilogy. While malevolent forces are seeking their destruction, Will and Lyra crisscross universes, surer than ever that they must join Lord Asriel's fight to overthrow the repressive Authority and set the lost children free from the Land of the Dead. All the time they are unaware that

**Philip Pullman** has been favorably compared to the master fantasist, J. R. R. Tolkien, for his ability to create a complex and believable "secondary universe." Even so, he has publicly scorned Tolkien's friend C. S. Lewis's work as "sheer dishonesty" and "ugly and poisonous." In His Dark Materials trilogy, Pullman inverts the *Paradise Lost* epic—and, therefore, the creation story of Genesis—boldly taking his stand with the rebels against Authority. Lyra/Eve's fall, by extension, is truly a "fortunate fall," not as because, as Milton argued, sin necessitated a savior, but because she "fell" into experience, both intellectual and sexual. This experience is the hallmark of independent, moral, choice-making personhood. Dust, one of the primary images of the novels, represents this kind of experience.

Pullman's writing is brilliant. For example, the creation of each person's daemon as his or her alter ego is unique in literature. However, Pullman's ideological purpose undermines the overall effectiveness of the stories. His unsubtle categorization of everything religious as evil and everything which revolts against religion as good is a contemporary version of the ancient heresy of Manichaeism.

Interestingly, nevertheless, Pullman, though he loathes the biblical narrative so explicitly, cannot help but depend upon it for his own positive images. For example, the No-Name Harpy loved the nourishment of *true* stories but not the lies that fell so easily from Lyra's lips. When Mrs. Coulter tried to explain that she really loved her daughter Lyra, she admitted that she didn't know the source of that love but that it came to her "like a thief in the night." Finally, when Lyra mourned her loss of ability to read the alethiometer, she was told that she had read it "by grace." Pullman cannot escape the Grand Narrative of Redemption however much he protests against it. Therefore, though his cosmology is blatantly naturalistic and his god is the autonomous Self of modernism, the series of books can be worthwhile to read and discuss together as a family. They will reward examination, helping you to understand the mind-set of Western culture.

The title of the series comes from this passage from Book II of *Paradise Lost*:

> *Unless the almighty maker them ordain*
> *His dark materials to create more worlds,*
> *Into this wide abyss the wary fiend*
> *Stood on the brink of hell and looked a while,*
> *Pondering his voyage. . . .*

their destinies are even more deeply embedded in the age-old story of good and evil and entwined with each other.

RECOMMENDATION: Will and Lyra's moment of sexual awakening heralds the new Fall—this time recognized in Pullman's universe as the ultimate good, not evil. This makes sense of all that went on before, but is it convincing? Lyra and Will are their own saviors. Despite all their bravery and experience in battle, are they up to the job? How do you evaluate their great personal sacrifice at the end? **MT, LT**

AUTHOR: **J. K. Rowling**

TITLE: ***Harry Potter and the Sorcerer's Stone*** (1998)

DESCRIPTION: Harry, an orphan, lives with his Uncle Vernon, Aunt Petunia, and cousin Dudley, who take pleasure in making his life as miserable as possible. On his eleventh birthday, he receives owl-delivered and then giant-delivered messages telling him to report to the Hogwarts School of Witchcraft and Wizardry. There he learns that he is famous in the wizard world for having foiled the attempts of Voldemort, the most wicked wizard, to kill him at the time he had cursed his parents with death. Harry settles happily into school, with its classes and friendships and sports, but Voldemort is not finished with him.

RECOMMENDATION: Wonderful characterizations, rollicking fun, spoofs on British school life, undergirded with a morally coherent battle between good and evil: all these make the first Harry Potter a hit with kids. In this story, what central metaphor for Christ's love can you see? **ET, MT**

AUTHOR: **J. K. Rowling**

TITLE: ***Harry Potter and the Chamber of Secrets*** (1999)

DESCRIPTION: Harry Potter, Ron, and Hermione return to Hogwarts for their second year, there to face new classes (Hermione loves these), batty professors, and Slytherin Draco Malfoy's attempts to make their lives unhappy. A Quiddich tournament and a fifty-year-old mystery surrounding Hogwart's Chamber of Secrets challenge their understanding of how life should work.

RECOMMENDATION: Harry continues to learn whom to trust and whom to fight as he grows in discernment and accepts his role as defender of the good in the world. **ET, MT**

AUTHOR: **J. K. Rowling**

TITLE: ***Harry Potter and the Prisoner of Azkaban*** (1999)

DESCRIPTION: Their third year at Hogwarts beckons Harry, Ron, and Hermione. The trio faces more wryly humorous situations, but they—

and especially Harry—must look within themselves for the resources to combat the prisoners of Azkaban who have escaped. Are Sirius Black and the Dementors, hired to protect Harry, who they seem to be? How about Professor Snape and Professor Lupin?

RECOMMENDATION: Harry must face his past as well as figure out his future as he grows up throughout this year. The forces of evil are more complex, and so Harry must grow in understanding to be able to prevail against them. **ET, MT**

AUTHOR: **J. K. Rowling**

TITLE: ***Harry Potter and the Goblet of Fire* (2000)**

DESCRIPTION: After watching the exciting Quidditch World Cup final match between Ireland and Bulgaria, Harry returns to Hogwarts for his fourth year. Instead of the usual inter-school Quidditch rivalry, this year there is a Triwizard Tournament among three schools, each represented by a champion, including Bulgaria's whiz Quidditch player. After Cedric Diggory was chosen to represent Hogwarts, why did the Goblet of Fire

**J. K. Rowling**, who has authored the most astonishing series in the history of children's publishing, causing many former non-readers to take up her Harry Potter books, has said that she has been deeply influenced by C. S. Lewis. That's one reason there will eventually be seven books in the Harry Potter series, just like the Narnia Chronicles. They are so wildly popular because they work well on several levels—as laugh-aloud books with word-plays, jokes and spoofs of British boarding school life, and as an introduction to a thoroughly real set of true-to-life characters who have their own quirks, foibles, and endearing charms paralleling our own. Except for the stereotypical mean stepfamily, the Dursleys, there are no cardboard, predictable characters. These include elves, giants, ghosts, animals, and oddball teachers of all sorts. Most importantly, Hogwarts is a complete world unto itself, a believable sub-creation in which the characters take chances, grow, fail, are forgiven, and learn discernment as they join the fight for the life-giving good against the life-destroying evil. Though Rowling is not a Christian believer, we can see the C. S. Lewis influence on her work in how she has created a "moral world that is consistent with biblical revelation of the nature of good and evil" (Neal, 176). Our recommendation, if you hesitate to let your children read Harry Potter because of the many claims that the books promote witchcraft as a positive lifestyle, is to read them yourselves first. Then explore the issue further with the well balanced, in-depth discussion in Connie Neal's *What's a Christian To Do With Harry Potter?* (WaterBrook Press, 2001). You must be fully convinced in your own mind, but exercise that mind prayerfully and with all the facts. You may become convinced, as we are, that not only are the books excellent fantasy, but that God can use them for redemptive conversations within your family and with the larger culture.

ET—Early Teens
MT—Mid Teens
LT—Late Teens
AA—All Ages

call Harry's name as well? Harry must complete three impossible tests as well as—horrors—lead the revelry at the Christmas Ball.

RECOMMENDATION: Harry's battle with Lord Voldemort both broadens its stage and deepens its consequences. How do Harry and Hermione and others' attitudes toward social differences, both across international boundaries and within the hierarchy of Hogwarts, impact the battle? How does the protection of the sacrifice Harry's mother had made for him extend its benefits even to the most evil Lord Voldemort? What parallels to the gospel do you see here? **ET, MT**

AUTHOR: **Robert Siegel**

TITLE: *Whalesong* (1981)

DESCRIPTION: First in a triology that includes *White Whale* and *Ice At the End of the World*. Hruna is a humpback whale whose size and courage mark him for a great destiny among the sea creatures. Humbly he submits to a visit to the Great Whale at the ocean's bottom, where he learns his place in the scheme of the universe as well as his true name. Skirmishes with man, the polluter of the oceans and the whale's most fierce enemy, prepare him to lead a final climactic battle for the survival of his pod.

RECOMMENDATION: Even those of you who know little about the life of sea animals will be fascinated by the lyrical (music is the primary motif) story of one humpback whale. You may read it as an absorbing adventure and as a fable about the need of all creatures—human included—to find their proper niches in the whole fragile and enchanted structure of the created ecology. What is our relationship to the created order? **AA***

AUTHOR: **Gloria Skurzynski**

TITLE: *What Happened in Hamelin* (1979)

DESCRIPTION: This is a fascinating retelling of the Pied Piper of Hamelin based, says the author, on historical evidence from medieval Germany. The events are seen primarily through the eyes of one of the older children, Geist, a baker's servant, who longs for the freedom that the Piper promises him.

RECOMMENDATION: One of the most intriguing features of this book is its exploration of medieval Christian views of human nature. With Geist you will wonder if Gant, the Piper, is evil. Is he a Christian (who isn't in that society)? Does he cause the evil that flows forth in others? This book should allow great family discussion. **ET**

AUTHOR: **J. R. R. Tolkien**

TITLE: ***The Hobbit*** (1937)

DESCRIPTION: Bilbo Baggins must leave his comfortable home in Bag End, Underhill, Hobiton, The Shire to help the dwarves recover their lost gold from a fire-breathing dragon. As he is in the midst of this adventure, he discovers a ring that has the power to make him invisible.

RECOMMENDATION: *The Hobbit* began as a bedtime story for Tolkien's children, but those who know their literary history will discover in it echoes of Wagner's *Ring Cycle* and *Beowulf.* Its theme is the common one of maturation as Bilbo goes on a quest to gain a treasure, but the achievement of that theme and that maturity is uncommon indeed. **AA***

AUTHOR: **J. R. R. Tolkien**

TITLE: ***The Lord of the Rings*** (1954, 1955)

DESCRIPTION: The trilogy consists of *The Fellowship of the Ring, The Two Towers,* and *The Return of the King.* The ring that Bilbo found in *The Hobbit* must now be lost—destroyed—because the ring, which Sauron,

**J. R. R. Tolkien** not only singlehandedly generated the contemporary revival of the fantasy or epic romance with *The Hobbit* and *The Lord of the Rings,* but he set the standard for fantasy that all who have followed him have tried to meet. Amazon.com has estimated that an astonishing 10 percent of all paperback books published are indebted in someway to Tolkien! Obviously then, his preferred form of art, fantasy based on the older mythological literatures of many cultures, has many riches to offer generations of readers. Tolkien knew loss as a child with the death of his parents and he knew gain with his own loving family, his Catholic faith, and his work as a professor of Anglo Saxon at Oxford. Because of these personal factors, he was not afraid of the charge that he wrote escapist literature, for who would not want to escape from the world as it is if it means escaping to a better world, a heightened reality, the world as its Creator meant it to be. He believed that a writer is a "sub-creator," doing in miniature what God did in creating the world, and no one has accomplished that creation of a sub-world better than he. Stephen Lawhead, another fantasy writer, says that Tolkien's works are a "celebration of life in all its myriad elements. . . .nothing less than a praise hymn to creation." The story of Middle Earth, he says, "paints a convincing portrait of Goodness, Beauty, and Truth." It's no wonder that Tolkien has so many imitators.

the Dark Lord, had made, is at the epicenter of the epic struggle between good and evil. Bilbo's nephew, Frodo, who has inherited the ring, is engaged in a battle much bigger than for his own life and the Shire. Nothing less than the survival of civilization and nature itself is at stake. The wizard, Gandalf, and the hobbits are attempting to destroy the ring before it destroys them. All must make choices as to which force he or she will serve, choices that shape who they are and what will become of the lands they inhabit.

RECOMMENDATION: The plight and the quest of these so-human creatures with their full range of emotions and motivations will become your own as you come under the spell of enchantment that Tolkien so skillfully weaves by his language that borders on poetry. Mythologies and literatures weave through these volumes as well, but the biblical truth of losing one's life to find it forms the very heart. You should become better yourself for having journeyed with Frodo through Middle Earth. **MT, LT***

AUTHOR: **Vivian Vande Velde**

TITLE: *The Rumplestiltskin Problem* (2000)

DESCRIPTION: This slim volume gives six alternative tellings of the Rumplestiltskin fairytale.

RECOMMENDATION: Each of these humorous, insightful tales probes the motivations of at least one of the characters involved. Delightful read-alouds that can foster fun discussions. **ET, AA**

AUTHOR: **Walter Wangerin, Jr.**

TITLE: *The Book of the Dun Cow* (1978)

DESCRIPTION: Chaunticleer the Rooster gives the barnyard world he rules over "direction and meaning and a proper soul" in part by his daily canonical crows. He knows his own importance. What he does not know is that this proper soul is keeping the diabolical Wyrm imprisoned beneath the earth as well. In a neighboring land, a prideful rooster reaches for more power than is rightfully his and in so doing gives birth to the monster-Rooster, Cockatrice. The Wyrm exploits that situation to break away. The battle lines are drawn, but Chaunticleer learns that, though he can win a fearsome battle, yet without the mysterious Dun Cow and the ordinary Mundo Cani (the barnyard mutt), he cannot win the war.

RECOMMENDATION: You will recognize many people you know—with all their mixture of gracious loveliness and frustrating faults (dare you think, sins?)—in the delightfully endearing animals that people this fantasy-fable. Perhaps you will also recognize the biblical account of proper living, of real lostness, and of undeserved salvation in it as well, and hold its truths more dear for recognizing them in this form. **LT***

AUTHOR: **John White**

TITLE: ***The Tower of Geburah* (1978)**

DESCRIPTION: Sequels in the Archives of Anthropos series published by InterVarsity Press are *The Iron Sceptre, The Sword Bearer, Gaal the Conqueror,* and *Quest for the King.* In the C. S. Lewis tradition, John White has created three children who enter another land, Anthropos, through an object, a TV, in their own world. There they discover that the rightful king, Kardia, is imprisoned; that the drought-stricken land is under the control of evil powers; and that the Shepherd, Gaal, is rumored to be near. Wesley, Lisa, and Kurt are drawn into the battle but must choose which side to aid and, in their very stubborn humanity, do not automatically make the best choices. It's good for them and for Anthropos that Gaal is near.

RECOMMENDATION: As one of Gaal's servants tells the children, "True wisdom cannot be seen from the outside, only from within." This book allows you to get on the inside of both wisdom and some very exciting adventures. You will be glad that the last line of the first volume promises more. **ET, MT***

AUTHOR: **Charles Williams**

TITLE: ***All Hallows Eve* (1945)**

DESCRIPTION: Charles Williams explores familiar themes of substitutionary love and the coequal realities of the natural and the supernatural. After World War II no more terror should fall from the sky, but even so a pedestrian, Lester Furnival, is killed in a plane accident. From her position in purgatory, Lester goes about unfinished business on earth, appearing to her husband, Richard, asking forgiveness of old friends, and, most particularly, helping to unshackle Betty from the grasp of the greedy spiritualist, Simon the Clerk, whose magic he has matched against Lester's love. The climax comes on a rainy London Halloween, "All Hallows Eve," when Williams shows again that the only wholeness people can have is through love.

RECOMMENDATION: Although this novel is by no means easy, Williams will reward your efforts if you attempt to read and understand him. **LT**

AUTHOR: **Charles Williams**

TITLE: *Descent into Hell* (1937)

DESCRIPTION: Peter Stanhope has written a play, which his neighbors decid
to put on. Only Pauline Anstruther understands its significance, but sh
is terrorized by ghostly fears. Stanhope encourages her to let him "sub
stitute" for her; he will take over her burden of fear through love
Relieved of that burden, Pauline can now bear the burdens of the othe
actors. Some of them grow in grace with her and others refuse to.

RECOMMENDATION: Charles Williams, a friend of C. S. Lewis and J. R. R
Tolkien, did not write a typical fantasy by which his characters and you
his readers, are transported to another world that those with less spiri
tual insight cannot see. Rather, you see the supernatural invading th
natural, for according to Williams's Christian theology, the two alway
coexist, either easily or uneasily, either for good or for evil. It may seen
surrealistic or spooky, but it makes theological sense. **LT**

AUTHOR: **Patricia Wrightson**

TITLE: *Moon Dark* (1987)

DESCRIPTION: Blue, Mort the fisherman's dog, knows that the Australia
wildlife—the bush rats, bandicoots, koalas, kangaroos, flying foxes, an
wild dingos—with whom he shares nocturnal adventures, are uneas
and hungry. Since building had begun in their backwater scrub, ther
doesn't seem to be enough food for everyone. Now the bush rats an
the bandicoots are openly at war. With the help of Keeting (Who is thi
ancient magical singer?) and by dint of the animals' own exhaustin
efforts, the ecological balance is restored.

RECOMMENDATION: *Moon Dark* may well become one of your favorite sto
ries; perhaps you will want to share it aloud with your family. Withou
humanizing the animals, Patricia Wrightson has captured their distinc
tive—memorable—personalities. She has woven Australian myth
throughout, as in all her books, enriching the story's action and mean
ing. And the very lack of stridency in her ecological message underscore
its urgency. **ET**

# Chapter 15

# Historical

AUTHOR: **Margot Benary-Isbert**

TITLE: ***The Ark* (1953)**

DESCRIPTION: In devastated Germany after World War II, the refugee Lechow family—or what was left of it, for Margret's twin had been killed and Father was in a camp in Russia—was ordered to reconstruct their lives at 13 Parsley Street in Mrs. Verduz's two attic rooms. Across the hard months from October 1946 to December 1947, the Lechows do come back to life by sharing their meager stores, watching them multiply with love. They open their hearts to other refugees, including Matthias's musical friend, Dieter, and impish Joey's orphan friend, Hans Ulrich. Only Margret does not have someone special, but she does have the offer of a job as kennel maid for Mrs. Almut. She and Matthias rebuild an old railway car into an Ark for their family and are renewed and restored by working on the land. Margret and Matthias's story continues in *Rowan Farm*.

RECOMMENDATION: Never a book to shy away from the harsh realities of war, *The Ark* is even more a book about the greater realities of love and courage and faith. You will be blessed to find these qualities so real among the people you may have thought of as the enemy. Most of Benary-Isbert's books are out of print now, unfortunately, but most libraries still carry copies so that new generations can benefit from these wonderful books. **ET, MT***

AUTHOR: **Gillian Bradshaw**

TITLE: ***A Beacon at Alexandria*** (1986)

DESCRIPTION: Charis's father engages her to Ephesus' cruel new governor. In order to escape, she disguises herself as a eunuch, Chariton, and goes to Alexandria to study medicine. No one will take her on except an old Jewish doctor, but from him she learns not only the Hippocratic skills and theories but also compassion for her patients. Alexandria is the most intellectually exciting city in the Roman empire, where all ideas clash, including the doctrines of various Christian factions. Because she has caught the keen eye of the godly Archbishop Athanasios, she is engulfed in the riots that follow his death and has to escape once more, this time to Thrace, at the northern border of the empire. There she is assigned to be an army doctor, while the Goths begin to harass and finally to conquer the once invincible Romans. Though she feared she would have to wait until heaven, it is in Thrace that Charis can at last become whole: a Roman, a doctor, and a woman.

RECOMMENDATION: Gillian Bradshaw's vivid panorama captures both the splendor and the squalor of a little-known period of history—the declining years of the Roman empire. It does so through the eyes of a most unusual heroine, a brilliant young girl who longs against all possible reason to become a doctor. Many philosophies clash in idea-obsessed Alexandria, but the ones that allow Charis and her love, Athanaric, to be true to their own best selves come from a humble Jewish doctor and an archbishop who loves God more than he loves power. Reading *A Beacon at Alexandria* is a wonderful way to be swept up in their struggle, for it is yours too. Another book by Bradshaw set in this time period is *The Bearkeeper's Daughter*. Look also for *Horses of Heaven, Sand Reckoner,* and *Island of Ghosts.* **LT***

AUTHOR: **Sue Ellen Bridgers**

TITLE: ***All Together Now*** (1979)

DESCRIPTION: Casey must spend her twelfth summer with her grandparents while her father is away in the Korean War and her mother is working. An odd assortment of people combine to make her time there unforgettable: Dwayne, a thirty-three-year-old retarded baseball fanatic; Hazard, a charming but unemployed dancing-man-waiter who is still courting Grandmother's friend, Pansy, after twenty-five years; and Uncle Taylor who would rather race cars and flirt with Gwen than work in Grandfather's lumberyard.

RECOMMENDATION: Casey senses that this will be the only time she will be able to deceive Dwayne into believing that she is the boy-companion he longs for. In doing so, she gets caught up in the small but significant battles in the empty lot, on the racetrack, and in the courthouse, to preserve for him the space he needs to be himself when his brother wants to commit him to an institution. This is a book about what people can do—even to determine by sheer will that others get well as the polio epidemic touches their small town—if only they will take the responsibility for each other. **ET**, **MT**

AUTHOR: **Michael Cadnum**

TITLE: *The Book of the Lion* (2000)

DESCRIPTION: Edmund, rescued from prison by a knight, learns how deeply honor and cruelty are intertwined as he accompanies his rescuer on the Crusades. King Richard the Lionheart's forces battle the Saracens at the Siege of Acre and the Battle of Arsuf.

RECOMMENDATION: In many ways the Christian Middle Ages is just as distant a world from ours as is the ancient Mayan civilization *(Heart of a Jaguar)* or current Mozambique *(A Girl Named Disaster)*. Cadnum, who is known more for his almost bitter young adult contemporary novels, brings the religious devotion and the almost casual disregard for life and other cultures to sensitive realization in Edmund and his companions. What threads connect Edmund's world to your own? **MT**

AUTHOR: **Christopher Paul Curtis**

TITLE: *Bud, Not Buddy* (1999)

DESCRIPTION: Newbery Medal, 2000. Ten-year-old Bud is motherless and on the run in Flint, Michigan, in 1936. Tired of living in a home for orphaned children, he finds a flyer that he thinks may lead him to his father, a flyer that advertises Herman E. Calloway and his famous band, the Dusky Devastators of the Depression. He sets out across the state on his own, with his tattered suitcase and, through miracles, human kindness and incredible luck laced with wisdom, Bud finds people who care about him.

RECOMMENDATION: The story is full of humor and wonderful characters, hitting the high notes of jazz and the low notes of coping with the Great Depression. Also see Curtis's award-winning novel, *The Watsons Go to Birmingham*. **ET***

AUTHOR: **Karen Cushman**

TITLE: *Catherine, Called Birdie* (1994)

DESCRIPTION: Newbery Honor. As Cadnum's *Book of the Lion* brings alive a boy's life in the cruel Middle Ages, so Cushman's *Catherine* gives flesh and blood to a girl's existence. Of course, her heroine is no "typical" girl mastering feminine skills and waiting passively for marriage. Rather she is a feisty modern longing for her freedom. Or do all people in all times and places long for it as well?

RECOMMENDATION: "In the illimitable sweep of time, what will it signify? What will you signify?" Perhaps this musing of Catherine's is the key question of this book—what does human life, particularly a girl's, mean in 1290? How would you characterize their faith in an omnipresent God? Does it seem more like a modern kind of faith, the kind you would observe today? Compare to Barbara Dana's *Young Joan* (the story of Joan of Arc) for a picture of family life saturated in faith. One of the most intriguing features of Cushman's novel is the saints' days headings for Catherine's journal. **ET**

AUTHOR: **Anne De Vries**

TITLE: ***Journey through the Night* (1984)**

DESCRIPTION: The De Boers, and especially their teenage son, John, resisted all that Hitler stood for when the Germans invaded Holland because they served both their fellow human beings and a higher King who controls all history.

RECOMMENDATION: De Vries is a Dutch author who, better than almost anyone else, captured on paper the essence of World War II. Translated into English and published first in 1984 by a Canadian publishing house, *Journey Through the Night* recently has been reprinted by Inheritance Publications. If your library does not have it, buy it while it is still in print. It is worth every penny! **MT, LT\***

AUTHOR: **Lloyd C. Douglas**

TITLE: ***The Robe* (1942)**

DESCRIPTION: Marcellus, son of a Roman senator, is banished to the edge of the Roman empire, where he is in charge of soldiers performing a crucifixion. It has left him with a bad taste in his mouth and the victim's robe in his possession. That robe, with its unusual power to affect its handler's mind, causes Marcellus's mental sickness and then his recovery so that he—along with his Greek slave, Demitrius, and eventually his beloved, Diana, a favorite of two cruel emperors—is led to discover the truth about Jesus.

RECOMMENDATION: This is a classic piece of historical fiction. **MT, LT\***

AUTHOR:  **Tony Earley**

TITLE:    ***Jim The Boy*** (2001)

DESCRIPTION:  Jim's father died just days before he was born. Raised in the depression-era in small-town North Carolina by his devoted mother Cissy and three bachelor uncles, Jim's tenth year is a year of firsts: his first trip to the ocean, his first best friend, his first baseball glove, his first encounter with a bully, and his mother's first suitor. He deals with the anxiety of starting at a new school and the threat of polio and confusion over his moonshiner grandfather who lives in the mountains and will have nothing to do with him.

RECOMMENDATION:  This book is luminous, a gem of a novel, a universal story about growing up, told in simple language and style, but handling complex issues of life. In some ways it is a children's book for adults. Don't let the fact that the protagonist is ten years old keep you from reading this! **LT**

AUTHOR:  **Allan Eckert**

TITLE:    ***Incident at Hawk's Hill*** (1971)

DESCRIPTION:  Based on an event in 1870 near Winnipeg, Canada, *Incident at Hawk's Hill* is a moving account of a reclusive little boy, more attuned to animals than people, who gets lost on the vast Canadian prairie and for two months lives with an injured mother badger until his family finds him at last. The visiting archbishop tells the MacDonalds that the return of their son, Ben, is a modern parable of the faithfulness of God.

RECOMMENDATION:  Eckert has an uncanny ability to get right inside the lives of lonely Ben, his anxious father, their cruel trapper neighbor, and the mother badger herself. This is a story worth reading aloud as a family. Many critics have judged that Eckert's sequel, *Return to Hawk's Hill*, is not of the same quality as the beloved first book, but fans will want to check it out for themselves. **ET, MT***

AUTHOR:  **John Fischer**

TITLE:    ***Saint Ben*** (1993)

DESCRIPTION:  Ben, the youngest son of the new pastor at Pasadena's Colorado Avenue Standard Christian Church, knows more ways to get into mischief than anyone else, especially when paired with his new buddy, Jonathan. Their love of the 1958 Edsel draws them together in unforgettable ways that test the depths of their different kinds of faith.

RECOMMENDATION: The phrase attributed to Pascal, "There is a God-shaped vacuum in every human heart," shapes the theme of this luminously true book about faith, hypocrisy, and friendship. Not to be forgotten, this book is best shared. **MT, LT, AA***

AUTHOR: **Esther Forbes**
TITLE:    ***Johnny Tremain* (1943)**

DESCRIPTION: Newbery Medal, 1944. If Johnny's story were not exciting enough—he is a young but skilled silversmith's apprentice whose hand is burned in molten silver because the other apprentices resent his pride and ability—it gets mixed up in Boston's 1773 struggle to force the issue of taxation with the British. Both Johnny and America learn what it means to "stand up" in freedom and responsibility.

RECOMMENDATION: Everyday citizens and famous people from your history textbooks come alive on these pages that some teens have been known to read again and again. **ET, MT***

AUTHOR: **Kathryn Forbes**
TITLE:    ***Mama's Bank Account* (1943)**

DESCRIPTION: Mama dips into her Little Bank at home to keep her Norwegian immigrant family solvent so that she doesn't have to go to the Big Bank in downtown San Francisco. Only after her daughter Katrin sells her first story twenty years later and gives the money to her mother, does she learn that Mama had invented the Big Bank so that her children would not worry.

RECOMMENDATION: Your entire family will enjoy this account of Katrin's growing up years. **AA***

AUTHOR: **Paula Fox**
TITLE:    ***The Slave Dancer* (1973)**

DESCRIPTION: Newbery Medal, 1974. Jessie is kidnapped from New Orleans onto a slave ship going to Africa to pick up cargo. His job will be to play his flute so that the slaves can dance and therefore get the exercise they need to stay alive. Though white, he is little more than a slave himself, and through him you can realize secondhand the horrors of slavery.

RECOMMENDATION: This is Paula Fox's most famous and most controversial book. Many feel that it is racist—demeaning to black people—and others think it is among the best books ever written for youth. If you let yourself go into Jessie's life, you may experience some little bit of what it meant to be a slave, and that may change you. Though the book does not have a hopeful ending—Jessie cannot ever listen to music again—ask yourselves what hope any slave can have—then or now. **ET, MT***

AUTHOR: **Rudolf Frank**

TITLE: ***No Hero for the Kaiser*** (1983)

DESCRIPTION: On Jan's fourteenth birthday, September 14, 1914, a German artillery unit destroys his Polish village on its way to a "quick" victory over Russia. Having nowhere to go, Jan and a dog named Flox become mascots to the unit and with the common soldiers learn the common horrors and camaraderies of war. The men soon regard their quick-witted "Panie" as good luck. After fighting with him on both the eastern and western fronts, they want to reward him with German citizenship, knowing that it would make good war propaganda as well. How Jan responds to this honor is the moving conclusion to this powerful novel.

RECOMMENDATION: The story of what happened to this book is as stirring as Jan's story itself. First published in Germany in 1931, it was widely praised, but when Hitler came to power in 1933 it was publicly burned and Rudolf Frank was put in jail. After it was republished in the '70s, it won many prizes, including the prestigious Heinemann Peace Prize in 1983, the year it was translated into English. The German-speaking Polish boy, Jan, is a boy for all peoples. The English version is out of print now, but search library shelves for a copy. **MT**

AUTHOR: **Louann Gaeddert**

TITLE: ***Friends and Enemies*** (2000)

DESCRIPTION: William, a preacher's kid, moves to a new town in Kansas as he begins high school on the eve of World War II. The only fellow to befriend him is Jim, a Mennonite, but as patriotic feelings swell in the community after the bombing of Pearl Harbor, Jim is ostracized for refusing to contribute to the war effort. William is caught in the middle of the conflict—literally—as he sorts through the meaning of friendship, patriotism, and courage, and in so doing leaves behind the days when he could "think as a child."

RECOMMENDATION: This fine novel explores important questions about loyalties, both temporal and eternal, and of just how we must love our neighbors—the very questions facing William, Jim, Clive, and the other kids in Plaintown's high school. **ET**, **AA***

AUTHOR: **Alan Garner**

TITLE: ***The Stone Book*** (1978)

DESCRIPTION: This and the next three books make up *The Stone Quartet*. On the day that "changed Mary for the rest of [her] days," she climbs up to the top of the spire her stonemason father is finishing and down to a hidden cave with him to "see and know" the prehistoric markings there.

She asks for a book to carry to chapel and he lovingly makes her a stone book whose fossils have "all the stories of the world and the flowers of the flood." In *Granny Reardun*, Joseph skips the last day of school to help his grandfather build a wall, trying to get up the courage to tell him that he doesn't want to apprentice to him. Robert *(The Aimer Gate)*, like his father before him, is searching for a trade. He wishes he could be a soldier like his Uncle Charlie, home on leave from World War I, though he also helps care for Faddock Allman, who lost his legs in that war. In *Tom Fobble's Day*, Grandfather, a smithie who that day is retiring, makes William a new sled with metal and wood from an ancient family loom. Riding farther on it than any of the boys dare and lighted by the searchlights looking for German planes, William feels "a line through hand and eye, block, forge and loom to the hill."

RECOMMENDATION: Each of these exquisite short stories can be savored by itself, yet, as the introduction to each states, "together they form a saga tracing four generations of a working class family in Chosley, a small town in Cheshire, England." Don't be deceived by the large print and simple woodcut illustrations. "Simple" in this case means elemental and deep, like the Greek drama or mythology that influences all of Garner's writing. If you have ever wondered about the origin of the universe or about what you should do with your life or how your ancestors affected you, then your wondering will be enriched by *The Stone Quartet*. **AA\***

AUTHOR: **Esther Hautzig**

TITLE: ***The Endless Steppe*** (1968)

DESCRIPTION: A privileged ten-year-old Polish girl is exiled to Rubtsovsk on the steppes of Siberia, with her adored father, her mother, and grandmother. There, unlike other Jews, she survives World War II. There in that cold alien environment she comes to maturity amid deprivation and squalor, supported by the love of her family, the companionship of hard-won friends, a mind ignited by the teaching of other exiles, and the protection of her God. When she can leave at age sixteen, Esther discovers that Siberia has become her home.

RECOMMENDATION: Esther Hautzig told this story of her girlhood, reminiscent of the way Laura Ingalls Wilder told hers. She will help young people discover that the ingredients of surviving teenage years with dignity intact are the same the world over. **ET, MT\***

AUTHOR: **John Hersey**

TITLE: ***A Bell for Adano*** (1944)

DESCRIPTION: A U.S. army major, Victor Joppolo, described by his author as "a good man, though weak in certain attractive human ways," is left behind as the mayor of Adano after the American invasion of Italy in

World War II. There he meets many people, most good and all weak, who have been repressed by decades of fascism. He tries, through being a servant, not a dictator, to show them the meaning of democracy.

RECOMMENDATION:  A warm, human account. **LT**


AUTHOR: **John Hersey**
TITLE:    ***The Wall*** (1950)

DESCRIPTION:  Through the eyes and pen of a nosey little Jewish scholar, Noach Levinson, you share a daily record of Jews forced first to relocate to the Warsaw ghetto in November 1939, and then to be trapped there behind the wall they were forced to build around it, and finally to be hunted down and exterminated there by May 1943.

RECOMMENDATION:  Many consider *The Wall* John Hersey's masterpiece. Noach and a few neighbors around Sienna 17 are not just Jews but Everyman in extreme circumstances. They display not only all the petty vices of jealousy and greed and bitterness but also all the reserves of faith and courage and love. Their defeats and ultimate triumphs of spirit will become your own. **LT**


AUTHOR: **Karen Hesse**
TITLE:    ***Out of the Dust*** (1999)

DESCRIPTION:  Newbery Medal, 1998. Don't let the simplicity of this book's format fool you. This is a novel for grown-ups. The diary of fourteen-year-old Billie Jo records what happened to her family during the terrible drought and dust storms of the early 1930s in the panhandle of Texas. Such a sorrow over the literal loss of land doesn't come suddenly. "But now, sorrow climbs up our front steps, big as Texas, and we didn't even see it coming," Billie Jo writes. What happens to the land is bad enough, but when her father mistakenly places a pail of kerosene next to the wood stove, the stage is set for tragedy.

RECOMMENDATION:  Written in powerful poetic prose, this is a beautiful book about overcoming adversity and the triumph of the human spirit. **MT, LT***


AUTHOR: **Karen Hesse**
TITLE:    ***Stowaway*** (2000)

DESCRIPTION:  A page-turner story of eleven-year-old Nicholas Young based on an actual stowaway aboard the legendary Captain Cook's ship, *Endeavor.* Although little is known about this boy, Hesse makes him a living, breathing person who runs away from the cruelties of his father and his employer by stowing away on a ship that takes him on a three-year voyage of discovery and adventure.

RECOMMENDATION:  The tale is rich in history, geography, and adventure. **MT, LT**

AUTHOR: **Jamake Highwater**

TITLE: ***Anpao: An American Indian Odyssey* (1977)**

DESCRIPTION: Newbery Honor. In this native America "odyssey," Anpao must seek the permission of the Sun to marry Ko-ko-mik-e-sis, undergoing many trials and adventures in the process. He travels through time and space and history—even the tragic history concerning the encounters of native Americans with the white invaders.

RECOMMENDATION: Highwater states that one of his purposes in compiling the stories of Native Americans in this new form is to provide "a personal journey for readers who wish to sail from one world to another." That other world is the "fundamental reality in the Indian concept of nature and of man's place in the cosmos." These huge worldview issues can become quite personal for you as you apply the questions (pp. 84–89) to the lively journey of Anpao and enter into his world. **MT, LT, AA**

AUTHOR: **Irene Hunt**

TITLE: ***Across Five Aprils* (1964)**

DESCRIPTION: Jethro Creighton is nine in April, 1861, when, on his family's farm in southern Illinois, he receives news that Fort Sumter has been fired on. He is thirteen in April 1865, when he learns that his idol, President Lincoln, has been assassinated. In between he grows to an early manhood as his brothers and cousin and schoolteacher go off to fight in the war, one on the side of the Confederacy. His family is attacked for Bill's "disloyalty," he hides a deserter and writes Lincoln for advice, and he learns the meaning of courage and maturity as he shoulders the work of the farm.

RECOMMENDATION: More than any other novel for young people set in the Civil War era, *Across Five Aprils* brings the war to life and into perspective in all its horrors and significance because you see it through the eyes of Jethro, a fine young man for whom human life is never cheap and decency is never to be mocked. **ET, MT***

AUTHOR: **Mollie Hunter**

TITLE: ***A Sound of Chariots* (1972)**

DESCRIPTION: Nine-year-old Bridie is devastated by the death of her passionate Socialist father and the grief of her deeply religious mother. Across the years, until she is fifteen and must leave home to make her living, she comes to terms with the realization that she too will die someday, with her heightened awareness of the beauty of life and the flight of time and with her own opportunity to live for what her father had believed.

RECOMMENDATION: Though about death, Bridie's story surges with life; though about grief, it is filled with honest hope and sensitive beauty. Bridie is her father's girl, one who would "find it much more exciting to ride to Heaven on [Marx's] coattails than to get there by crossing over from the Sinners to the Saints." However, her mother's Brethren faith is viewed lovingly and honestly, though limited by a child's incomplete understanding. **ET**

AUTHOR: **Mollie Hunter**

TITLE:  *Hold on to Love* (1984)

DESCRIPTION:  In this sequel to *A Sound of Chariots*, on the brink of World War II, Bridie pursues her dream of being a writer even as she works long hours in her grandfather's Edinburgh flower shop. Bridie learns, as her dying grandmother warns, "Hold on to love!" but will that love be of her passionately chosen craft, or will it be of a fine young man named Peter whose possessiveness may interfere?

RECOMMENDATION: Bridie's story is really Mollie Hunter's own and as honestly told as her retellings of Scottish history and folklore. Bridie has a turning point experience in which she realizes that God exists and though he may be her antagonist—someone to argue with—he is quite thoroughly mixed up in Bridie's life. **ET, MT**

**Mollie Hunter** says she has a philosophy of life that compels her to write for young people, and which permeates her historical novels, contemporary novels, and folklore-fantasies, all set in Scotland. She believes in the "triumph of human love over the dark powers of the soul-less ones" and in "a one-to-one contact between man and God, and between man and man." Her splendid story-telling abilities bring these themes to life; they are not preachy bits tacked on. Her books are so varied that whether you like stories about today's teens, fantasy, or historical romance, you will find something of hers to suit you.

AUTHOR: **Anne Isaacs**

TITLE:  *Torn Thread* (2000)

DESCRIPTION:  Though she is the younger, Eva is the stronger of two Jewish sisters who are forced into hard labor at a Nazi-controlled labor camp in Czechoslovakia. She follows her beloved father's advice to make the choices that will keep her and Rachel alive for one more hour.

RECOMMENDATION: Books based on personal Holocaust experiences are beginning to multiply as the Holocaust survivors are growing old. All are not equal, but each is an important piece of the puzzle that must continue to plague us about the enormity of evil and the incredible value of each individual life. Eva and Rachel's story of survival—of life and of faith—is one such moving title that compels us "never to forget." Of what value is hope to the girls—in outside circumstances, in the character of fellow prisoners, and in the God who seems not to care about them? **MT**

AUTHOR: **Brian Jacques**

TITLE: *Castaways of the Flying Dutchman* **(2001)**

DESCRIPTION: In 1620 Neb, a young boy serving as cook's helper, and his dog Denmark are washed from the deck of the Flying Dutchman into the Atlantic Ocean during a terrible storm as the ship recedes into the darkness under the curse of God. Reaching shore against all odds, they are blessed by an angel who sends them off on their own eternal journey, equipped with special gifts for the good work assigned to them. After centuries of braving winds and waves and countless perils, their travels take them to Chapelvale, a sleepy nineteenth-century village whose very existence is at stake. Using the will of the people and their own insights, the special dog and boy go to work to save this town.

RECOMMENDATION: After fourteen popular novels about the inhabitants and battles of Redwall, Brian Jacques takes a bold and creative step in writing about the legend of the never-ending voyage of a fatal ship. He gives the legend new depth and new meaning, combining suspense, fantasy, and unforgettable characters. **ET, MT, AA**

AUTHOR: **Jan Karon**

TITLE: *At Home in Mitford* **(1996)**

DESCRIPTION: Father Tim Kavanagh, bachelor rector of the picture-perfect Episcopal Church in Mitford, North Carolina, gives himself to his lovable but eccentric town and parish folk. Even so there is a hollow spot in his heart. Then along comes an altogether too large dog (who responds only to scriptural commands), an eleven-year-old boy without a functioning family but with lots of potential, and children's book writer and illustrator who moves next door. Somehow, life isn't so lonely anymore, or it wouldn't be if Father Tim will risk falling in love.

RECOMMENDATION: Laugh and cry and share the best lines—there are many—of this book and its several sequels *(Light in the Window; These High, Green Hills; Out to Canaan;* and *A New Song)*. You will love the people, who are by no means perfect but who are willing to grow through the pain and joys that come their way. You'll love how Tim and Dooley and Cynthia and (fill in the name of your favorite character) grow towards becoming the people God meant them to be. You'll love your own responses to the challenges of everyday life that these wonderful books make so vivid. Great for read alouds. **LT, AA***

AUTHOR: **Kathryn Lasky**

TITLE: *The Night Journey* **(1981)**

DESCRIPTION: Rache lives with her parents and great-grandmother. An ordinary teen, she finds reciting ordinary school events to Nana Sachie boring until, in return, Sachie starts sharing about the dangerous escape she and her Jewish family made from Czarist-controlled Russia.

RECOMMENDATION:  In this tender yet funny family book, times shift between contemporary America and pre-communist Russia, tied together by two families' love and "laced with the bright filaments of memory that in turn linked two people at opposite ends of life for a vital moment in each one's existence." Illustrated by Trina Schart Hyman. **ET**

AUTHOR:  **Stephen Lawhead**

TITLE:      **The Pendragon Cycle (1987)**

DESCRIPTION:  This set includes *Taliesin, Merlin, Arthur, Pendragon,* and *Grail.* The King Arthur saga is one of the foundational epics of Western culture, and Stephen Lawhead retells it with breathtaking sensitivity and detail. His span reaches back to the lost city of Atlantis from which the beautiful and good Charis escapes with her life only to find herself in the realm of squabbling Celtic chieftains. She meets the fabled bard-prince, Taliesin, who first envisions the righteous Kingdom of Summer where love, justice, and mercy reign; and then bears Merlin. Merlin must bring his father's vision to reality through suffering many strenuous trials that nearly destroy him and by nurturing the young Pendragon, Arthur, to become the High King. Arthur has battles of his own, for the petty chieftains around him value their own skins more than a visionary kingdom that could bring peace to all the peoples of Britain. And lurking in the mists and shadows around Taliesin, Merlin, and Arthur is the hate-filled sorceress, Morgian.

RECOMMENDATION: Many are the retellings of the Arthur story, and deservedly so, for his tale is a wellspring of much that is good in our culture. What sets Lawhead's splendid interpretation apart is his careful integration of Christian faith and truths into the lives of his characters. And why not? What is the Kingdom of Summer, after all, but an attempt to actualize the kingdom of Heaven on earth? If you find that these fire your imagination and spirit, and you want to read other Arthur stories, try the romances of Mary Stewart *(The Crystal Cave, The Hollow Hills, The Last Enchantment,* and *The Wicked Day)* or the histories of Rosemary Sutcliff *(Sword at Sunset,* and the trilogy, *Sword and the Circle, Light Beyond the Forest,* and *Road to Camlann)* or the definitive and best-loved version of them all, based on Mallory's *Morte d' Arthur,* T. H. White's *The Once and Future King.* Another Lawhead historical fiction to try is *Byzantium.* **MT, LT***

ET—Early Teens
MT—Mid Teens
LT—Late Teens
AA—All Ages

AUTHOR: **Gail Carson Levine**

TITLE: ***Dave at Night* (2001)**

DESCRIPTION: It's 1926. Dave's beloved father is dead and his stepmother doesn't want him. Only the Hebrew Home for Boys will take him in. HHB—Hell Hole for Brats. When he hears the door slam behind him, he vows he will escape. It doesn't prove to be that simple. Dave is no ordinary kid; he does escape regularly, and returns from a whole new world he discovers at night.

RECOMMENDATION: Most of all, this is a story about friendship, about New York City's Lower East Side, about the hope and magic of the Harlem Renaissance where he meets great and wondrous characters. In the end, Dave transforms the HHB. **ET, MT.**

AUTHOR: **Sonia Levitin**

TITLE: ***The Return* (1987)**

DESCRIPTION: Full of pathos, yet laced with humor, this is the story of Desta, an Ethiopian Jewish teenage girl, who was secretly airlifted from a refugee camp in the Sudan to redemption in Israel during the 1984 Operation Moses rescue mission.

RECOMMENDATION: Because of the richness of Sonia Levitin's re-creation of both Desta's warm Ethiopian family and village life and of her Jewish beliefs, you will enter fully into the girl's profound losses as she escapes her village as well as her gains of freedom, learning, and personal choice. This is a wonderful book! Check out other Levitin titles in the Contemporary and Science Fiction sections. **ET, MT\***

AUTHOR: **Catherine Marshall**

TITLE: ***Christy* (1967)**

DESCRIPTION: Christy Huddleston, a sheltered nineteen-year-old girl seeking "life piled on life" comes to the mountains of Cutter Gap, Tennessee, in 1912 to teach school for the American Inland Mission. It is life she finds, but life in its rawest forms—poverty, disease, ignorance, revenge shootings, drunkenness—enough to disillusion the most idealistic and shake the faith of the most genteelly religious of girls. But she also finds among the people and her coworkers deep longings for beauty and truth, steadfast loyalty, and self-sacrificial love, all coming to a head during a typhoid epidemic.

RECOMMENDATION: Marshall wrote this story based on her mother's first year in the Smoky Mountain Mission. It truly teems with life, the "life piled on life" that Christy found because she gave hers away. Fairlight, Opal and Tom, Bird's Eye, Lundy, David, Miss Alice, and Dr. Neil all will become your friends too on this marvelous adventure of faith. If you liked *Christy*, you will probably also enjoy *Julie* by Marshall. She turned from her mother's history to her own in *Julie*, which is about living through the Johnstown Flood. **MT**, **LT***

AUTHOR:  **Harry Mazer**

TITLE:      ***The Last Mission*** **(1979)**

DESCRIPTION:  Jack Raab is fifteen in 1944 when he sneaks his brother's birth certificate and enlists in the Air Corps in order to fulfill his daydream of killing Hitler, who had killed all the Jews, his people. He quickly discovers that war isn't as glamorous as he had thought, but still he and his bomber crew complete twenty-five missions unscathed. In late April 1945, with rumors of the war's end circulating, they make an unusual run over Czechoslovakia and are hit. Jack survives to be taken prisoner by the retreating Germans.

RECOMMENDATION:  While not as profound as Rudolf Frank's *No Hero for the Kaiser*, also about a too-young boy in combat (which is no longer in print), *The Last Mission* has a high degree of adventure and a standard anti-war theme. There is a sprinkling of the predictable barracks language as well as a sense of naiveté that clings to Jack all through his incredible experiences, based on Mazer's own. **ET**, **MT**

AUTHOR:  **Carolyn Meyer**

TITLE:      ***White Lilacs*** **(1993)**

DESCRIPTION:  Rose Lee's responsibilities as her gardener-grandfather's helper expand in 1921, and so she is among the first to learn that the whites in Dillon, Texas, plan to turn their "colored" Freedomtown neighborhood into a new park.

RECOMMENDATION:  Seen through the eyes of a young girl who was profoundly affected by it, this tale of an obscure—yet real—historical injustice (it really happened in Denton, Texas) is simple, powerful, and true. **ET**

AUTHOR:  **Gloria Miklowitz**

TITLE:      ***Masada: The Last Fortress*** **(1998)**

DESCRIPTION:  Two men, so different from each other yet so similar in their unswerving commitment to the beliefs that have formed them, tell the true story of how the Romans conquered the last Jewish stronghold, Masada, in A.D. 72. Teenage Simon ben Eleazar is an aspiring physician, the son of the Zealot leader of the Jewish community holed up in the seemingly invincible fortress, and hopelessly in love with Deborah, who loves his best friend. Flavius Silva, the commander of the Roman Tenth

Legion, masterminds the incredible strategy that finally breaks the Jewish defenses even though he despises strength without honor.

RECOMMENDATION: The story alternates between the Jewish and Roman points of view, building up to its inevitable tragic end. Parents may want to read this first because the account does not fudge the historical reality to spare its readers' emotions. **MT, LT**

AUTHOR: **Margaret Mitchell**

TITLE: *Gone with the Wind* (1936)

DESCRIPTION: Has there ever been a novel (or movie) more popular than *Gone with the Wind*? Many think not. Margaret Mitchell drew strong characters in Scarlett O'Hara, the belle of a plantation devastated when Sherman marched through Georgia; in Ashley Wilkes, the gallant but weak-willed southern gentleman she adored but could not have; Melanie, the sweet girl who married Ashley and could see only good in all people; and Rhett Butler, the charming scoundrel in whom Scarlett met her match. They are so strong that the actors who played them in the movie were forever identified with them.

RECOMMENDATION: The panorama of the Civil War era will come alive for you on these 1000 pages, but you may also want to compare *Gone with the Wind* to Margaret Walker's *Jubilee* (see review in this section) for another point of view about these events for which our country is still paying a price. **MT, LT**

AUTHOR: **Lucy Maud Montgomery**

TITLE: *Anne of Green Gables* (1908)

DESCRIPTION: No girl, or for that matter, no boy should grow up without meeting Anne Shirley, the carrot-haired, imaginative, accident-prone, talkative orphan who wins over the hearts of a spinster sister and bachelor brother, Marilla and Matthew, who run a small farm outside Avonlea on Prince Edward Island. They'd hoped to get a boy to help them but instead take in Anne, who was sent to them by mistake. Avonlea, as Diana and Gilbert can testify, was never the same afterward.

RECOMMENDATION: You'll be glad to know that many other books follow in the series that takes Anne's story right through her children's lives. And if you still do not tire of these genuine PEI folks, Montgomery has also written the Emily of New Moon series. **ET, MT***

AUTHOR: **Gilbert Morris**

TITLE: *Edge of Honor* (2000)

DESCRIPTION: Quentin Laribee is a surgeon in training, being groomed to take over a fashionable practice of a New York City doctor and to marry his socialite daughter. However, he finds himself face to face with a surrendering Rebel soldier in the last days of the Civil War—and kills him. Thrown into despair by his guilt, he determines to make restitution to the dead man's family and is drawn into their lives and into their Arkansas community.

ECOMMENDATION: Christy Award for Historical Fiction. You will learn about the final days of the Civil War in this story and about some of the hardships the South faced under reconstruction. However, the story's central theme is forgiveness and restitution, and it never wavers from being the kind of romance Morris is well known for writing. If you are interested more in the history than the romance, try Michael Shaara's *Killer Angels*, which is an account of the Battle of Gettysburg from the point of view of various generals. Some A.P. History classes require students to read *Killer Angels*. As might be expected if soldiers are telling their stories, there is some swearing, but it is remarkably restrained compared to today's "standards." **LT**

UTHOR: **Farley Mowat**

TTLE:   ***The Dog Who Wouldn't Be*** (1957)

)ESCRIPTION: Farley Mowat was a boy lucky enough to grow up on the edge of a Canadian prairie with a mutt and various wildlife as his companions, a tolerant mother, and a father full of schemes that took them camping, hunting, and sailing (miles from any water!).

ECOMMENDATION: You can share Farley's luck if you read this gently humorous account of his boyhood, focused primarily around the escapades of his dog, Mutt, who regards himself as too good for a dog's station in life—in fact, he believes he is nearly human. **MT**, **LT**

UTHOR: **Janette Oke**

TTLE:   ***Love Comes Softly*** (1979)

)ESCRIPTION: First of a trilogy including *Love's Enduring Promise* and *Love's Long Journey* published by Bethany House. Marty's young husband is killed on their covered wagon journey west. The same day that she buries him, in desperation she marries Clark, a widower with a child— a union in name only that is merely a convenience for both of them. Across the fall and winter months until she can leave Clark on the first wagon train going east, Marty learns to be a pioneer housewife, learns to care for Missie and her own Clem's baby, and learns to love Clark's God and—surprisingly—Clark.

ECOMMENDATION: This simple romance begins a highly popular series that has spawned other series, and you will be charmed by its simple but true values. Janette Oke says that pioneer life appeals to her because in those uncluttered days "only what [was] of true worth was accepted and cherished," including spiritual values. Even if you have had trouble getting into other books, you will probably find Oke's many prairie romances right for you. **ET, MT\***

AUTHOR: **Ruth Park**

TITLE: *Playing Beatie Bow* (1980)

DESCRIPTION: Fourteen-year-old Abigail watches a neighbor boy play a game called "Beatie Bow" and follows a strange girl, also watching, into her own city of Sydney, Australia, but a century before. There she encounters the Bows and Talliskers, "poor as dirt, but full of vitality," who compel her to stay until she fulfills her role in preserving their family gift of foresight and healing—and until she learns what it is to love.

RECOMMENDATION: The characters in Park's fine slip-time book make Victorian New South Wales come fully alive. How Abby is smitten with love for Judah, whose time she longs to escape, is as well described as any first love. But it is what she comes to realize about sacrificial love and the significance of each human's life that makes her experience worth sharing. **ET**

AUTHOR: **Katherine Paterson** (See author overview on page 154.)

TITLE: *The Master Puppeteer* (1975)

DESCRIPTION: Jiro hates the exacting work of puppet-making almost as much as he hated to go hungry with his mother and father during the famine in eighteenth-century Osaka, Japan. He apprentices himself to the puppet theater, where he quickly masters the intricate art of moving the large puppets. He also makes friends with Kinshi, the son of the demanding master puppeteer, and cheers the exploits of the Robin Hood-style bandit, Saburo. Jiro and Kinshi both learn that compassion for the hungry exacts a price, one that must be paid by many members of the Hanaza Puppet Theater.

RECOMMENDATION: Katherine Paterson is something of a master puppeteer herself, bringing to vivid life Jiro, Kinshi, and the family troupe at the Hanaza Puppet Theater in poverty-stricken, riot-torn Osaka, Japan. Though these two genuine boys are true to their times, their appeal lies partly in their universal characteristics of ambition, jealousy, loyalty, compassion, and humor. Kinshi's self-sacrifice nearly makes him a Christ-figure. **MT, LT\***

AUTHOR: **Katherine Paterson**

TITLE: *Lyddie* (1991)

DESCRIPTION: Their father having abandoned them and their mother going mad, Lyddie and Charles leave their Vermont farm. Lyddie becomes indentured as a coach house servant. From that position, she makes her way to Lowell, Massachusetts, to work in the mills, trying to earn enough money to pay their farm debts and to gain both literacy and independence.

RECOMMENDATION: Paterson paints a realistic picture of the conditions of the poor working mill girls in the 1840s with her finely conceived heroine, Lyddie. **MT**, **LT**

AUTHOR: **Katherine Paterson**

TITLE: *Rebels of the Heavenly Kingdom* (1983)

DESCRIPTION: Wang Lee is kidnapped off his parents' farm by despicable bandits during the drought of 1851. When his freedom is bought by a member of the God-fearers, his fortunes become tangled up with this idealistic Heavenly Kingdom of Great Peace. They are driven by their own versions of pacifist and celibate Christian doctrines but also by a great hatred for the corrupt and unjust Manchu government. Because their leaders believe that they have been given the Mandate of Heaven to inaugurate a new era of righteousness, they take up arms to drive the Manchu out. Wang Lee, and his savior, Mei Lei, and their companions slowly become hardened warriors until they must confront the fact that their ideals have been lost.

RECOMMENDATION: Wang Lee and Mei Lei may seem light years away from your contemporary existence, but Paterson skillfully brings their complex and fascinating (and historically true) situation to life. These young people in a distant time and place face the same dilemmas as all ethical young people—how not to be corrupted when the evil that surrounds you tempts you to use less than noble means to justify noble ends. **MT\***

AUTHOR: **Richard Peck**

TITLE: *A Long Way from Chicago* (2000) and *A Year Down Yonder* (2000)

DESCRIPTION: *A Long Way from Chicago*, a Newbery Honor book, is full of adventures in a small town in southern Illinois where Joey and Mary Alice go to visit their gun-toting Grandma Dowdel. Grandma Dowdel is not a good influence, which is why Joey likes to visit her. In A *Year Down Yonder* (Newbery Medal, 2001), her parents send Mary Alice to

ET—Early Teens
MT—Mid Teens
LT—Late Teens
AA—All Ages

live with Grandma Dowdel since the Great Depression necessitates the parents moving into a single room in Chicago. Mary Alice is sure it will be horrible to live in Grandma's hick town now that she is fifteen, but she ends up having a hilarious time learning from Grandma, who manages to shake up the local populace, keep her outhouse from being tipped over at Halloween, and purloin someone's pumpkins to make pies for the school party.

RECOMMENDATION:  These stories are touching, funny, and as one teenage boy said, "I cried. Hey, I'm sensitive!" **ET, MT**

AUTHOR:  **Eugenia Price**
TITLE:     ***The Beloved Invader* (1965)**

DESCRIPTION:  First of a trilogy that includes *New Moon Rising* and *Lighthouse*. The true story of Anson Dodge, a wealthy young New Yorker who gave up a typical career to minister to the forgotten people of St. Simons Island after the Civil War's devastation, is told as a romance. Dodge married two women: his beloved cousin, the joyous and glamorous Ellen whose tragic death he mourns for years, and the island's own Anna, who kept house for him for many of those years and who with him learns that God makes redemptive use of everything in our lives.

RECOMMENDATION:  You'll be glad to know that Price is a prolific writer of historical fiction, all from a Christian perspective. **LT***

AUTHOR:  **Eugenia Price**
TITLE:     ***Savannah* (1983)**

DESCRIPTION:  First of a quartet of books that includes *To See Your Face Again, Before the Darkness Falls,* and *Stranger in Savannah*. In 1812 Mark Browning makes his way to Savannah, the raw young town aspiring to gentility that contains the secrets of his birth and—he hopes—the key to his future. He meets the merchant Robert Mackey who invites him into his home and office, and so Mark's life becomes entwined with that prominent family (including its beautiful wife and mother) and all the intrigues and pleasures that come to an astute young businessman with a dark past. Mark's story and that of his descendents continues in the sequels that take you through the Civil War era.

RECOMMENDATION:  The setting, both of time and of place, is all-important in this book as it is in any good historical fiction—and Eugenia Price's stories stand with the best. Many of these characters really lived, though you may find some of them too beautiful, too intelligent, and too passionate to seem quite real. The Savannah stories are also loosely tied to Price's *Don Juan McQueen* series. **LT***

AUTHOR: **Slavomir Rawicz**

TITLE:    ***The Long Walk: The True Story of a Trek to Freedom*** (1997)

DESCRIPTION: In 1941 the Polish author of this book and a small group of fellow prisoners escaped a Soviet labor camp, finding their way out of Siberia, marching across Mongolia and the Gobi Desert, through the mountains of China and Tibet and over the Himalayas to British India. Fear, uncertainty, hunger, endurance, determination to be free, all thread through this amazing recounting of a man whose country was cruelly devastated by the decisions of world leaders.

RECOMMENDATION: This is surely one of the most amazing and heroic stories of our time, an authentic look into history. **LT**

AUTHOR: **Ann Rinaldi**

TITLE:    ***The Second Bend in the River*** (1997)

DESCRIPTION: This retelling of the real Rebecca Galloway's growing up in the wilderness of western Ohio at the turn of the nineteenth century brings pioneer circumstances alive. Rebecca meets and falls in love with the courageous Indian chief, Tecumseh, and if she marries him, thousands of lives might be saved.

RECOMMENDATION: Careful research, lively writing, and perceptive insights into human nature are hallmarks of this book. Rinaldi has written many novels set in America's past. If you like this one—and it would be hard not to—you will have many more to choose from. **MT**

AUTHOR: **Kenneth Roberts**

TITLE:    ***Northwest Passage*** (1937)

DESCRIPTION: Major Robert Rogers not only led the 1759 expedition against the Indian village of St. Francis but also had a dream to find an overland passage to the Pacific. Pursuing it, he travels to London to find financial backing and then to Michigan, where he becomes governor of Fort Michilimackinac. Roger's story is told through the eyes of his friend, Langdon Town, who has a desire of his own to be able to paint the Indians as they really are.

RECOMMENDATION: There is enough humor, suspense, romance, adventure, and excitement to satisfy the most demanding of readers. Families have been known to enjoy reading this book aloud. Roberts has written many other fine historical fiction novels, which appeal particularly to male readers. You might particularly enjoy *Rabble in Arms, Arandel,* and *Oliver Wiswell. Arundel* is the story of Benedict Arnold's march on Montreal and *Oliver Wiswell* is the story of a Tory family who stayed loyal to the British during the American Revolution. **LT***

AUTHOR: **Margaret Rostkowski**

TITLE: ***After the Dancing Days*** (1986)

DESCRIPTION: When thirteen-year-old Annie's army doctor father comes home from World War I, things don't settle back to normal. How could they? Her mother's beloved brother Paul had been killed. Her mother is determined to forget the war even though her father decides to work at a veteran's hospital. Annie is drawn to a bitter, disfigured soldier there, despite her own misgivings, and despite her mother's disapproval. From Andrew she learns much about courage, about heroism on and off the battlefield, about meaning in the face of senselessness, and about living by her own beliefs.

RECOMMENDATION: Even in a thoughtful, loving family there can be grave disagreements over values. Annie's father and mother choose different ways to put the horrors of WW I behind them—bury the painful memories, or support the veterans who make them remember. Annie must decide her own way and in the process has her shining ideals of heroism shattered. But the truth she gains in the process is worth so much more—it is a truth she can grow and live by. **ET**

AUTHOR: **Patricia St. John**

TITLE: ***If You Love Me*** (1982)

DESCRIPTION: Teenage Lamia and her family are middle-class Arab Christians who find themselves caught up in the destruction of Lebanon in 1973, which still has its repercussions in the continuing Middle East crisis.

RECOMMENDATION: St. John is much loved for her children's books set in Europe and North Africa. Redemption in the midst of ashes is her powerful theme. In England, Scripture Union titled this book *Nothing Else Matters* when it came out in 1982, and in the United States, Moody Press (Chicago, Ill.) gave it the title *If You Love Me*. Unfortunately it is no longer in print, but find it if you possibly can in a church library or bookstore or online. **ET, MT***

AUTHOR: **Graham Salisbury**

TITLE: ***Under the Blood-Red Sun*** (1994)

DESCRIPTION: Tomi and Billy are eighth-grade best friends, intent on improving Billy's range of pitches, starting their science projects, and avoiding the local bully, during the idyllic fall of 1941 in Honolulu. Their joy in simple pleasures is shattered the day Japan bombs Pearl Harbor, when Tomi's grandfather mistakenly unfurls his Japanese flag and American soldiers destroy his father's fishing boat, killing his young assistant and taking him away to detention.

RECOMMENDATION: War forces two young American boys—one under suspicion for his Japanese origins—to grow up faster than they otherwise would have and to decide where their loyalties lie. The author deftly weaves in baseball lore and Japanese customs to make this a believable and heart-tugging story. **ET, MT**

**ET**—Early Teens
**MT**—Mid Teens
**LT**—Late Teens
**AA**—All Ages

AUTHOR: **Dodie Smith**

TITLE:    ***I Capture the Castle*** (1940)

DESCRIPTION: Seventeen-year-old Cassandra Mortmain tells the story of her slightly zany family, which lives in not-so-genteel poverty in a ramshackle old English castle. Her witty and insightful journal chronicles not only her hopes and dreams, but also the family troubles as they wait for their father to overcome his writer's block and produce something to help the family stay alive. Meanwhile their new mother sells off pieces of furniture to hold life together. Hope comes alive when the family encounters the estate's young and handsome landlord and love blooms.

RECOMMENDATION: People smile when they recommend this book because they are sure you've never met anyone quite like this family, and Cassandra is a heroine to love. Written in 1940, this book is back in print in a new edition—a delightful tale of romance, adventure, and pluck. **LT**

AUTHOR: **Mary Stolz**

TITLE:    ***Cezanne Pinto*** (1994)

DESCRIPTION: A former slave boy, freeman, and cowboy tells the story of his young life, which is the story of nineteenth-century America.

RECOMMENDATION: Terrible yet beautifully wrought as it is with love and grace and faith (and doubt) and knowledge, and fine, fine language, this book is as large in its vision as the indomitable human spirit. Do you agree with Cezanne's assessment that the freedom project is not yet finished? This book is a wonderful read-aloud. **ET, AA\***

AUTHOR: **Irving Stone**

TITLE:    ***The Agony and the Ecstasy: A Biographical Novel of Michelangelo*** (1961)

DESCRIPTION: Michelangelo's passion for sculpture, for his city of Florence, and for God personifies the turbulent era of the fifteenth- and sixteenth-century Italian Renaissance. Though the artist's problems with the several popes he outlived, the wars of the city states, and the daily struggle just to eat and work may seem far removed from today, you may find

yourself caught up in his overwhelming desire to create as God had cre
ated. If you have ever wondered about the origin of the word "human
ism," you will find it here as you see Michelangelo wrestling to unite th
best of the Greek view of the body with the true Christian vision of th
spirit.

RECOMMENDATION:  Stone has the rare ability to bring a whole era to lif
through a focus on one genius. If you enjoyed *The Agony and the Ecstasy*
you may also enjoy other books by Stone, including *Lust for Life*, his fic
tional biography of another artist, the tortured Christian of a later era
Vincent Van Gogh. A couple of American women who marrie
Presidents have their own books—Rachel Jackson in *The President
Lady* and Mary Todd Lincoln in *Love is Eternal*. The search by Henr
and Sophia Schliemann for the mythical city of Troy, which develope
into the field of archeology, is described in *The Greek Treasure*. **LT**

AUTHOR:  **Harriet Beecher Stowe**
TITLE:      ***Uncle Tom's Cabin*** (1852)

DESCRIPTION:  Abraham Lincoln told Harriet Beecher Stowe that she "wrot
the book that made this great war." Though it may seem sentimenta
now, over 300,000 Americans bought it during its first year in print
Besides influencing an era, it has contributed unforgettable figures t
our cultural memories: the old Uncle Tom; the little Topsy who wasn'
born, just "grow'd"; the slave girl Eliza who jumps from ice floe to ic
floe in her effort to escape across the Ohio River; and the cruel over
seer, Simon Legree.

RECOMMENDATION:  If you are interested in this era of history, you will wan
to compare this classic with the more contemporary but excellen
*Jubilee*, by Margaret Walker. **MT**

AUTHOR:  **Rosemary Sutcliff**
TITLE:      ***The Eagle of the Ninth*** (1954)

DESCRIPTION:  Marcus, a new Roman cohort commander, is wounded in hi
first battle with the rebellious British and must recuperate in his uncle'
home, where he impulsively buys a British gladiator as his slave. Late
having freed Esca, Marcus and his new friend travel, disguised, int
Caledonia (Scotland) to search for the eagle standard of the Nint
Legion with which his father had disappeared years before.

RECOMMENDATION:  Rosemary Sutcliff, who has dozens of books to he
credit, has the rare ability to breathe life into "dead" history, and she i
at her best in the era of Roman Britain, though the later kings and leg
ends of Britain concern her as well. (Any title you can find in you

library or bookstore will be excellent.) You'll count the Roman Marcus and the British Esca among your friends and yearn for them to understand the values of the other's way of life. **ET, MT***

AUTHOR:  **Rosemary Sutcliff**
TITLE:    *Song for a Dark Queen* (1978)

DESCRIPTION:  The real person in this book is Queen Boadicea, the matriarch of the Iceni, who in A.D. 60 led a nearly successful revolt against the conquering Romans. You see her through the eyes of the harpist, Cadwan, who observed everything so that he could turn it into songs that praised the queen he loved and the life of the tribe she stood for.

RECOMMENDATION:  Rosemary Sutcliff says that "real people, lost behind their legends, have always fascinated" her; she, in turn, makes them fascinating for you. **ET, MT**

AUTHOR:  **Marc Talbert**
TITLE:    *Heart of a Jaguar* (1995)

DESCRIPTION:  Balam is caught between boyhood and manhood just as his Mayan village, in the grips of a two-year drought without the life-giving maize, is caught between death and life. Even though they are careful to follow all the prescribed rituals, Balam and his village are helpless as disasters multiply. They reluctantly conclude that they must give the Lord Sun the ultimate sacrifice he demands. The question that baffles them is why the gods don't realize that their own welfare is dependent on the welfare of the village.

RECOMMENDATION:  To read this book is to enter into a strange, even horrifying, yet beautifully coherent culture and once there to close the door of escape behind you because you empathize so completely with the boy-man Balam. Yet part of your mind will continue to keep its distance and to ask and seek answers to the questions this ancient Mayan worldview raises. What are the surprising similarities to your own and what are its fatal flaws? A book worth talking about with your family. **MT, LT**

AUTHOR:  **Mildred Taylor**
TITLE:    *Roll of Thunder, Hear My Cry* (1977)

DESCRIPTION:  Newbery Medal. Cassie Logan tells the compelling story of how her proud, hard-working, land-owning black family "faced adversity and survived" in Mississippi during the Depression by love and understanding and respect for all, themselves and even their racist oppressors.

ET—Early Teens
MT—Mid Teens
LT—Late Teens
AA—All Ages

RECOMMENDATION: We will all be poorer if we do not meet the Logans. After all, Americans have all been shaped by the events that Cassie recounts so truly (which is really the story of Taylor's father's family). Many teachers know this and so often introduce *Roll of Thunder, Hear My Cry* and its successor, *Let the Circle Be Unbroken,* to children in elementary school. However, usually boys and girls need the added maturity that comes with age and experience to comprehend with Cassie both the power of racism to cripple us and the power of love to overcome it. Parents would profit from reading these books with their teens. Other companion volumes include *The Friendship* (for younger readers), and *The Well: David's Story, Mississippi Bridge, Song of the Trees,* and (new in the fall of 2001) *The Land* (about Cassie's grandfather, the son of a plantation owner and slave). **ET, MT***

AUTHOR: **Mildred Taylor**

TITLE: *** The Road to Memphis* (1990)**

DESCRIPTION: "Powerful" is the best word to describe this sequel by Mildred Taylor about the Logan family. Cassie and her brothers and friends are older now, on the verge of adulthood. Cassie is in her last year of high school in Jackson and looking forward to college and law school. Stacey, Clarence, and Moe are aware that, with a war economy gearing up, they might do better than work in the box factory, and Sissy wants only for Clarence to marry her. They have changed by the fall of 1941, but their southern community does not seem to have changed at all.

RECOMMENDATION: If you want to experience prejudice secondhand (yet powerfully), then become part of what happened in three explosive days to Cassie, her friends, and the white boy, Jeremy, with whom they have always shared an uneasy friendship. Feel your personhood demeaned, trust a hurting white person with your very life, learn what your own responses might be as you move outside the strong protection of your loving family, and yet stand for one last time in the circle of that family united in prayer. **MT**

AUTHOR: **Bodie Thoene**

TITLE: **The Zion Chronicles (1987)**

DESCRIPTION: Includes *The Gates of Zion, A Daughter of Zion, The Return to Zion, A Light in Zion,* and *The Key to Zion.* The months before Israel became a nation in May 1948 are played out in all their drama and suspense through the lives of a Jewish archaeologist, Moshe Sachar; an emotionally scarred survivor of the Nazi death camps, Rachel Lebowitz; an American photojournalist, Ellie Warne; and the American World War II flying ace, David Meyer. Among many others who touch their lives for good or ill are Gerhardt, a former S.S. man, twisted by his hatred of the Jews; Sarai, the sister of one of Gerhardt's Arab henchmen; an old rabbi and other Haganah defending the walls of the Old City of Jerusalem, as well as people whom you will recognize from your history books. There are narrow escapes through labyrinth sewers or over burning rooftops, smuggled weapons and food and partisans, plots and counterplots, agents and double agents, bombings and rescues, enough to keep you turning the pages of this wonderful five-volume series. But threaded throughout the intrigue of "the miracle that is Israel" is a strong, sure belief in the redeeming power of Yeshua, the Messiah of Israel, who can heal both individuals and nations.

RECOMMENDATION:  This religious vision puts the Zion stories in strong contrast to the more famous *Exodus* by Leon Uris, which equals its drama. However, Uris's characters' main motivation is the powerful but secular desire for freedom. Uris's Ari Ben Canaan says, "The only Messiah that will deliver [us] is a bayonet on the end of a rifle." However, *Exodus* also paints a broader picture of the birth of Israel through flashbacks in various characters' lives, stretching from the steppes of Czarist Russia to the ovens of Auschwitz to the deck of the rescue ship *Exodus* to the kibbutzim carved out of the desert. If The Zion Chronicles hooks you on this period of history, as well it might, you may want to give *Exodus* a try. Thoene herself has written a series of "prequels" to the Chronicles called Zion Covenant *(Vienna Prelude, Prague Counterpoint, Munich Signature,* and *Jerusalem Interlude, Danzig Passage,* and *Warsaw Requiem)* in which she follows the fortunes of several minor characters in the Israeli series during the years of World War II. As you might guess from the titles, music plays an important role in them, but they are as suspenseful and faith-infused as the books set in Israel. Most recently, The Zion Chronicles continues in another series entitled The Zion Legacy. **MT, LT***

AUTHOR:  **Margaret Walker**

TITLE:  ***Jubilee* (1966)**

DESCRIPTION:  Based on the lives of her great-grandparents, Margaret Walker tells a compelling story of blacks in the south, from slavery days when Vyry was the bastard daughter of a Georgian plantation owner and Randall was a free black blacksmith in the nearby town of Dutton. The story continues through the years of the Civil War and the Ku Klux Klan years of reconstruction that followed.

RECOMMENDATION:  Vyry's husband once realized, after a final confrontation with her past, that Vyry was "touched with a spiritual fire and permeated with a spiritual wholeness that had been forged in a crucible of suffering." You too will quickly perceive that whole human greatness that makes her story so remarkable. **MT, LT**

AUTHOR:  **Gloria Whelan**
TITLE:    ***Miranda's Last Stand*** (1999)

DESCRIPTION:  This carefully researched book is set in the late 1800s against the backdrop of Custer's Last Stand. Miranda's father is killed in the battle with Sitting Bull, and from her experiences at the fort, where her mother works as a laundress, she comes to believe that Indians are inherently evil. Later Miranda and her mother join the traveling company of the Buffalo Bill Show, ultimately experiencing many adventures and friendships with the young Indians in the show. Slowly her prejudice and anger dissolve.

RECOMMENDATION:  Whelan is a consistently fine writer. In an interview, she said, "It isn't that I write books where kids always do the right thing; it's that at some point in the story they understand or it becomes clear to them what the right thing is." See more of Whelan's stories in a trilogy set on Mackinac Island: *Once on This Island, Farewell to the Island,* and *Return to the Island.* **ET, MT**

AUTHOR:  **Laurence Yep**
TITLE:    ***The Star Fisher*** (1991)

DESCRIPTION:  Joan Lee's story of moving to a West Virginia town in 1927 where she and her family are the only Chinese is really Yep's grandmother's story. There she faces both prejudice and offers of friendship.

RECOMMENDATION:  Yep is known for his honest yet heart-warming novels about the Chinese-American experience both historical and contemporary. **ET, MT**

# Chapter 16

# Mystery

AUTHOR: **Avi**

TITLE: ***The Man Who Was Poe*** (1989)

DESCRIPTION: Eleven-year-old Edmund, his twin sister, and Aunty Pru arrive in Providence, Rhode Island, in 1848 after receiving an urgent message from his missing mother. Within weeks his aunt and sister have also disappeared under sinister circumstances. He turns, unwillingly, for help from a stranger who calls himself Auguste Dupin and who sometimes has great insight into Edmund's plight. At other times, however, he is both drunk and indifferent. What Edmund does not know is that "Dupin" is really that fictional character's creator, Edgar Allan Poe, who sees Edmund's real life as a possible plot for a new story. But if he writes it, Sis will have to die.

RECOMMENDATION: You may find yourself fascinated not only by the clever unraveling of Edmund's plot—a mystery in itself—but by this fictional peek into the unstable mind of America's greatest writer of horror stories, Edgar Allan Poe—yet another mystery. **ET**

AUTHOR: **Lynne Reid Banks**

TITLE: ***Melusine: A Mystery*** (1988)

DESCRIPTION: When Roger and his family vacation at an old French chateau, they stumble into an odd situation. The owner seems strangely evil and his daughter, Melusine, seems strangely surreal. Roger wants to help Melusine, but as he does so, he unearths a long-buried mystery.

RECOMMENDATION:  A clue to the mystery is the historical associations surrounding Melusine's name. You should dissect Roger and his father's theological discussion about Melusine/Eve, the meaning of faith and suffering. Is faith "believing without questions"? What is God's relationship to the events in the crumbling castle? **MT**

AUTHOR:  **G. K. Chesterton**

TITLE:     ***Father Brown*** (1911)

DESCRIPTION:  Father Brown is the most unlikely of detectives, and his methods of analysis are more psychological than the forensics used by Sherlock Holmes. You may therefore find yourself even more fascinated to have the chance to sleuth along with the outwardly bumbling priest who "tries to get [himself] inside the murderer. Till," as he says, "I really am the murderer. And when I am quite sure that I feel exactly like the murderer myself, of course I know who he is." **MT, LT***

AUTHOR:  **Agatha Christie**

TITLE:     ***Murder on the Orient Express*** (1934)

DESCRIPTION:  An evil-eyed American asks famed detective Hercule Poirot to prevent his murder. Poirot refuses because he doesn't like the American's demeanor. However, while traveling from Tokatlian to Calais on the Orient Express, the man is stabbed to death. One of the passengers must be guilty.

RECOMMENDATION:  The intrigue of an Agatha Christie murder mystery— and there are many of them—is watching the mastermind of deduction at work. **MT, LT**

AUTHOR:  **Tom Clancy**

TITLE:     ***Red Storm Rising*** (1986)

DESCRIPTION:  *Red Storm Rising* envelops you in the Soviet Union's critically desperate plot for Middle Eastern oil because a Muslim fanatic has destroyed its major refinery. To ensure that NATO countries will not retaliate for its seizure of that oil, military and diplomatic intrigue is launched on a giant scale. You see events unfold through the eyes of Soviets and Westerners, both key strategists and common soldiers.

RECOMMENDATION:  Clancy is the cleanest of the writers of international intrigue; you can read his novels without fear of embarrassingly steamy sex scenes and continuous streams of foul language. **LT**

AUTHOR:  **Peter Dickinson**

TITLE:  ***The Seventh Raven*** (1981)

ET—Early Teens
MT—Mid Teens
LT—Late Teens
AA—All Ages

DESCRIPTION:  One hundred and one children participating in a dress rehearsal for the annual church opera are taken hostage by three Latin American terrorists who had bungled kidnapping the boy playing the role of the seventh raven—the son of their Mattean ambassador to England.

RECOMMENDATION:  Just because this suspense takes place in a church, don't expect that the characters are religious. Instead, you'll discover the relevance of the Elijah-Baal stories—as well as art—to today's unjust political situations. You will also empathize with Doll over her growing awareness of her guilt and her calling in the context of a needy world. Besides being a terrific story, this book gives you lots to think about. Danny, one of the terrorists, says at one point, "I have heard you sing in your opera the song of the King in the Middle [Ahab]. This king in your story is a traitor to the God in your story. So in this world, this real place, which is not a story, you, you, and you, and you are traitors. You are traitors to Man." Are you? **MT**

AUTHOR:  **Rosey Dow**

TITLE:  ***Reaping the Whirlwind*** (2000)

DESCRIPTION:  Trent Tyson has moved to sleepy Dayton, Tennessee, after being fired from his detective job in Chattanooga for exposing a ring of bootleggers. Work as the town's new deputy sheriff is slow until he suspects that an old woman's death isn't from a heart attack after all, but poisoning. Then he overhears a group of local businessmen in the town's drugstore plotting to create a challenge to Tennessee's new law prohibiting the teaching of evolution. They hope that a trial might put Dayton on the map. It does!

RECOMMENDATION:  The two mysteries—a string of unexplained deaths and the ins and outs of the arguments concerning evolution and law during the Scopes "Monkey" Trial in 1925—intertwine in intellectually and emotionally satisfying ways as the townspeople reap what Darwin has sown. You will be glad to meet the skeptical Tyson and his new neighbors and to question with them the facts and meanings of their dilemmas. **MT, LT***

AUTHOR:  **Sir Arthur Conan Doyle**

TITLE:  ***The Adventures of Sherlock Holmes*** (1887)

DESCRIPTION:  Sherlock Holmes, who is, according to his companion, Dr. Watson, "the most perfect reasoning and observing machine that the world has ever seen," is therefore one of the world's greatest detectives; in fact, tourists try to find 221 Baker Street in London, when really the famous lodgings and the famous lodgers are just figments of Sir Arthur Conan Doyle's imagination.

RECOMMENDATION: Put your own reasoning powers to work as you trace with Holmes "the scarlet thread of murder that runs through the colorless skein of life." **ET, MT***

AUTHOR: **P. L. Gaus**
TITLE:  ***Blood of the Prodigal: An Ohio Amish Mystery*** (1999)

DESCRIPTION: Professor Michael Branden, Pastor Cal Troyer, and even their old friend Sheriff Bruce Robinson team up to find the kidnapped grandson of one of Holmes County's strictest Old Order Amish bishops. His own father, whose rebellious teenage behavior ten years before had caused the Bishop to shun (excommunicate) him, had taken Jeremiah Miller. Will rescue come in time for repentance and grace?

RECOMMENDATION: This is a story that is not only intriguing in itself but which gives sensitive insight into a complex culture outside the American mainstream. Rich indeed! This is the first of a proposed series, including *Broken English* and *Clouds without Rain*. **MT, LT**

AUTHOR: **Dorothy Gilman**
TITLE:  ***The Amazing Mrs. Pollifax*** (1970)

DESCRIPTION: A grandmother who volunteers at the hospital, pours tea at the garden show, and takes karate lessons—she is the amazing Mrs. Pollifax, and she's off to Istanbul to help the CIA spirit an old counteragent to safety.

RECOMMENDATION: The characters are so genuine and the plot both so swiftly moving and right that the triumph of virtue can't be in doubt. What do you think of Emily and Magda's discussion about the "karma" that brought them together? (A few characters swear.) Mrs. Pollifax has many more adventures to satisfy her legion of fans. **MT, LT**

AUTHOR: **Virginia Hamilton**
TITLE:  ***Sweet Whispers, Brother Rush*** (1982)

DESCRIPTION: Newbery Honor. The suspense in this story that takes place both on the rough city streets and in rural poverty is not so much the ghost who appears on the first page but in the battle for Dab's life and Tree's security. The mystery, again, is not so much the ghostliness but in figuring out how the past affects the present.

RECOMMENDATION: Grimly realistic, this story is about a fourteen-year-old girl essentially abandoned by her parents to bring up her older retarded brother alone. Nonetheless, you may find strands of love and flashes of hope. **ET, MT**

AUTHOR: **Tony Hillerman**

TITLE: ***The Blessing Way*** (1970)

DESCRIPTION: Luis Horseman, "another poor soul who didn't quite know how to be a Navajo and couldn't learn to act like a white," has been suffocated to death. Did someone think he was the Navaho Wolf, a vengeful witch? Or was it the Wolf who was the killer? Joe Leaphorn of the office of Law and Order puts together the physical evidence and the cultural clues to solve the crime. Meanwhile a cynical anthropology professor must adjust his rationalistic theories about witchcraft to fit the facts of the case.

RECOMMENDATION: The title refers to a Navaho rite of passage. Hillerman's many mysteries—*The Blessing Way* being his first—are multilayered, working well on the suspenseful story level and also on the cultural level. To understand the Navaho worldview is to gain insight into the right—and wrong—workings of Joe Leaphorn's world. Some adult language. **LT**

AUTHOR: **Laurie R. King**

TITLE: ***The Beekeeper's Apprentice*** (1996)

DESCRIPTION: Sherlock Holmes, long retired from his detective work, is studying honeybee behavior on the Sussex Downs when he meets Mary Russell, a very modern fifteen-year-old whose intellect and audacity matches his own. Under Holmes' tutelage, Russell hones her talent for deduction, disguises, and danger.

RECOMMENDATION: An imaginatively crafted mystery sends the two sleuths on the trail of a murderer who scatters meaningless clues and who is seemingly without motive. This time the hunters are the prey in a wonderfully suspenseful and fun mystery. **LT**

AUTHOR: **John LeCarré**

TITLE: ***The Spy Who Came in from the Cold*** (1963)

DESCRIPTION: Alec Leamus has just watched the destruction of his spy network so carefully built up during the years just following the erecting of the Berlin Wall. He returns home to England, supposedly to retire in disgrace, but really to attempt one last time to defeat his East German Communist counterpart. Or is it Leamus who is being manipulated by him?

RECOMMENDATION: LeCarré's most famous spy story is not only an espionage thriller with twists that will keep you reading past your bedtime but it provides a careful and compassionate examination of the central moral dilemmas of spying: Do the ends justify the means? Are a few people worth sacrificing to save many? Do you agree with the experienced but jaded spy, Leamus, that killing is despicable but necessary in a world gone mad? Or with the idealistic but confused Communist, Liz, that though truth is absolute (built into historical processes more important than individuals), individuals are ultimately significant? Or have you formulated a worldview different from either of theirs? **MT**, **LT**

AUTHOR: **Alistair MacLean**
TITLE: *The Guns of Navarone* **(1957)**

DESCRIPTION: Against impossible odds, a hand-picked group of five Allied saboteurs are sent off into the Aegean Sea to make their way to the fortress island of Navarone. They must destroy the German guns that control that strategic crossroad and prevent the British from evacuating 1200 soldiers from Kheros. Among them are two mountain climbing experts, the New Zealander leader, Mallory, and an inwardly fearful British soldier, Stevens. To accomplish their goal, they must scale a sheer precipice never climbed before. A giant Greek, Andreas, who has seen his family and village slaughtered; an American explosives expert, Miller; and Casey Brown, who can fix any engine, make up the rest of the party.

RECOMMENDATION: Besides being a story of compelling action that you won't be able to put down, *The Guns of Navarone* explores the qualities of courage, the notions of what kinds of killing can be justified in a desperate wartime situation, and the common humanity among enemies that makes their lives worth living and sacrificing. Although many of MacLean's later books do not live up to the standard he set in *Navarone*, you do not want to miss this one. **MT**, **LT**

AUTHOR: **Walter Dean Myers**
TITLE: *Tales of a Dead King* **(1983)**

DESCRIPTION: John Robie and Karen Lacey, two American teens chosen to help John's great-uncle, Dr. Leonhardt, with an archaeological dig in Egypt, arrive there to discover that he is missing. In their week-long search for him, they encounter snakes planted in Karen's room, daggers thrown at them in the marketplace, and capture by kidnappers in a deserted village.

RECOMMENDATION: There is action enough for all in this easy-to-read mystery and a gently understated message that "worshiping gold" is not worth the price. **ET**

AUTHOR: **Frank Peretti**

TITLE: ***The Veritas Project: Hangman's Curse* (2001)**

DESCRIPTION: When three star athletes at Baker High School must be hospitalized because they are hallucinating—literally losing their minds—just as the football team is sure to qualify for the state tournament, the Springfield family of the Veritas Project—including teen twins Elijah and Elisha—are called in to search for the truth *(veritas)* in order to solve the mystery of the hangman's curse.

RECOMMENDATION: Although it stretches credulity to imagine these events happening at an ordinary high school, the murders at Columbine High School were unbelievable too. *Hangman's Curse* is an exciting, even scary, mystery as well as a compassionate look at high school life in and out of the classroom. The book does convey high school stereotypes, but it does so in order to break them down with love and truth. Highly recommended. (This book can be fruitfully compared to *The Body of Christopher Creed*.) How can you practice the Truth behind the facts? **ET, MT\***

AUTHOR: **Frank Peretti**

TITLE: ***This Present Darkness* (1986)**

DESCRIPTION: A typical small town is the unlikely place that the Prince of Darkness has chosen to orchestrate his final assault on Christianity by establishing a world religion, Universal Consciousness. The newly arrived newspaper editor, the pastor of a troubled and divided church, and a brilliant but bitter professor of psychology are some of the key figures in this vast spiritual drama that moves back and forth between the physical and spiritual realms where devils and angels alike plot their strategies. It also moves to a tightly controlled climax and has exciting scenes of exorcisms, intriguing glimpses of New Age thinking, and vivid pictures of diabolical plots and angelic counterplots.

RECOMMENDATION: This book has remained very popular because it highlights themes of commitment and purity that are important at the turn of the century. There are cautions that must be noted, however. First, you should keep in mind that, though it is classified here as "suspense" (Peretti has been called the Christian Stephen King!), it could also be classified as "fantasy." It must not be taken literally, any more than Madeleine L'Engle's stories or C. S. Lewis's *Screwtape Letters*, even though it may well convey actual truth, as all stories attempt to do. Second, you must evaluate as you read. Who has power to act in this book—people, or angels and devils, or both? Are people just puppets, reacting as programmed by good and evil forces, or do they exercise a true freedom of will? If you decide primarily for the former view, you may find yourself uneasy at several critical points in the novel. **LT**

AUTHOR: **Ellis Peters**
TITLE:    *A Morbid Taste for Bones* (1978)

DESCRIPTION: Ellis Peters has dozens of mysteries to her credit, but probably the best loved are her medieval ones revolving around a Benedictine monastery in Shrewsbury. Her sleuth is Brother Cadfael, a worldly, traveled man who has retired to the monastery to raise herbs. In this first one, when Brother Columbanus is cured of his madness by a vision of the Welsh St. Winifred, he declares that the saint wants her bones to enhance the prestige of Shrewsbury Abbey. The delegation sent off to retrieve her remains discovers that the Welsh villagers are not anxious to part with them. Even so, they are horrified when their main opponent is found dead. Evidence points to the victim's English suitor, Engelard, but Br. Cadfael is not so sure. He and Sioned, the daughter, contrive both to discover the true murderer and to ensure that St. Winifred rests where she belongs.

RECOMMENDATION: With all the puzzles and suspense of a mystery, these Brother Cadfael stories also reveal a shrewd yet sympathetic insight into human nature. Mercy is as apparent as greed and pride. You will find yourself nodding with agreement when Br. Cadfael argues that we must "meet every man as you find him, for we're all made the same under habit or robe or rags. Some made better than others, and some better cared for, but on the same pattern all." Look also for *Sanctuary Sparrow* as well as many others. **MT**, **LT***

AUTHOR: **Ellen Raskin**
TITLE:    *The Westing Game* (1978)

DESCRIPTION: Newbery Medal, 1979. Sixteen oddly matched people move into Sunset Towers next to the mysterious old Westing mansion. They learn one of them could be heir to the fortune of the newly dead multi-millionaire, Samuel Westing. The catch is that the one who inherits the money must first figure out who killed him.

RECOMMENDATION: Full of word plays and puns and zany visual clues, this mystery is an enjoyable one with which to test your observational skills. Like the sixteen potential heirs, you may discover that cooperation has its rewards! What do you make of the eleventh clue? "Death is senseless yet makes way for the living. Life, too, is senseless unless you know who you are, what you want, and which way the wind blows." Is Raskin just saying this tongue in cheek, or is it a viable philosophy of life? **ET**

AUTHOR: **Dorothy Sayers**

TITLE: ***Strong Poison*** (1930)

DESCRIPTION: Sayers wrote twelve mysteries and in *Strong Poison*, Harriet Vane, a writer of detective stories, has been accused of poisoning her former lover with arsenic. Because her latest book concerns an arsenic poisoning, she is considered an expert on the subject. The case seems airtight to everybody but Lord Peter Wimsey.

RECOMMENDATION: Wimsey, the amateur detective made famous by Sayers, says that "in detective stories virtue is always triumphant. They're the purest literature we have." Do you agree? From time to time you'll be able to see a Lord Peter Wimsey mystery on public television. Try *Nine Tailors* too. Critics disagree whether it or *Strong Poison* is Sayer's best novel. **MT, LT**

AUTHOR: **Josephine Tey**

TITLE: ***The Daughter of Time*** (1951)

DESCRIPTION: Inspector Alan Grant of the Scotland Yard is bored beyond belief as he lies day after day in a hospital with a broken leg. To pass the time, he studies portraits of famous people, using his detective's eye for detail and evidence to discern something of their personalities. King Richard III's portrait intrigues him because history books claim he was one of England's worst villains, killing his young nephews to secure his throne. Yet his face is kindly and sensitive. Could the truth of the 1485 murder be known? Grant is determined to find out.

RECOMMENDATION: Many consider Josephine Tey's *The Daughter of Time* to be one of the best mysteries ever written. It is only one of many Elizabeth MacIntosh wrote about Inspector Grant under her Tey pen name or under the name Gordon Daviot. The book takes you right inside the reasoning processes of a master detective, a fascinating place to be. If you've ever wondered how historians, who should be merely detectives themselves, separated by time from their flesh-and-blood evidence, determine what really happened, this lets you into the secret of truth-finding. Do you agree with the old proverb of the title, that "truth is the daughter of time"? **MT, LT**

# Chapter 17

# Nonfiction

AUTHOR: **Joy Adamson**

TITLE: ***Born Free*** (1960)

DESCRIPTION: Elsa is a lioness raised from birth by Kenya game warden George Adamson and his wife, Joy, but also trained by them to be able to take her place confidently in the wild, her true home. This story is of their four years together in which Elsa achieved the impossible: both freedom to be a natural wild animal and a friend to humans. You'll learn many fascinating facts about African wildlife while this lioness captivates you as she did the Adamsons. ET*

AUTHOR: **Jennifer Armstrong**

TITLE: ***Shipwreck at the Bottom of the World*** (1998)

DESCRIPTION: Intent on becoming the first to cross the Antarctica in 1914–1915, an English expedition under the leadership of Sir Ernest Shackleton instead became trapped in the ice a hundred miles from the South Pole for nine months. Finally, massive ice floes crushed *The Endurance* and the twenty-eight men somehow had to make their way across the frozen wastelands toward possible rescue against impossible odds. Armstrong's book contains unbelievable, exciting narrative and compelling actual photographs saved from the expedition. If you liked this book, try Peter Lerangis's novel, *Antarctica: Journey to the Pole.* ET

AUTHOR: **Misty Bernall**

TITLE: ***She Said Yes: The Unlikely Martyrdom of Cassie Bernall* (1999)**

DESCRIPTION: "P.S. Honestly, I want to live completely for God. It's hard and scary, but totally worth it." Cassie Bernall wrote this note the night before she was gunned down at Columbine High School. This is her story . . . of all the steps and missteps and retraced steps she took which led her to face the point of a gun in her school library and to affirm her faith in God. (Included in her mother's account are titles of several books her youth group had been studying.) **AA**\*

AUTHOR: **Paul Brand and Philip Yancey**

TITLE: ***In His Image* (1984)**

DESCRIPTION: A hand surgeon famous for his work with leprosy patients around the world teams up with a professional writer to explore the wonders of the human body. Then they apply the fascinating tidbits and patterns of information metaphorically to the spiritual body of Christ in this richly layered book, a companion volume to their *Fearfully and Wonderfully Made*. Dr. Brand and Yancey want "to throw across" (the literal meaning of the word "symbol") a bridge between the natural visible world of the body to the invisible world of the spirit, because they stand in the tradition of Copernicus, Kepler, Galileo, and Newton, the great scientists of the past who believed the created world revealed God's nature to his people. Dorothy Clark Wilson has written a biography of Dr. Brand's work in India, reconstructing the hands of lepers, *Ten Fingers for God*. **LT**\*

AUTHOR: **Ross Campbell and Dave Lambert**

TITLE: ***Getting a Clue in a Clueless World* (1996)**

DESCRIPTION: The problems that face teens today can be overwhelming, but Ross Campbell, a psychologist, and Dave Lambert, an editor at Zondervan, have teamed up to give teens solutions in this book of sixty devotions that will lift their spirits and ground them in the Bible. For a lighter, more humorous devotional book, try *Jumper Fables* by Lambert and Ken Davis. *Completely Alive* is a year's worth of devotions that cover such topics as self-esteem, dating, peer-pressure, success, families, and faith, written by a Campus Life editor, S. Rickly Christian. **ET, MT, LT**

AUTHOR: **Ben Carson with Cecil Murphey**

TITLE: ***Gifted Hands: The Story of Ben Carson* (1990)**

DESCRIPTION: Raised in inner-city Detroit by a mother with a third-grade education, Ben Carson lacked motivation and had a pathological temper. Then his mother decided that her two sons would read books, not watch TV. Today Carson is a world-famous pediatric neurosurgeon whose story will inspire you to try to beat any odds that may be facing you, as he beat the odds facing him. **MT, LT\***

AUTHOR: **Bruce Catton**

TITLE: *The Civil War* (1960)

DESCRIPTION: The leading historian of the Civil War, Bruce Catton won a Pulitzer prize citation for this vivid narrative of the years of the war that divided and demoralized the United States. The American Heritage Press edition contains 200 photographs and illustrations. Look for other books by Catton on various aspects of the conflict, including *Mr. Lincoln's Army, A Stillness at Appomattox, A Terrible Swift Sword,* and *Never Call Retreat*. **MT, LT\***

AUTHOR: **Elias Chacour**

TITLE: *Blood Brothers* (1984)

DESCRIPTION: Any book that is dedicated to the Jews who died at Dachau and the Palestinians who died in refugee camps is sure to give you a unique view of the history of the Palestinian/Israeli conflict. Elias Chacour, a Palestinian Melkite Christian priest, tells his own story of how he learned to love the Jews who sent his family from their ancient farms and learned to serve the disheartened Palestinian villagers, his blood brothers. This was not with acts of terrorism or by passive acceptance but the third way of active reconciliation and justice. **LT**

AUTHOR: **Padraic Colum**

TITLE: *The Golden Fleece, and the Heroes Who Lived Before Achilles* (1921)

DESCRIPTION: Newbery Honor. Many of the strange and wonderful stories of Greek mythology, including those of Jason and the Golden Fleece, Persephone in the Underworld, Prometheus and the creation of fire, Hercules and his twelve labors, and the battle of wits between Theseus and the Cretan Minotaur are woven into one splendid tale by this master Irish storyteller. Whether you are already a lover of mythology or whether these timeless tales are new to you, Colum is sure to delight you. **AA\***

AUTHOR: **Don Cormack**

TITLE: *Killing Fields, Living Fields* (1997)

DESCRIPTION: Don't read this book, which some call one of the greatest of all stories in church history, unless you are prepared to weep and to pray for the persecuted church. Telling the story from the perspective of the Cambodian Christians themselves, Cormack recounts the history of their church from its earliest days in remote villages, through the brief years when it experienced an explosion of young urban believers in the days just preceding the takeover of the Khmer Rouge. Then followed the decade of genocide in which ninety percent of the church died at the hands of the unspeakably brutal revolutionaries who killed over thirty percent of all their countrymen. But God had not abandoned his precious people, and he resurrected a vibrant church out of their suffering and sacrifice. This is a book that can change your life if you let it. **LT***

AUTHOR: **Annie Dillard**
TITLE:    ***Pilgrim at Tinker Creek*** (1974)

DESCRIPTION: Pulitzer prize, 1974. Though this journal of a year's natural cycle at Tinker Creek in Virginia is loaded with biblical and literary allusions and scientific minutiae, it really is an attempt by the author to look so closely (and without blinking) at both the horrors and beauties of nature that she can determine if she should praise God for them or reject him. (Unlike the teenager in Gary Paulsen's *The Island*, you understand from Dillard what intense yet exhilarating work this looking is.) One image of horror—a giant waterbug sucking the life out of a frog—and one of beauty—a sycamore tree coming alive in a flame of thousands of birds—recurs until she resolves the question whether "all things live by a generous power and dance to a nightly tune; or . . . all things are scattered and hurled, that our every arabesque and grand jéte is a frantic variation on our one free fall."

Annie Dillard is an author highly praised in literary circles and much appreciated by those in thoughtful religious circles who know her. *Pilgrim* will reward anyone who puts in the effort it takes to read and understand it, especially those who have been disturbed by the problem of natural (not man-made) evil. And if you like *Pilgrim*, you may also enjoy her *American Childhood*, which chronicles her rebellious teenage years. **LT***

AUTHOR: **Gerald Durrell**
TITLE:    ***Birds, Beasts and Relatives*** (1969)

DESCRIPTION: This is a companion volume to Durrell's hilarious *My Family and Other Animals* about the five years just prior to World War II that his zany family lived on the idyllic island of Corfu. Five outspoken individualists reside with even more individualistic animals, including a donkey, barn owl, five baby hedgehogs, and a spade-footed toad. Odd neighbors and house guests make their appearances as well. All manage to keep life in an uproar, yet ten-year-old Gerry persists in collecting the wildlife of the island. **MT**, **LT***

AUTHOR: **Freeman Dyson**

TITLE:    ***Disturbing the Universe*** (1979)

DESCRIPTION: A wonderfully literate physicist, who after World War II worked with the physicists famous for inventing the atomic bomb, examines the significant moral dilemmas that science and technology raise for sensitive, compassionate people. He does so by tracing his own scientific life from a young boy genius in England to his richly productive adult career in the United States and even projects us into a future of space colonization. This complex but very readable book is for you if you are passionate about science and literature and willing to think hard about the relationships between them and the great moral dilemmas of our day. **LT**

AUTHOR: **Joni Eareckson**

TITLE:    ***Joni*** (1976)

DESCRIPTION: Joni was an active athlete of seventeen when a diving accident made her a quadriplegic for life. She tells in her book about her accident and the months and years that followed as she adjusted to never being able to move again. Well-meaning people told her just to have faith that God would heal her, but she gradually discovers the spiritual significance that her life could have through art and a ministry to others. Joni's story has been made into a movie, and she has written other books about her life and overcoming handicaps in God's power. **ET, MT***

AUTHOR: **Loren Eiseley**

TITLE:    ***All These Strange Hours: The Excavation of a Life*** (1975)

DESCRIPTION: The language and imagery in anthropologist Loren Eiseley's autobiographical *All These Strange Hours* sing both true and steel-hard as he describes his days as a drifter, as a thinker, and as a doubter in which his philosophy of "behind nothing/before nothing/worship it the zero" is confirmed. He takes you deep into his mind as a naturalist who has faced the implications of his worldview honestly. It will be a dangerous yet poignantly compelling journey for you if you are a patient and mature reader interested in cultures and science. **LT**

AUTHOR: **Elisabeth Elliot**

TITLE:    ***Shadow of the Almighty*** (1958)

DESCRIPTION: Elisabeth Elliot draws on her first husband's journals to tell the gripping story of how God shaped him into a man he could use during his college years at Wheaton. There God called him to seek out the savage stone-age Auca Indians of Ecuador who had never heard the gospel. Jim and four others died at the Auca's hands in 1956, and their martyrdom has inspired thousands with the truth of what Jim wrote: "He is no fool who gives what he cannot keep to gain what he cannot lose." **MT, LT***

ET—Early Teens
MT—Mid Teens
LT—Late Teens
AA—All Ages

AUTHOR: **Tom Feelings**

TITLE: ***The Middle Passage* (1995)**

DESCRIPTION: The old proverb, "A picture is worth a thousand words," certainly holds true for this incredibly moving retelling of a defining event in American history: the Middle Passage through which African slaves passed on their way to bondage in America. Were you aware that of the 60,000,000 (that's sixty million!) who were captured and put on slave ships, only one-third survived? Prepare to be moved to horror and to commitment to fight racism wherever it raises its sinful head. Talk together about how you can do that. Also, you will inevitably find yourself discussing how the past is intertwined in the present. Are we guilty today for our forefathers' sins? Can we make up for them? Tom Feelings introduces his paintings with an essay discussing how he created this book to "journey back in order to move forward." Dr. John Clarke briefly outlines the historical context of the Atlantic slave trade. **ET, AA**

AUTHOR: **Anne Frank**

TITLE: ***Anne Frank: The Diary of a Young Girl* (1947)**

DESCRIPTION: If you haven't read Anne's story in school, then you'll want to meet her now. The irrepressible Jewish teenager is hidden in a "secret annex" in Amsterdam with seven others for two years until the Nazis discover them and take her off to Bergen-Belsen. Cherishing the privacy that her diary alone can give her, Anne explores all the emotions common to adolescents everywhere, yet they are especially clarified by her particularly difficult circumstances. Do you agree with the words she wrote just before her capture? ". . .in spite of everything I still believe that people are really good at heart." **ET, MT**

AUTHOR: **Robin Graham and L. T. Gill**

TITLE: ***Dove* (1972)**

DESCRIPTION: At the age of sixteen, Robin Graham quit school and set off to sail across the Pacific Ocean alone in the Dove. Two years later he has accomplished his goal, exploring the lands and peoples along the route, and is determined to continue on around the world. Even the beautiful Patti with whom he had fallen in love on the Fiji Islands could not deter him, nor could dramatic storms nor seductive voices whispering to wreck the boat. Even though he is guided and protected by God, Robin forgets the One who on occasions calms the seas for him. He arrives back in Los Angeles five years after his departure. *Home is the Sailor* continues his story when, restless, bored, and unfulfilled after his voyage, he and his wife, Patti, seek new adventure in the untamed wilderness of Montana and the God who could fill their spiritual void. **LT**

AUTHOR: **Brian Greene**

TITLE:    *The Elegant Universe* (1999)

DESCRIPTION: Against the backdrop of the two most significant results of twentieth-century physics, Einstein's theory of relativity and quantum mechanics, Brian Greene tells the story about the relatively recent discovery of string theory, which is the current candidate for the "theory of everything." Behind his description is the assumption that there is such a theory—be it string theory or something else to be found in the future—and when scientists find it, it will be correct because it describes what is really in the universe. Although string theory is mathematically quite complex, he describes its basics in clear language with a minimum of technical details and with many examples from everyday experience. This makes the book suitable not just for trained scientists, but also for anyone interested in the current understanding of how the world works. If you could overhear a group of Christian physicists discussing this book, how do you think they would evaluate it? Is God in a "theory of everything" even if he isn't mentioned? **LT**

AUTHOR: **John Howard Griffin**

TITLE:    *Black Like Me* (1960)

DESCRIPTION: In 1959 John Howard Griffin, an expert in race relations, decided that he really didn't know the Negro's real problems, and the only way to correct that was to experience them as a Negro. *Black Like Me* is the journal, raw and real, of the six weeks that he was "cast on the junkheap of second-class citizenship" so as to tell "the real story . . . the universal one of men who destroy the souls and bodies of other men (and in the process destroy themselves) for reasons neither really understands." **MT**, **LT**

AUTHOR: **John Gunther**

TITLE:    *Death Be Not Proud: A Memoir* (1949)

DESCRIPTION: The writer, famous for his travel guides, gives you this memoir of his son, Johnny, who died of a brain tumor when he was seventeen, but "not so much a memoir . . . in a conventional sense as the story of a long, courageous struggle between a child and Death." Because Johnny was so exceptionally bright and good and brave and loved, his special qualities infuse this book with a radiant joy. The title is from a wonderful poem by John Donne, quoted in the beginning, as is Johnny's own "Unbeliever's Prayer," at the end. **MT**, **LT**

AUTHOR: **Philip Hallie**

TITLE: ***Lest Innocent Blood Be Shed*** (1980)

DESCRIPTION: What happened in the small French Heugonot village of Le Chambon has been called a miracle of goodness. Though under the surveillance of the Nazis, two pastors lead the whole town in a conspiracy to save thousands of Jews. This book tells the compelling story of Le Chambon and Pastors Trochme and Theis as well as examines in a more philosophical way how such goodness could happen in a world where evil is rampant. **LT**

AUTHOR: **Virginia Hamilton**

TITLE: ***Anthony Burns: The Defeat and Triumph of a Fugitive Slave*** (1988)

DESCRIPTION: Hamilton places "an oppressed slave, a common man, . . . at the center of his own struggle" to be free. Anthony Burns was that man, the focus of a riot and court battle in Boston between abolitionists and slave owners after he had escaped and was recaptured. But instead of being just the slave these impersonal forces struggled over in 1854, in this biography Burns becomes a young man keen for freedom in his own right. And, as Hamilton comments, "As long as we know he is free, we too are liberated." **ET***

AUTHOR: **Virginia Hamilton**

TITLE: ***In the Beginning: Creation Stories from Around the World*** (1988)

DESCRIPTION: Newbery Honor. A master storyteller retells twenty-five creation myths from around the world, including Babylonian, Greek, and the Genesis accounts. Hamilton says that myths are stories about "a god or gods . . . superhuman beings . . . and the first people on earth [which are] truth to the people who believe in them and live by them." You may be interested in figuring out for yourself similarities and differences between the stories she includes. Especially look at the character of the creator-god and whether he or she makes mistakes in creation. **AA**

AUTHOR: **Joshua Harris**

TITLE: *I Kissed Dating Goodbye* (1997)

DESCRIPTION: Harris provides a refreshing and biblical—though controversial—perspective on dating. He argues that dating leads to intimacy, but not to commitment. Intimacy, he says, is rightly a reward of commitment. Harris calls for teens to make friendships in which they practice skills of relating, caring, and sharing their lives with others. He also encourages them to wait and trust and "redeem the time" by serving God and others in their purposeful singleness. This is not an anti-relationship book, but instead strives to give teens a healthy and realistic view of friendships, intimacy, purity, singleness, and marriage. Many teens and twenty-somethings have found his advice helpful. There is a companion study guide and a sequel called *Boy Meets Girl*, which he wrote with the woman who became his wife. **MT**, **LT**

AUTHOR: **Torey Hayden**

TITLE: *One Child* (1980)

DESCRIPTION: Torey Hayden is an educational psychologist who teaches the throwaway children whom no one else wants. *One Child* is the true story of six-year-old Sheila, abandoned by her mother, and terribly abused by her uncle and her alcoholic father. She refuses even to talk. Underneath, Hayden discovers a brilliant child with a loving heart who can be healed. Hayden has written books about other children she has worked with as well. **MT**, **LT**

AUTHOR: **Jeanne Wakatsuki Houston and James Houston**

TITLE: *Farewell to Manzanar* (1973)

DESCRIPTION: This is a true story of one ordinary American family's internment for three and a half years during World War II in Manzanar—just because, like the 10,000 others, they happened to be Japanese. It brings to life a too-little known shameful episode in American history. Even though they were surrounded by barbed wire, searchlights, and armed guards, they did not stop being American. Cheerleaders, Boy Scouts, sock hops, baton twirling lessons, and high school yearbooks all had their place in the camp. Jeanne's family survived the indignities with their dignity intact, but she shares with you honestly the high price they paid for that survival. **MT**, **LT**

AUTHOR: **Peter Jenkins**

TITLE: *A Walk Across America* (1979)

DESCRIPTION: Peter Jenkins was a young man disillusioned about his country and his future when he started walking across America with his dog,

Cooper. Meeting ordinary people of all races, working side by side with them, moving on to the next place, from New York state through the Appalachian Mountains to New Orleans, each rich in history and heritage, restores his faith in himself, his country, and his God. The second book Jenkins wrote, about the rest of his walk to the Pacific Ocean, this time with his new wife, Barbara, is called *The Walk West*. **MT**, **LT***

**ET**—Early Teens
**MT**—Mid Teens
**LT**—Late Teens
**AA**—All Ages

AUTHOR: **Phillip E. Johnson**

TITLE: ***Defeating Darwinism by Opening Minds*** (1997)

DESCRIPTION: Phillip Johnson, a professor of law at the University of California at Berkeley, has long engaged the scientific elites in debates about the validity of evolution and naturalism. In this book he simplifies and focuses his arguments so that high schoolers and those who work with them can understand and argue against the faulty logic that undergirds the culturally accepted theories of evolution. A book for thinkers! **LT**

AUTHOR: **Peter Kreeft**

TITLE: ***Between Heaven and Hell*** (1982)

DESCRIPTION: The same day that John F. Kennedy was assassinated on November 22, 1963, two other famous men died—C. S. Lewis and Aldous Huxley. Kreeft imagines the three of them engaging in a dialog that Socrates would have approved of in their life together after death. He sees Kennedy as a modern humanist; Lewis, a Christian theist; and Huxley, an Eastern pantheist. Their dialogue hinges, as does that of all history, on the identity of Jesus Christ. Even if you've never had to think as a philosopher before, you'll find the style of this book intriguing and the ideas stretching. If you like it, there are several other Kreeft titles, including *Socrates Meets Jesus* and *The Unaborted Socrates*. **LT***

AUTHOR: **Julius Lester**

TITLE: ***To Be a Slave*** (1968)

DESCRIPTION: Who better to tell what slavery was like than the slaves themselves? Lester has gathered together their stories, from capture in Africa to eventual emancipation during the Civil War, adding his own commentary as a bridge between them. Tom Feelings (see *The Middle Passage* on page 233) beautifully illustrated the Scholastic edition. **ET**, **MT***

AUTHOR: **C. S. Lewis**

TITLE: ***The Screwtape Letters*** (1941)

DESCRIPTION: These letters from veteran devil Screwtape to his novice nephew Wormwood shed more humbling light on the spiritual weaknesses of people than they do on the state of supernatural beings. Wit and wisdom combine to aid us all to discern better the traps of the Evil One. There' plenty more of Lewis's clear apologetic writings for those who ar intrigued by Screwtape. **MT, LT***

AUTHOR: **Doris Lund**

TITLE: *Eric* (1974)

DESCRIPTION: Eric was a seventeen-year-old star soccer player ready to g off to college when he learned that he had leukemia. His mother tell the story of his four-year feisty fight against that disease and his four year love affair with life, learning, and love itself. **MT, LT**

AUTHOR: **Robert Massie**

TITLE: *Nicholas and Alexandra* (1967)

DESCRIPTION: Over the vast and disintegrating empire of the Russias in th turbulent early twentieth century, Nicholas II reigned as Tsar. For household of a wife, Alexandra, and four lovely daughters, he was a lov ing husband and father. Then on August 12, 1904, his long-awaited son Alexis, was born—born with hemophilia—and that "moment . . . th two disasters"—hemophilia and a disintegrating empire—"were inter twined." Under the hypnotic influence of the Siberian mystic, Rasputir who she thought could heal her son, Alexandra refused to allow th Romanov regime to be reformed. And so the stage was set for th Russian Revolution and the murders of all whom she loved. Massie' biography of the last Tsar and Empress is crowded with fascinatin details about one of the most fascinating periods of European history. **L**

AUTHOR: **Gavin Maxwell**

TITLE: *Ring of Bright Water* (1960)

DESCRIPTION: Gavin Maxwell writes about the remote Scottish Hebride island of "Camusfearna," where he lives, and about its "intense and var ied" beauty of landscape and animals—the otters whom he adopte after the death of his dog, the geese and swans, the whales, the stag; the wildcat—with a "transcendent touch of love [that] summons [his world into being." **LT**

AUTHOR: **Brian McClaren**

TITLE: *Finding Faith* (2000)

DESCRIPTION: This is a book that doesn't speak in religious language eve though it is about a religious search—for faith, for truth, for God. Usin the words of such media giants as Bob Dylan, Alanis Morissette, "Th

X Files," and "Touched by an Angel," McClaren investigates, not so much the "what" of faith, but the "how" of a faith that engages both intellect and emotions.

RECOMMENDATION: McClaren says that genesis of this book lay in his own teenage questions and searchings. Teens may find it more accessible than their parents, but both can use it to understand how we can live out a real and relevant faith in our pluralistic, skeptical (yet longing to be spiritual) postmodern culture. **LT**

AUTHOR: **Milton Meltzer**

TITLE:      ***Never to Forget*** (1976)

DESCRIPTION: "The heaviest wheel rolls across our foreheads/to bury itself deep somewhere inside our memories," says Mif, a child in the Terezin ghetto (1944). To remember the Holocaust, writes Milton Meltzer, is to "think of what being human means." He helps you do that in this book by gathering together the words of many Jews, from their days in the ghettos of Europe's great cities to the early days of harassments, to Kristallnacht, and finally to the concentration camps. There they went to death or, for some few, to cling tenaciously to life, both with great dignity. He allows you to see the Holocaust, not as a matter of appalling statistics but of haunting personal suffering and victories, and to think thereby of what being human means. **ET, MT***

AUTHOR: **Milton Meltzer**

TITLE:      ***The Rescue*** (1988)

DESCRIPTION: As a companion volume to *Never to Forget*, Meltzer has told the stories of "righteous Gentiles" throughout Europe who risked what they had to help the Jews. Sometimes a person acted individually, like Frau Schmidt, who left baskets of food for the Jewish woman for whom she had formerly washed clothes. Sometimes they were a network of resistance, like the one Joop and Will belonged to in Holland, or whole communities like Le Chambon (see also *Lest Innocent Blood Be Shed*), or a whole country like Denmark. While inspiring you with hope for the human race, the book also reminds you that God gives each of us the opportunity to "choose good, choose life" in the face of evil. **ET, MT***

AUTHOR: **Neil Postman**

TITLE:      ***Amusing Ourselves to Death*** (1985)

DESCRIPTION: TV has affected every part of American society, not only how families relate to each other but also how politicians run for office, how news is conveyed, how teachers teach, and how preachers preach. Neil

ET—Early Teens
MT—Mid Teens
LT—Late Teens
AA—All Ages

Postman, a professor of communications, explores just how television is causing the American people to lose its freedoms not due to censorship of ideas or external political pressures but due to trivial and irrelevant images and internal emotional pleasures. We are, he claims, "amusing ourselves to death." Postman writes clearly and provocatively about serious ideas. No one escapes his probe—not the educators who created *The Voyage of Mimi* you may have seen in school, not the makers of *Sesame Street*, and certainly not the televangelists. He will surely cause you to think as well as he disturbs the waters of the cultural medium in which you swim. **LT**

AUTHOR: **Don Richardson**
TITLE: *Peace Child* (1975)

DESCRIPTION: Don and Carol Richardson traveled deep into the jungles of New Guinea to work as missionaries to the Sawi headhunters, among whom deceit and death were a way of life. Love for the people and careful observation of their culture lead the Richardsons to discover within the Sawi customs a "redemptive analogy" to the Christian story of forgiveness through Christ. He is called the Peace Child. One of the best missionary stories ever. **MT, LT**

AUTHOR: **James W. Sire**
TITLE: *Chris Chrisman Goes to College* (1993)

DESCRIPTION: Chris goes off to Hansom State where he finds challenges to his Christian faith in the dorm and in the classroom. With new friends Bill and Bob and Susie, he begins to search for and apply the truth to his life and studies. Some of those challenges have names, such as relativism, individualism and pluralism, all of which can be tamed by Christian truth, community, and tolerance. This book, written by the author of *The Universe Next Door*, is a must read for everyone going to college—and everyone who wants to understand American culture at the turn of the millenium. **LT.***

AUTHOR: **Corrie ten Boom**
TITLE: *The Hiding Place* (1971)

DESCRIPTION: A Dutch watchmaker and his two "old maid" daughters are the unlikely heroes in the cosmic battle between good and evil as it was focused on Nazi-controlled Holland. Always willing to hide Jews in the name of the Lord Jesus, Corrie, her sister Betsy, and their father are finally betrayed and captured. Corrie and Betsy are taken to Ravensbruck concentration camp where Betsy eventually dies a brutal death, but together the sisters bring hope and peace to their sister inmates. Corrie herself discovers "that it is not on our forgiveness any more than on our goodness that the world's healing hinges, but on [God's]. When He tells us to love our enemies, He gives, along with the command, the love itself." A book not to be missed. **MT**, **LT***

AUTHOR: **James Thurber**
TITLE: ***The Thurber Carnival* (1944)**

DESCRIPTION: Thurber once described his drawings as "having reached completion by some other route than the common one of intent" but his writings as having been actually written since "it is impossible to read any of them from the last line to the first without experiencing a definite sensation of going backward." This collection of his essays, stories, and cartoons is a good introduction to an American humorist. **LT**

AUTHOR: **Malcolm X as told to Alex Haley**
TITLE: ***The Autobiography of Malcolm X* (1964)**

DESCRIPTION: Before he was killed by an assassin in 1965, Malcolm X was the best-known leader in the black separatist movement of Elijah Mohammed's Nation of Islam. He worked for blacks to come out from the cesspool of white immorality that controlled ghetto life, find redemption and identity in Islam, and create their own culture. To Alex Haley he tells the story of his own life—of sinking to the depths of that cesspool before meeting Allah in prison—and his role of articulating black America's rage. A New York newspaper reporter who knew him as well as perhaps any white person knew him says the book is "a testimony to the power of redemption and the force of human personality." **LT**

# Chapter 18

# Science Fiction

AUTHOR: **Douglas Adams**

TITLE: ***Hitchhiker's Guide to the Galaxy* (1979)**

DESCRIPTION: Series continues with *The Restaurant at the End of the Universe; Life, the Universe and Everything;* and *So Long and Thanks for All the Fish.* Douglas Adams's quartet of books are not conventional science fiction despite their computers and spaceships. Enormously popular with teens and young adults, they are an off-the-wall, zany trip through time and space with four oddball companions thrown together by the incomprehensible "perversion of physics." Among their discoveries is the fact that Earth is really a computer that was unfortunately destroyed to make way for an interstellar freeway bypass five minutes before its makers (two mice) determined the ultimate question of life's meaning. The answer is 42; the question, reconstructed by the end of the second volume, is "What is 6 x 9?"

RECOMMENDATION: Adams responds to the meaninglessness of twentieth-century life as he sees it—and projects it—not with serious pronouncements but with a Monty Python kind of humor. Just every once in a while as you read—and laugh—you'll discover that he cannot maintain the mask. For example, the award-winning computer designer of Earth's fjords says, "What does it matter? Science has achieved some wonderful things, of course, but I'd far rather be happy than right any day." "And are you?" "No, that's where it falls down, of course." For insight into the controlling culture of Western teenagers, these books are must reading. **MT, LT**

AUTHOR: **Isaac Asimov**

TITLE: ***The Bicentennial Man and Other Stories*** (1976)

DESCRIPTION: Most of the stories in this collection revolve around robots and consider from various intriguing angles, such as communications, triage, autism, genetic engineering, what it means to be human in a technological society where machines can do more than some people.

RECOMMENDATION: Isaac Asimov, the prolific writer best known for his science fiction, collected for this anthology some of the stories he wrote in the 1970s. In the introduction that he writes for each story you can see an enormous ego at work! Though the notion of creation does not enter Asimov's stories, the central matters of humanity—free will and determinism, and self-sacrifice, for example—are explored over and over. **MT, LT**

AUTHOR: **Isaac Asimov**

TITLE: ***Foundation*** (1951)

DESCRIPTION: First of series, continued by *Foundation Empire* and *Second Foundation*. Isaac Asimov preaches in the first of his famous Foundation series a sophisticated religion of science whose chief characteristic is "that it really works." As the old Galactic Empire is dying, Hari Seldon, a psychohistorian, creates the Foundation, a fringe society of Encyclopedists, cataloging all knowledge so as to foreshorten the inevitable period of barbarism that follows the death of an empire. More importantly, this will allow them to create the Second Empire.

RECOMMENDATION: Old questions of free will and determinism, science and religion, take on clever new twists in the 12,000th year of the Galactic Empire. Asimov is perhaps the best-known science fiction writer of our age, and he does not attempt to disguise his belief system, a rational, humane scientism. **LT**

AUTHOR: **Isaac Asimov and Robert Silverberg**

TITLE: ***Nightfall*** (1990)

DESCRIPTION: Imagine a planet with six suns that hasn't experienced the terrifying reality of night for over 2000 years. That planet is Kalgash. Religious fanatics predict that night will come as the judgment of the gods while scientists predict a dreadful, long night resulting in madness and chaos. Whom will the people believe?

RECOMMENDATION: Questions to ponder as you read this book are: How does science account for data contradicting established theories? Science fiction writers often pit science and religion against each other. Is this a

**ET**—Early Teens
**MT**—Mid Teens
**LT**—Late Teens
**AA**—All Ages

valid conflict—in this book and in reality? Who should be blamed for Nightfall? This novel is an expanded version of a short story by the same name that Asimov published in 1941. **MT**, **LT**

AUTHOR: **Ray Bradbury**

TITLE: ***The Martian Chronicles*** (1946)

DESCRIPTION: In a series of short stories that don't relate to each other at first glance except that they follow the various missions to Mars in chronological order, Ray Bradbury paints a picture of an ancient and marvelous civilization that, although it resists in ingenious ways, is destroyed by invaders from earth who are already destroying their own planet.

RECOMMENDATION: Spender is an example of a character who dissents from the goals of the mission, and as such, he provides a telling commentary on what people are really like and how we have allowed science to control us. Calvin Miller, author of the Singer poetry trilogy published by InterVarsity Press, said that when he was a teen, reading Bradbury nurtured his hope. **MT**, **LT***

AUTHOR: **Orson Scott Card**

TITLE: ***Ender's Game*** (1994)

DESCRIPTION: Andrew, or Ender, is selected for the elite Space Battle School, where children are trained in readiness for the coming war with an alien species. The novel is less about the battle itself and more about the lives of the gifted children as they are thrown into this challenging environment.

RECOMMENDATION: One adult reader, who isn't such a sci-fi fan but loves this book (and first read it at the recommendation of her younger "gifted" brother), observes that Card captures much of the turmoil of children. He brings to life their alternating self-doubt and exuberant confidence, the oppression and support from peers, and the first inklings that adults may not be infallible. Coarse language but not enough to spoil your reading enjoyment. **LT**

AUTHOR: **John Christopher**

TITLE: ***The Prince in Waiting*** (1970)

DESCRIPTION: Series continued in *Beyond the Burning Lands* and *The Sword of the Spirits*. Luke wins a tournament through skill and luck and thereby guarantees that he will be Prince in Waiting of Winchester, a medieval city set in an England of the future, after an ecological holocaust. In so doing, though, he becomes an unwitting tool of the Seers, the priests of the Spiritists, who under cover of their magic, are hoping to restore a civilization based on the now-banned science and technology.

RECOMMENDATION: In these three fine books, you will explore with Luke the human costs of pride and jealousy as well as the larger theme of when the ends—in this case, the restoration of a beneficent society— justify the means—of deception and treachery. Luke's battle to become the Prince of Winchester parallels the larger battle of the Seers. And always on the edges of both stories are the despised outcasts, the Christians, who show them all another way. ET*

AUTHOR: **John Christopher**

TITLE: *The White Mountains* (1967)

DESCRIPTION: Series continued in *The City of Gold and Lead* and *The Pool of Fire*. Will should have been looking forward to his Capping by the Tripods, the ceremony that signaled his transition to adulthood. He is instead approached by a man posing as a crazy vagrant, who confirmed his worst fears about the event. With his despised cousin, Henry, and later a French boy, Beanpole, he runs away from his English town toward Switzerland where a few free men have banded together to fight their domination by the Tripods. In the books that follow, you will find Will and a German boy winning an athletic contest for the "privilege" of serving the Tripods behind a walled city of gold and lead. There they learn that the gruesome masters come from another planet and are planning the extinction of the human race by altering the environment. Finally the freedom fighters bravely attack the three cities but find themselves divided as to how to use and preserve their hard-won freedom.

RECOMMENDATION: Will is a very human hero, flawed by a quick temper and a tendency to take the easy, undisciplined way. Nevertheless, he and his friends take a daring stand for what it means to be human because they have "the vital spark of defiance" against evil repression. You will find yourself cheering them on through all their dangers. ET*

AUTHOR: **Arthur C. Clarke**

TITLE: *2001: A Space Odyssey* (1968)

DESCRIPTION: The computer, Hal, has been created "innocent; but, all too soon, a snake enters his electronic Eden." Therefore, he betrays his two human fellow astronauts, Poole and Bowman. Bowman nevertheless continues on *Discovery* to one of the rings of Saturn, there to determine if the evolution of the whole human race had been programmed by an extraterrestrial, TAM–1. Hal may have been created, but soon Bowman is re-created—to be master of his old world.

ET—Early Teens
MT—Mid Teens
LT—Late Teens
AA—All Ages

RECOMMENDATION: Clarke is a prolific writer of science fiction, and this is his most famous story, really based on the movie of the same name. Even without all the special effects of the screen version, you will sense the arrogance of science without God even as you are compelled to keep turning the pages of this story. **LT**

AUTHOR: **Peter Dickinson**

TITLE: ***Eva* (1988)**

DESCRIPTION: The intriguing "What if?" behind this thought-provoking book is "What if a human brain were transplanted into a chimp's body?" Would the chimp/person who resulted be an animal or a human or both? Thirteen-year-old Eva's body was killed in an auto accident, and her father, a primate researcher on an overcrowded planet, eagerly allows the procedure to take place. Her mother agrees only reluctantly in order to keep her only child alive. But in this decaying society in which people are losing their will and their hope, will chimps be able to survive at all? Could Eva's presence among them make the critical difference?

RECOMMENDATION: This book raises more important questions about what it means to be human than any average library shelf of titles. Several to discuss together are: Is Eva born again? What is a person? What makes you *you*? How do minds and bodies relate to each other? Can advancing scientific knowledge justify the death of an animal? Of a human? Equally so? Are humans animals? What is our place in the animal world? How should species relate to each other? How do you think your answers compare to the ones implicit in Dickinson's book? He is one of Britain's most respected writers of adolescent literature. Look for some of his other titles. (One character swears.) **ET, MT, AA**

AUTHOR: **Nancy Farmer**

TITLE: ***The Ear, the Eye and the Arm* (1995)**

DESCRIPTION: Newbery Honor. In gang-infested Harare, Zimbabwe, of 2194, the chief of security uses all the technology he has to keep his children safe at home. They, however, long for adventure. What they get once they break out of the family's fortress is an excursion into the Zimbabwean past and present and an opportunity to grow in grace and courage. So do the three odd but lovable detectives—Ear, Eye, and Arm—who search for them.

RECOMMENDATION: This book strains the boundaries of the science fiction genre into which it is placed, but as the past, present, and future Zimbabwe weave together, you can ask—with Tendai—many questions about cultures (Are they "whole cloth" or can we pick and chose among them what we'd like? Are they redeemable?) and about personal virtues and vices (Why, for example, does She Elephant act as she does? How are courage and truth related?). Thirteen-year-old Tendai is the most fully realized character, but all are genuine and intriguing in their complexity. **ET, MT**

AUTHOR: **Frank Herbert**

TITLE: *Dune* (1965)

DESCRIPTION: First of a six-volume series. Frank Herbert was one of the first of the great modern science-fiction writers to create an alien world that captured the imagination of millions of readers. *Dune* is about the forbidding desert planet, Arrakis, where the mind-altering and life-lengthening spice needed by the rest of the universe is harvested. The House of Atreides is headed by Duke Leto, with his fifteen-year-old son, Paul, and his concubine, Lady Jessica. She is trained in the sisterhood, Bene Gesserit, to total mental and physical mastery not only of her own life but of the whole human race's through genetic breeding. They must not only work out their own precarious destiny but also prevent the evil House of Harkonnen from totally exploiting the planet. After the Duke's death and their escape into the harsh, waterless communities of the Freemen in the interior, it is Paul and his mother who fulfill—or is it manipulate?—the prophesies of a Messiah rescuer.

RECOMMENDATION: If you're intrigued by questions of power and purpose, knowledge and destiny, you'll be glad to explore them with Herbert. And you may find it ironic that in a person-created world of great complexity, where his characters' every gesture can "move a gigantic lever across the known universe," Herbert has one of his most appealing characters realize just before his death that, "his father and all the other scientists were wrong ... the most persistent principles of the universe were accident and error." **LT**

AUTHOR: **Stephen Lawhead**

TITLE: *Empyrion* (1985)

DESCRIPTION: Winner of a Campus Life fiction award. Orion Treet, a journalist down on his luck, is kidnapped and then offered a huge sum of money to record what he can discover on Empyrion, a planet secretly colonized by a multinational corporation. Colonists had been sent several years before but have never communicated with home base. To get there with any speed, he must travel through a wormhole. Get there he does, but millennia in the future, and what he discovers is two civilizations so different from each other that it is hard to believe they came from the same stock.

RECOMMENDATION: There is adventure aplenty for all in this book. There are questions to ask as well, and the one that presses the most for answers is why the two groups have evolved so differently. Orion continues his adventures in *The Siege of Dome* in which he must prevent the two civilizations from going to war. **MT, LT**

AUTHOR: **Ursula LeGuin**

TITLE: ***The Left Hand of Darkness*** (1969)

DESCRIPTION: You may not know that Ursula LeGuin, who is famous for her children's fantasy series, is also an author of adult science fiction. In this award-winning book, she wonders, *What if . . . ?* What if men and women were androgynous (both male and female) so that sexuality did not determine our cultural patterns (women having babies, for example, and being primary care-givers), a very "hot" question today indeed! She sets her androgynous society on an ice-age planet on the edge of the galaxy in the Ekumenical Year, 1490. Genly Ai is the lone Envoy from the confederation of civilized planets with the job of persuading the Karhides to join them. The only person who seems to trust him is the Prime Minister, Estraven. Or does he? Therein lies the story. Perhaps more than anything else, it is about the possibility of friendship between different peoples.

RECOMMENDATION: LeGuin defines science fiction as a thought experiment ("What if . . . ?") that does not predict the future but describes the present. It is a metaphor, she says in her introduction to *The Left Hand of Darkness*, based on the contemporary realities of science, technology, and a mindset that says there is no absolute truth. Read the introduction, as interesting as the story itself, if you'd like to explore how novelists are lying to tell the truth. **LT**

AUTHOR: **Sonia Levitin**

TITLE: ***The Cure*** (1999)

DESCRIPTION: Gemm 16844 believes that "conformity begets harmony" that ultimately leads to universal good. This is the mantra of his utopian society. Even so he finds the forbidden music irresistible, to the horror of his twin, Gemma 16844. Instead of being recycled for his deviance, Gemm is offered the Cure, which sends him back into the life of Johannes, a Jewish boy in Strasbourg, Germany in 1348. Johannes's love of music brings him both supreme pleasure and dreadful pain.

RECOMMENDATION: This fine book works on so many levels. As science fiction, it explores the same question that Lois Lowry's *The Giver* does about the inherent defects in too-perfect conformist utopias (compare also to the less satisfying adult fantasy *A Villain by Necessity*, by Eve Forward). As historical fiction, it is the best of the many medieval-based reality novels or fantasies in its recreation of the whole of medieval life, belief and unbelief, good and evil, beauty and terror. (If you are interested in Jewish life in the Middle Ages, try *The Cross by Day, The Mezuzzah by Night* by Deborah Spector Spiegel.) The characters in *The Cure* are fully realized and well rounded. It raises many questions worth discussing about conformity and freedom, even the freedom to choose to do evil; about the role of art in fostering or hindering individuality, diversity, and tolerance; and about the feasibility of people being able to change and to love everyone. **MT, AA***

AUTHOR:  **C. S. Lewis**

TITLE:  *Out of the Silent Planet* (1938)

DESCRIPTION:  Series continues with *Perelandra* and *That Hideous Strength*. Out on a walking tour, a professor, Ransom, is kidnapped by two evolutionary scientists, who take him to Malacandra as an offering to a strange species, the sorns. If they are successful, they can continue their plans to take the gold and prepare to defy death by planting a civilized colony there. Ransom escapes only to fall in with some hrossa who are astonished that he is from the silent planet that has been abandoned by their ruler, Malaldil. For his part, he is astonished to find that the hrossa's instincts "so closely resembled the unattained ideals" of man. The struggle between Ransom and Weston continues in the subsequent volumes.

RECOMMENDATION:  Like most science fiction writers, C. S. Lewis (of Narnia fame) is holding up a mirror on contemporary society as much as he is projecting a possible future. You will recognize echoes of a theistic worldview as well as barbed satire of a science that tries to be independent of God. **MT, LT***

AUTHOR:  **C. S. Lewis**

TITLE:  *Perelandra* (1943)

DESCRIPTION:  In the second of the Lewis's Space Trilogy, Ransom does not travel back to Malacandra, which is an ancient planet that has withstood temptation; instead, he is sent by Oyaran to Perelandra (Venus), which is about to face temptation. There he must help the Green Lady combat powers and principalities to preserve the purity of her planet. His old enemy, Weston, shows up to engage the battle for the Bent One.

RECOMMENDATION: Many critics consider this the best of the Space Trilogy. As you discover parallels to the Genesis story, be sure to compare notes with your family. Just enjoy the lush descriptions of an unfamiliar world as well. **LT***

AUTHOR: **C. S. Lewis**

TITLE: *That Hideous Strength* (1945)

DESCRIPTION: The location of Lewis's third science fiction novel shifts from far-away, fantastical planets to the very earthy world of England where all the truths that Ransom learned on his journeys must be put to the test of day-to-day living. Make no mistake, however! The battle between good and evil is just as fierce. Here, the playing field is petty politics and scientific and social engineering by N.I.C.E. (The National Institute for Coordinated Experiments). Ransom calls on Merlin for the decisive help he needs for victory.

RECOMMENDATION: As the setting changes, so does C. S. Lewis's tone. He uses sharp satire, which feels far removed from myth and romance that suffuse the previous volumes. However, his tone allows us as readers to gain a critical eye on our own fallen society. How does Merlin, then, fit into this drab, everyday picture? How do Mark and Jane Studdock make the choices they do? In the more than fifty years since the trilogy was published, it has not lost is relevance. One critic says that Lewis "is one of those rare writers who leaves us different from what we were before we read him" because he "gives us words and phrases by which we grasp vital ideas. . . ." Do you agree? **LT***

AUTHOR: **Lois Lowry**

TITLE: *The Giver* (1993)

DESCRIPTION: Newbery Medal, 1994. In Jonas's perfect society where there is no reason for anyone to have negative emotions—or negative any-thing—twelve-year-olds receive their life assignments in a yearly cere-mony. Jonas is chosen to become the next Giver, a rare honor. During his training from the old man, Jonas receives the society's memories—of color, of historical experiences, of a range of emotions, causing him to question everything on which he has based his life.

RECOMMENDATION: In this splendidly written story, Lowry allows us to test our assumptions about what a good life and good society are. Are com-fort and safety and congeniality the highest goods? Or are choices, feel-ings, and love with its risk of hatred? What is the "meaning of everything" that the Giver and Jonas debate while they make their fate-ful choice? Many teachers use this book for fruitful classroom discussion. It would create rich family discussion as well. Another dystopian novel that tenderly examines individual freedom versus collective needs as well as the important way memory links the past and the present is Lowry's *Gathering Blue* (2000). Who would we be if we did not know our past? Who is God (god) in each of these books? **ET, MT***

ET—Early Teens
MT—Mid Teens
LT—Late Teens
AA—All Ages

AUTHOR: **Daniel Quinn**
TITLE: *Ishmael* (1992)

DESCRIPTION: A sour, disillusioned man surprises himself by answering a newspaper ad placed by a teacher seeking a pupil who wants to save the world. He is even more surprised to discover that the teacher is a gorilla, Ishmael, who communicates by way of mental telepathy. They begin a dialogue about how the world has gotten into its terrible condition and how this state of affairs might be changed.

RECOMMENDATION: This book beat out thousands of competitors for the $500,000 Turner Tomorrow Fellowship prize. That Ted Turner was so enchanted by the book gives you a clue as to its worldview. It is not a book for everyone. There is essentially no action. All the forward movement of the book is by way of Socratic questions and answers. But if you are interested in taking apart ideas and evaluating them, you may find fascinating Quinn/Ishmael's assertions about the differences between two possible forms of cultural evolution, one which will lead to a dead end and the other still open to the future. He calls these the Takers and the Givers. All of the worldview questions appear here. Who is man? What is our place in nature, in history, and in eternity? How did we get to be as we are? Can we be saved? Sometimes man and gorilla compare their answers directly to the biblical "myth." Ishmael's answers cannot be neatly categorized, and you will want to compare your analysis of them with others in your family. Do you think that, roughly, he is a New-Age pantheist? Or would you call him a garden variety naturalist? As might be expected of a sour, disillusioned man, the pupil swears from time to time. **LT**

AUTHOR: **Nevil Shute**
TITLE: *On the Beach* (1957)

DESCRIPTION: After the Third World War, an Australian naval officer and his wife and baby, an American submarine officer, and a young Australian woman must make their lives count for something, knowing that the radiation sickness is slowly creeping to their remote corner of the world. Shute quotes from a famous T. S. Eliot poem, "This is the way the world ends / Not with a bang but a whimper" as he explores just how that momentous event might be for rather ordinary people.

RECOMMENDATION: Some critics feel that the characters are so ordinary that they are flat, making it difficult to identify with or learn anything from them. What do you think? Perhaps a bang would be better than a whimper? **LT**

AUTHOR: **Kathy Tyers**

TITLE: *Firebird* (1998)

DESCRIPTION: This science fiction is premised on a "what if" of another universe, another rebel civilization, and another remnant faithful to their Creator's promise of redemption. Lady Firebird Angelo is a Netaian wastling, doomed to die after her oldest sister has two children. A fighter pilot, she chooses to die gloriously in an invasion of another star system. Captured and interrogated by Brennen Caldwell, who reads her very deepest thoughts by telepathy, Firebird must choose her political and religious allegiances. Brennen will not force them on her though he has the power to do so.

RECOMMENDATION: Taughtly and compellingly written, this first volume of the Firebird Series explores the existence and character of God from the viewpoints of a stoic pagan and a committed believer, both wondering about their roles and destinies in the Federacy. Other titles in the triology are *Fusion Fire* and *Crown of Fire*. **LT***

AUTHOR: **Jules Verne**

TITLE: *Twenty Thousand Leagues Under the Sea* (1870)

DESCRIPTION: Early in the twentieth century someone commented that "the advance of the peoples is merely living the novels of Jules Verne." So it would seem with his imaginative projection of submarine life and warfare. The mysterious Captain Nemo, who has some sort of grudge against society, commands the submarine *Nautilus* on which Pierre Aronnax, professor from the Museum of Paris, and Ned Land, expert harpoonist, find themselves captive.

RECOMMENDATION: Besides predicting scientific advances, Verne began a new kind of writing. He is considered by many to be the father of science fiction. **ET***

AUTHOR: **H. G. Wells**

TITLE: *The Island of Doctor Moreau* (1896)

DESCRIPTION: H. G. Wells, along with Jules Verne, is the second contender for the title: father of science fiction. His *Island of Doctor Moreau* is one of his most intriguing plots, especially in this day of genetic engineering. When Wells wrote about the experiments that the self-styled "god," Doctor Moreau, performed on his remote island to create man-like creatures from the beasts, he was exploring the dark side of the evolutionary theory he otherwise welcomed, because it seemed to free man from God. The question for him became "Can man create any better than God did?"

RECOMMENDATION:  You may be interested in comparing *Island* to Daniel Defoe's *Robinson Crusoe*, where a man is also isolated on a remote island but responds to his circumstances, particularly concerning his faith, quite differently. **LT**

AUTHOR:  **H. G. Wells**
TITLE:     ***The War of the Worlds*** (1898)

DESCRIPTION:  *The War of the Worlds* is not reread today so much for its literary value but for its historical value. Not only did it do much to form our popular conceptions of Martians, but when it was read aloud on the radio early in the 1900s, listeners panicked, thinking that Martians had really landed. **MT**

# Chapter 19

# Sports

AUTHOR: **Dave Dravecky with Tim Stafford**
TITLE: ***Comeback*** (1990)

DESCRIPTION: If baseball is a metaphor for the American dream, as Tim Stafford claims, then Dave Dravecky is the ultimate dreamer. His is the story of making it to the top as a major league pitcher against the odds, then being forced to quit because of a cancerous tumor in his pitching arm, and then—against all odds again—returning to pitch in a pennant-race game, only to break his arm yet again while pitching five days later. It will encourage you, or anyone, to come back against whatever odds are facing you. Dravecky's faith in God is the key to both his determination and his joy. **MT, LT***

AUTHOR: **Frank Deford**
TITLE: ***The Best of Frank Deford: I'm Just Getting Started*** (2000)

DESCRIPTION: Frank Deford's acerbic wit and penetrating intelligence have kept millions glued to their radios for his Wednesday morning sports commentaries on NPR and turning to his columns in *Sports Illustrated*. This collection contains many of those pieces. From sports fashion to pre-game shows to coaching styles, whatever the topic, you'll find yourselves chuckling (and reading aloud to someone across the room), and nodding your head (mostly) in agreement. Try acting out his hilarious "The Bard Goes to the Super Bowl" together next January to make a family memory that will last forever.

ECOMMENDATION: Deford is known as "the world's greatest sports writer." He is witty and urbane and doesn't worship sports. You won't necessarily always agree with him (for example, on legalizing betting for college sports, perhaps) but you will have plenty to discuss about the way sports represents its larger culture. **LT**

**ET**—Early Teens
**MT**—Mid Teens
**LT**—Late Teens
**AA**—All Ages

ᴜTHOR: **John Feinstein**

ᴛITLE: ***A Good Walk Spoiled: Days and Nights on the PGA Tour* (1995)**

ᴅESCRIPTION: John Feinstein joins the golfing circuit in order to give an insider's view on the most individual and most frustrating of sports. He follows people whose names you know as well as ones just trying to break into the pros, trying to convey what makes golfers tick.

ECOMMENDATION: Feinstein is a fine writer with many books to his credit. Perhaps you have seen him on TV sports talk shows or heard his weekly commentaries on NPR. He makes sports accessible to everyone. Try also his *The Last Amateurs* about college basketball. **LT**

ᴜTHOR: **Zane Grey**

ᴛITLE: ***Tales of Tahitian Waters* (1928, 1998)**

ᴅESCRIPTION: Although he is best know as a writer of westerns, Zane Grey was also an avid fisherman and traveled to far places in the world in search of the biggest and most exciting catch. This is a hair-raising tale of fishing in the shark-infested Pacific waters for marlin and wahoo, written in his traditional storytelling style.

ECOMMENDATION: With wit and wisdom, Grey pens these compelling and appealing stories, as winsome for today's readers as when they were first written in the early 1900s. See also *The Best Zane Grey Outdoorsman: Hunting, Fishing Tales* (Classics of American Sports Stories) which is a compilation of Grey's best works on hunting, fishing, and camping. **MT**, **LT**

ᴜTHOR: **G. Bruce Knecht**

ᴛITLE: ***The Proving Ground* (2001)**

ᴅESCRIPTION: The 1998 Sydney Hobart Races, the most demanding sailing races in the world, became the proving ground for sportsmen enduring unbelievable stress in eight-foot waves. One hundred fifteen boats started; forty-three finished the race. Six sailors lost their lives and fifty-five had to be rescued.

ECOMMENDATION: This riveting book, along with *Fatal Storm* by Rob Mundle, lets you feel the terrors and exhilaration of racing sailboats. If you like sea stories, you may also want to read *The Perfect Storm: A True Story of Men Against the Sea* by Sebastian Junger. **LT**

AUTHOR: **Jon Krakauer**

TITLE: *Into Thin Air: A Personal Account of the Mt. Everest Disaster* (1997)

DESCRIPTION: Krakauer, a mountaineering journalist writing an article about the commercialization of Mt. Everest, was a member of one of several teams attempting to reach the summit of the highest mountain in the world on May 10, 1996. Before the day was over, eleven had died. He explores the personalities and motivations of the people, both Westerners and Nepalese sherpas, who cross over the line from being driven to achieve a difficult goal to acting in a foolhardy way. (Where would you draw this line?) Another line that was crossed that fateful day was between the good and evil residing in all human hearts.

RECOMMENDATION: Be advised that adult language sprinkles this book. If this book intrigues you, check out one from a different perspective and for a younger audience, *The Ultimate High: My Everest Odyssey* by Goran Kropp. Krakauer has also written *Into the Wild* (1996) about a young man who tests his skills against the Alaskan Wilderness, exploring some of the same issues, set against complicated family dynamics, with disastrous results. **LT**

AUTHOR: **Ring Lardner**

TITLE: *The Annotated Baseball Stories of Ring Lardner: 1914–1919* (1997)

DESCRIPTION: Ring Lardner, a topnotch sports reporter later turned fiction writer, combines the best of both worlds in these stories published in the early 1900s. His reputation still commands respect and reading today as this collection edited by George Hilton attests. Twelve of these stories are about legendary Jack Keefe, a semiliterate, self-absorbed White Sox pitcher.

RECOMMENDATION: Lardner's vivid depiction of the game mixes fictional characters with well-known, real-life players. His style and his sense of humor make delightful reading for baseball fans. One avid sports reader commented, "I could read this book a hundred times and never tire of it." **LT**

AUTHOR: **David McCasland**

TITLE: *Eric Liddell: Pure Gold* (2001)

DESCRIPTION: If you have seen *Chariots of Fire*, then you know Eric Liddell as the Flying Scotsman who won the 1924 Olympic gold medal for the 400-meter race and as the Christian who refused to run his best event, the 100 meters, because he would have had to break the Sabbath to do so. Eric ran the distance, however, for two decades afterwards in China as a missionary with the London Missionary Society.

RECOMMENDATION: As this wonderful biography of him reveals, he won his crown of pure gold by his service in China and by his death while an internee in a Japanese prisoner of war camp during World War II. A must read aloud for any family with teens. **MT**, **LT**, **AA***

AUTHOR: **Bob Muzikowski and Gregg Lewis**

TITLE: ***Safe at Home: The True and Inspiring Story of Chicago's Field of Dreams*** (2001)

DESCRIPTION: Bob Muzikowski grew up in a hard urban environment himself and knows from experience the allure of drink and drugs. After he became a Christian, he began to form Little League teams in the most unlikely of places—the toughest big city housing projects. This book tells about the ones at Cabrini Green in Chicago.

RECOMMENDATION: Sports has always had a special ability to bring people together and to change lives for the better. You'll cheer these boys on when they win on and off the field; you'll cry when the forces of evil in the city overwhelm them. Most of all, you'll be encouraged to know that God can use anyone to bring light into dark places. **MT**, **LT**

AUTHOR: **Mike Plant and Scott Tinley**

TITLE: ***Iron Will: The Triathlete's Ultimate Challenge*** (1999)

DESCRIPTION: The Hawaiian Iron Man Triathlon consists of a 2.4-mile swim, a 112-mile bike race, and a full marathon 26.2-mile run—all done in one day. To read this book is to feel the emotions, pain, and triumph of the athlete.

RECOMMENDATION: Why would anyone put himself through this? Discover the answer to this question as well as the history of how triathlon went from a death-defying challenge to a full-fledged professional championship. The race between Scott Tinley and Dave Scott is the focus of much of the book, along with the endurance philosophy and lure of the sport. **LT**

AUTHOR: **Alfred Slote**

TITLE: ***Hang Tough, Paul Mather*** (1993)

DESCRIPTION: There isn't any kind of ball that Paul Mather can't throw. He lives, eats, and breathes baseball. He is good. Then he finds himself not feeling well and discovers that he has leukemia, which puts him in and out of the hospital. When the game of the year comes up, Paul is determined to pitch and win the game for his team.

RECOMMENDATION: This is a good book to share with ill children because there is a lot of grace and helpful emotion in the story. Paul's example of courage, character, and dignity make for good discussion. **ET**

AUTHOR: **Gary Soto**
TITLE:    ***Baseball in April*** (1990)

DESCRIPTION: This collection of short stories is about working class Latino kids who live in Fresno, California.

RECOMMENDATION: Many of Soto's books for older teens (such as *Burned Onions*) are grittily realistic, but this one introduces you to some kids with ordinary concerns whom young teens would probably be glad to call their friends. **ET**

AUTHOR: **Paul D. Staudohar, compiler**
TITLE:    ***Football's Best Short Stories*** (1997)

DESCRIPTION: This is a superb collection of classic and contemporary football fiction by respected authors. "The Trojan Horse" by Ellery Queen, "Sooper, Dooper" by Frank Deford, "Hold 'em Yale" by Damon Runyon, and "The Eighty-Yard Run" by Irwin Shaw give a taste of the good reading here. Other stories by John Updike, Grantland Rice, and many others will delight football fans. Some of the stories give glimpses into the physical toll of this game as well as the personalities of successful coaches.

RECOMMENDATION: These books are for teens to share with their fathers or uncles. Be prepared for every writer to have a different tone, just as in any short story collection. **LT**

AUTHOR: **Seth Swirsky**
TITLE:    ***Baseball Letters: A Fan's Correspondence with His Heroes*** (2000)

DESCRIPTION: There was no baseball to follow during the 1994 strike, so Seth Swirsky decided to write to some of his favorite players, whether they were stars or not. To his surprise, many, such as Cal Ripkin, Ted Williams, and Enos Slaughter, wrote back, sharing touching personal stories or game tips or insights into controversial moments on the field.

RECOMMENDATION: The ninety-seven letters in this book proved so interesting to readers that Swirsky followed with *Every Pitcher Tells a Story: Gathered by a Devoted Baseball Fan*, which includes letters from Roger Clemens, Dave Cone, Tom Glavins, Steve Carlton, and others. **LT**

# Chapter 20

# Tried and True

AUTHOR: **Chinua Achebe**

TITLE: ***Things Fall Apart*** (1959)

DESCRIPTION: Okonkwo, though he is the son of a weak man, has carved out a leadership role for himself in his tribe through hard work and determination. However, "things fall apart" for him—and, indeed, for all of precolonial West Africa—with the arrival of the white missionaries. Or did they fall apart for this proud man because his pride and fear of weakness led him to violate some of the tribe's most sacred traditions? The Nigerian Achebe takes you to the heart of another culture in this sympathetic yet unflinching examination of Okonkwo's village life. **LT**

AUTHOR: **Jane Austen**

TITLE: ***Pride and Prejudice*** (1813)

DESCRIPTION: "It is a truth universally acknowledged that a single man in possession of a good fortune must be in want of a wife." So opens Austen's most famous novel. But, of course, it is the single women (and their mothers) who need husbands. Whether Elizabeth Bennet and Fitzwilliam Darcy can overcome their individual pride and their social prejudices to become husband and wife is the crux of this ever-contemporary look at social hypocrisies. Much loved by generations of readers. The PBS Masterpiece Theater production is quite faithful to the text. **LT**

AUTHOR: **James Baldwin**

TITLE: ***Go Tell It on the Mountain*** (1953)

DESCRIPTION: *Go Tell It on the Mountain*, without wincing at all from the raw realities of Harlem life, tells the story of the salvation experience of a young, illegitimate black boy. John hates his hypocritical stepfather, the preacher Gabriel, who really only loves his "true" sons, the dead Royal, son of his mistress, and the weak Roy, son of John's mother. In all the vivid language and ceremony of the black church, you experience John's transformation by God's love on the mountain top, just as you experience the bondage (often explicitly sexual) that had held John as it held Gabriel, and the women in his life. For the most mature reader. **LT**

AUTHOR: **Ray Bradbury**

TITLE: ***Fahrenheit 451*** (1950)

DESCRIPTION: This classic explores what a society might be like that sends firemen, not to put fires out, but to burn books, those dangerous containers of dangerous ideas. Fireman Guy Montag is one such fireman until he meets Clarisse, who has such an unusual view of books. The title comes from the temperature at which paper burns. Bradbury himself says that the novel is about what happens when "a book-burner . . . suddenly discovers that books are flesh-and-blood ideas and cry out, silently, when put to the torch." Bradbury has written many other fine short stories and novels. **MT, LT**

AUTHOR: **Charlotte Brontë**

TITLE: ***Jane Eyre*** (1847)

DESCRIPTION: Long a favorite of many teenagers, *Jane Eyre* has the ingredients of a thrilling romance: a high-spirited orphan heroine determined to make her own way by training to be a governess; a wealthy, aloof master of an English country estate; mysteriously set fires, seances, and strange appearances by a madwoman; and a happily-ever-after resolution to the plot. **MT, LT***

AUTHOR: **Emily Brontë**

TITLE: ***Wuthering Heights*** (1847)

DESCRIPTION: *Wuthering Heights* is well named, for it definitely rises to stormy heights (wuthering means "stormy"). The cold sweep of the northern moors is an apt setting for the stormy intertwining of the Earnshaws and the Lintons and the brooding stranger, Heathcliffe, taken in by Mr. Earnshaw when Heathcliffe was only fourteen. Earnshaw's favoritism to the boy over his own two children, Hindley and Catherine, sets the stage for the jealousies that blow up into mismatched romances and revenge. These work themselves out into three generations who live at Wuthering Heights. All the passions of Emily Brontë's book run deeper and more violently than in her sister's *Jane Eyre.* **MT, LT**\*

AUTHOR: **Pearl Buck**

TITLE: ***The Good Earth* (1931)**

DESCRIPTION: Chinese peasants are tied to the natural cycle of the earth, which supplies their every need. So it is with Wang Lung, an ambitious peasant, who works hard and shrewdly takes advantage of the misfortune that natural disasters bring to others. He survives them but pays the price of living too far above the land as he attains wealth. His wife, O-lan, his children—the favored sons, the despised feeble-minded daughter—and the concubine of his wealthy days are all sympathetically drawn so that you can walk in the shoes of people who live a very alien way of life and thought from your own. **LT**

AUTHOR: **John Bunyan**

TITLE: ***Pilgrim's Progress* (1676)**

DESCRIPTION: While unjustly imprisoned in a British jail, Bunyan wrote this allegory of a pilgrim named Christian who is on a journey from this world to the next. Seeking the Celestial City from his home in the City of Destruction, Christian faces the Slough of Despond, receives bad advice, loses his burden in the House of the Interpreter, climbs the Hill of Difficulty, fights with the monster Apollyon, passes through the Valley of the Shadow of Death, is tempted in Vanity Fair, is troubled in Doubting Castle, and must cross the Dark River before he can reach his destination. There are many editions available, but one your whole family might especially enjoy is the 1985 Eerdman's edition, called *Dangerous Journey,* illustrated by Alan Parry, who animated the story for British television. **AA**\*

AUTHOR: **Albert Camus**

TITLE: ***The Plague* (1947)**

DESCRIPTION: *The Plague* is one of Camus's more readily understandable books. If you are willing to put in the effort to think deeply, Camus will take you on a rewarding journey exploring the existentialists' dilemma, in his own words, "Can one be a saint without God?" When the bubonic plague hits the North African port city of Oran, all the residents quarantined there are forced to react to the disaster according to their own principles. The book focuses on what meaning those who seek to help their fellow sufferers can wrestle out of life. Camus has won the Nobel prize for literature. **LT**

AUTHOR: **Willa Cather**

TITLE: ***Death Comes for the Archbishop*** (1926)

DESCRIPTION: Jean Marie Latour, French missionary to the Ohio regions i:
the 1840s, is made Vicar Apostolic of New Mexico. With Father Josepl
Vaillant, his boyhood friend, he makes his way across the vast continen
to the newly annexed region where lax Mexican priests and supersti

tious Navaho are not happy to see hin:
Nevertheless, they persist and over th
years build up a diocese to the poin:
where it could even support its ow:
cathedral. Not a fast-paced book but a:
calm and determined as the soul c
Latour, it unfolds the rewarding story c
the lives and devotions of these tw
priests as well as the land and peopl:
that so captivated them until deatl
comes for the Archbishop—Latou:
himself—many years later. **LT***

Illustration by W. T. Benda for Willa Cather's *My Antonia*,
reprinted by permission of Houghton Mifflin Company.

AUTHOR: **Willa Cather**

TITLE: ***My Antonia*** (1918)

DESCRIPTION: Jim Burden, an easter:
orphan who grew up on the vas:
prairies of Nebraska at his grandparent:
farm but who left to study at Harvarc
tells the story of an immigrant girl
Antonia Shimerda. Antonia helps he:
beloved father carve out a living from the prairie, learns English fror
Jim, joins the hired girls in the town of Black Hawk in their daytim
work and evening fun, decides what moral values she will live by, an
eventually returns (unlike Jim) to the soil that has nurtured he:
Typically American, Antonia's story is both lyrical and deceptively sim
ple and has been enjoyed for generations. **LT**

AUTHOR: **Joseph Conrad**

TITLE: ***Lord Jim*** (1900)

DESCRIPTION: Jim, a wanderer and an outcast, works various seaport job
until he finally arrives on the East Indian Ocean island of Patustan. Wha
he is running from is his self-hatred for abandoning a sinking ship fu:
of Muslim pilgrims after the captain and mates, drunkenly and cow
ardly, left him in charge. He had thus betrayed his own deepest moral

ity and could never escape a haunting sense of failure. On Patustan, however, he is trusted by the natives and finally earns an opportunity to redeem himself. **LT**

AUTHOR: **James Fenimore Cooper**

TITLE: ***The Last of the Mohicans*** (1826)

DESCRIPTION: The exciting plot of this tale of pursuit and captivity and rescue and siege during the French and Indian Wars has kept readers on the edges of their seats for over 175 years. Two British sisters are being escorted to the fort where their father is commander, when they are intercepted by some Indians aiding the French. Besides its vivid actions, *The Last of the Mohicans* is rich in description of Indian lore. **MT, LT\***

AUTHOR: **Stephen Crane**

TITLE: ***The Red Badge of Courage*** (1894)

DESCRIPTION: Some consider *The Red Badge of Courage* America's greatest Civil War novel. It certainly changed the way Americans wrote about war as it "ript away the gilt and glitter that had so long curtained [its] horror, and with a stern realism pictured for us the bloody grime of it all." The nameless youth of the brief story, however, emerges as a common man's hero who survives the blood of battle, not reduced to an animal but having grown to be a man who understands and loves his world. **LT**

AUTHOR: **Charles Dickens**

TITLE: ***Great Expectations*** (1860)

DESCRIPTION: Though *Great Expectations* does not have the comic relief of the typical Dickens character sketches, it has an absorbing enough plot to overcome its rather gloomy feeling. Pip is an orphan whose great expectations for life are intertwined with those of a vindictive, jilted old maid, Miss Havisham, and a mysterious, grateful, escaped prisoner, Abel Magwitch. Discovering the identity of the benefactor who enables him to gain a London education, his life's love, and the proper attitude with which to live satisfactorily—these make up Pip's story. **MT, LT**

AUTHOR: **Charles Dickens**

TITLE: ***A Tale of Two Cities*** (1859)

DESCRIPTION: Many teens who first read Dickens when *A Tale of Two Cities* is assigned in school should find it a satisfying story. It is full of true-to-life yet larger-than-life characters who act out their heroism and their deceit, their private sorrows and public political passions, against the

"Pip Leaves the Village"—illustration by F. W. Pailthorpe for Charles Dickens' *Great Expectations.*

huge panorama of the French Revolution of the late eighteenth century. The true love between Lucie Manette and the fine French aristocrat, Charles Darnay, who is made to pay for the crimes his family has committed against the common French people, and the sacrifice that the weak, alcoholic Sydney Carton has opportunity to make, join to form the structure of the book. If you only read one book by Dickens in your lifetime, perhaps this should be the one. **MT, LT***

AUTHOR: **Lloyd C. Douglas**
TITLE: ***Magnificent Obsession (1929)***

DESCRIPTION: Why is it that evil is so much more attractive than good in books? Many people believe it is almost impossible for authors to make good attractive. However, Douglas's *Magnificent Obsession* is an exception to that "rule": It is the chronicle of playboy Robert Merrick, whose life is saved at the expense of an eminent brain surgeon, Dr. Wayne Hudson. Challenged to make his own life worthwhile by taking Dr. Hudson's place, including accepting Hudson's belief in the Higher Power, Merrick enters medical school and eventually perfects techniques that save the life of Hudson's attractive young widow. **LT**

AUTHOR: **Daphne Du Maurier**
TITLE: ***Rebecca* (1938)**

DESCRIPTION: A dead woman, Rebecca, dominates the action and the thoughts of the characters of Daphne Du Maurier's classic romantic suspense novel. The narrator is the insecure and timid second wife of Maxim de Winter, owner of the magnificent Manderley estate. Rebecca was his adored first wife, or so it seems to the narrator as she feels the full force of the staff's resentment. Slowly the truth about Rebecca's character and death come to light and with them come both tragedy for the estate and resolution for the newly married couple. *Rebecca* is considered the supreme example of this favorite genre. **MT, LT**

AUTHOR: **Shusaku Endo**

TITLE: *The Samurai* (1980)

DESCRIPTION: In 1613 Hasekura, a lowly samurai from a desolate corner of Japan in the service of a powerful feudal lord, accompanies Velasco, an ambitious Franciscan priest who longs to be named Bishop of Japan, on a treacherous sea voyage to Mexico. From there they go to Europe, seeking to guarantee trading privileges in return for more missionaries—Franciscans, not the rival Jesuits. Hasekura is persuaded that he must outwardly embrace the emaciated Lord on the crucifix who so offends his sensibilities in order for the mission to succeed. But when he returns to Japan four years later, he discovers that Japan no longer wants corrupting outside influences, economic, political, or religious, and that Christians are being martyred. Hasekura was a real samurai who really made this journey, but Endo, considered one of Japan's finest novelists, has documented far more than a physical journey in this remarkable historical novel. Hasekura's spiritual journey to faith is portrayed with both its terrible costs and its high rewards. Joining Velasco's and Hasekura's journeys will surely enrich your own. For the reader ready to venture into new territory. If you found this Endo title compelling, try his more famous (but more difficult) *Silence*. **LT**

AUTHOR: **Edna Ferber**

TITLE: *Giant* (1952)

DESCRIPTION: In Texas, where everything is giant-sized—ranches, wealth, social and political hobnobbing, the gap between the haves and the have-nots—Leslie Benedict, her rancher husband, Bick, and two independent-minded children, Jordan and Luz, make the appropriate gestures to size. But is their lifestyle the very cause of everything that is coming home to haunt them? **LT**

AUTHOR: **Edna Ferber**

TITLE: *So Big* (1924)

DESCRIPTION: Pulitzer prize, 1925. Selina lives a hand-to-mouth but nevertheless whimsical life with her gambler father who has conveyed to her a sense of the joy in experiencing life. It is this intense sense that life is magic that Selina attempts to retain after she educates herself and finds a job—teaching in a Dutch farming community in Illinois. More than that, she wants her son, Dirk, to inherit that same zest. To her disappointment, he compromises with the material, corporate-ladder-climbing world and must ultimately decide where his values lie and whether he will only be "so big." **LT**

AUTHOR: **C. S. Forester**

TITLE: ***The African Queen*** (1940)

DESCRIPTION: In 1914 the Germans commandeered everything on the German Central African mission station where Rose Sayer had lived for ten years under the thumb of her now-dying missionary brother. She escapes with the British cockney miner, Charlie Allnutt, who irregularly delivered their supplies. Determined to damage Germany by destroying its ship blocking the only British entrance into German territory, Rose, with the befuddled Allnutt in tow, makes for the lake in his well-stocked *African Queen*. Never mind that she has never managed anything before in her life, never mind that the Ulanger River had never been navigated, and never mind that events strange and sinful enough to shock any missionary's soul would face them. A wonderfully tender story, though its amorality may bother you. Rose is not, by anyone's standards, a typical missionary. **LT**

AUTHOR: **C. S. Forester**

TITLE: ***Captain Horatio Hornblower*** (1937)

DESCRIPTION: Exciting sea battles, both won and lost, make up most of Captain Horatio Hornblower's fascinating story, first as commander of a frigate giving secret British aid to a Spanish American dictator who wants to be free from Spain's rule, and then of a larger frigate now allied to Spain against France. Taken captive at the Battle of Gibraltar, a disguised Hornblower later escapes from the French, returning to England as a hero and to a reward for having remained faithful to his sickly wife. **LT**

AUTHOR: **Paul Gallico**

TITLE: ***The Snow Goose*** (1940)

DESCRIPTION: This is a moving short story about a deformed artist who lives alone in a bird sanctuary, a girl from the nearby village, and the injured Canadian snow goose who brings them together. Meant to be read aloud. **AA***

AUTHOR: **Rumer Godden**

TITLE: ***In This House of Brede*** (1969)

DESCRIPTION: Philipa Talbot is a successful career woman in her forties when she decides to enter the Benedictine monastery for nuns called Abbey of Brede. There she can practice the unceasing cycle of prayer, praise, and work "without sloth or haste." Her former boss, the Permanent Secretary for the British government, predicts she will last six months, but the story takes us through Philipa's first seventeen years, moving through crises of faith to a final sacrifice. Or is it fulfillment? The story is as much about the Benedictine Order as it is about Philipa. **LT**

AUTHOR: **Rumer Godden**

TITLE: *Kingfishers Catch Fire* (1953)

DESCRIPTION: Sophie Barrington Ward, a genteelly poor young widow—against the advice of everyone, British and Indian—decides to remain alone in the primitive region of Kashmir with only her two children. Despite her good intentions to make her way among the peasants there, the dire warnings seem to be coming true. Finally even her daughter, Teresa, is in grave danger. Does Sophie have a duty to those who injured Teresa? The whole village is involved in the repercussions of the beating, as you will be. And you too will have "richer eyes" for having seen the kingfishers of Kashmir as only Godden can bring them to life. **LT**

AUTHOR: **Rumer Godden**

TITLE: *The River* (1946)

DESCRIPTION: Harriet, the second of four children of a British manufacturing family living in India, experiences both a death and a birth, both guilt and love, during one winter. As a result, there are "cracks in [the] wholeness of her unconsciousness" where she is reaching to understand the meaning of the flow of life. You will most likely see your own tentative understanding of the enormity of life and your own small yet significant place in it through this beautifully written book. **MT**, **LT**

AUTHOR: **William Golding**

TITLE: *Lord of the Flies* (1954)

DESCRIPTION: Did you know that "lord of the flies" is the English equivalent of Beelzebub, or the devil? It seems particularly appropriate for a fable or parable about the modern condition of the human race. But Golding's devil is not an external force—very modern, very psychological, it resides in the deepest part of our hearts. Golding sets his story on a remote island where a group of British schoolboys have crash-landed. In this "paradise" they have the chance to create a civilization from scratch, but their venture becomes a struggle between order and reason (Ralph) and anarchy and wildness in human hearts (Jack). This exploration of what most Christians call total depravity seems heightened because children, in contrast to adults, are supposed to be "innocent." Do you see yourself and your classmates in the behavior of these boys? Does Golding present any way out of this brutal situation he has created? (This book is often assigned in school even before teens may feel ready to handle it.) **LT**

AUTHOR: **Elizabeth Goudge**

TITLE:    *The Dean's Watch* (1960)

DESCRIPTION: The old humble artisan-watch repairman, Isaac Peabody, chances to meet the ugly, formidable Dean of the city's cathedral, Adam Ayscough, who is childless and only tolerated by his beautiful but cold wife. The meeting brought them not only the pleasure of an unexpected friendship, but also for the Dean the affection of his parishioners, and for Isaac faith in the God he has always doubted. This is a touching and profoundly beautiful book with clock symbolism worked naturally throughout. Other books by Goudge include *The Child From the Sea, The Castle on the Hill,* and *The Heart of the Family.* **LT***

AUTHOR: **Graham Greene**

TITLE:    *The Power and the Glory* (1940)

DESCRIPTION: Set in the poverty-stricken villages of Mexico, *The Power and the Glory* is about the tensions between the revolutionary police lieutenant and the last priest in the district, whom he is hunting down. This "whiskey priest" has failed in so many ways—particularly his drunkenness, his fathering a child—but stubbornly persists in his duties despite the persecution. Although the novel is gripping by virtue of its suspenseful plot, it is also compelling in its psychological probe of the motives and actions of a sinful saint. It was the novel that gave modern master Graham Greene the most satisfaction to write as he explored a paradox: "the idealistic police officer who stifled life from the best possible motives, [and] the drunken priest who continues to pass life on." For the mature reader. **LT**

AUTHOR: **Ernest Hemingway**

TITLE:    *Farewell to Arms* (1929)

DESCRIPTION: *Farewell to Arms* is Hemingway's novel about the Italian front of World War I. Frederic Henry is an American ambulance driver for the Italian army who meets a British nurse, Catherine Barkley. They fall in love and, after he is wounded, she nurses him and they consider themselves married. Just after he learns that "Cat" is pregnant, Henry must go back to the front but gets caught in a disorderly, harried retreat. The book might just be like dozens of other war novels except for those few passages where Henry, who doesn't like to think, does so anyway, reflecting on the meaning of it all. What do you think of his idea that "if people bring so much courage to this world, the world has to kill them to break them, so of course it kills them"? **LT**

AUTHOR: **James Herriot**

TITLE: ***All Creatures Great and Small*** (1972)

DESCRIPTION: You'll be delighted to meet James Herriot, who in the 1930s was a young vet apprenticed to Siegfried Farnon, a bachelor Yorkshire vet extraordinaire with "ideas both brilliant and barmy," which "came in . . . a constant torrent." You'll meet the dour and hardworking farmers; rich eccentric landowners (Mrs. Pumphrey, who indulges her Tricky Woo, is the classic example); Siegfried's Casanova younger brother, Tristan; gentle Helen with whom James falls in love; and a wide assortment of animals whose personalities are as distinctive as those of their owners.

Herriot is a master storyteller whose tongue-in-cheek style is just right to tell these marvelous tales. You'll cheer to know there are four wonderfully long "All Creatures" volumes to laugh and cry over; the other three are *All Things Bright and Beautiful*, *All Things Wise and Wonderful*, and *The Lord God Made Them All*. The PBS series that recreated them is very faithful to the books, but nothing will substitute for the pleasure of reading them. **MT**, **LT**, **AA**\*

AUTHOR: **James Hilton**

TITLE: ***Lost Horizon*** (1933)

DESCRIPTION: If you have always thought of Shangri-la as a lush, peaceful Paradise Island, you will be surprised to learn that it is an imaginary lamasery in Tibet. Hugh Conway, a competent but undistinguished consul at a remote British outpost, is being evacuated after putting down an uprising in 1931, when the plane carrying him, another consul, an American embezzler, and a missionary woman is diverted and then crashes in a high Tibetan valley. As the pilot dies, he calls out the name "Shangri-la," and so the survivors set out for it. They eventually learn that it is a Buddhist monastery (lamasery) headed by a 250-year-old former Catholic priest who wants to create a community able to reintroduce civilization after the coming World War. No one has ever been allowed to leave—the promise of long life beckons them anyhow—but when a chance comes, should Conway take it? **LT**

AUTHOR: **William Hudson**

TITLE: ***Green Mansions*** (1904)

DESCRIPTION: An old man, Abel, tells the story of his youthful adventuring in the South American jungles, where he patiently coaxes friendship from a strange, birdlike girl, Rima, hiding away from the Indians. A legend says that she is the daughter of the spirit Didi, but Abel knows her

ET—Early Teens
MT—Mid Teens
LT—Late Teens
AA—All Ages

to be an intensely lonely girl who longs to communicate in the fluttering, birdlike language she had learned from her long-dead mother. They set out to find that mother, but disaster strikes them both. Is Hudson saying in this legend that has become a classic, that nature herself is like Rima, longing to tell us of herself but unable to do so completely? **LT**

AUTHOR: **Victor Hugo**

TITLE: *Les Miserables* (1862)

DESCRIPTION: Revived in a highly popular stage version, this book is a very long but enthralling picture of life in post-revolutionary France. Jean Valjean is imprisoned for nineteen years for stealing a loaf of bread to feed his starving sister. Afterward, befriended by a bishop who gives Valjean the recovered silver he has stolen, the ex-convict disguises himself as a priest and opens a factory. In his new role as benefactor, he must evade the ever-vigilant policeman, Javert, and also help the blackmailed beauty, Fantine, and her daughter, Cosette. Powerful not only in its depictions of the miserable social conditions of the Parisian slums, *Les Miserables* is also considered one of the best stories of all times. **LT***

AUTHOR: **Kathryn Hulme**

TITLE: *The Nun's Story* (1956)

DESCRIPTION: Unable to marry the man she loves, Gabrielle becomes a nun and discovers more of the world than she could ever have dreamed as she nurses in an insane asylum on a mission station in the Congo, where uprisings of the "natives" ever threaten, and in the Belgian underground during World War II. As Sister Luke she struggles to keep her vows of poverty, chastity, and obedience to God. **LT**

AUTHOR: **James Joyce**

TITLE: *Portrait of the Artist As a Young Man* (1916)

DESCRIPTION: If you've ever wondered about whether your particular place in the cosmos is significant to anyone, you may well be hooked by the beginning of James Joyce's *Portrait of the Artist*, an autobiography (disguised as a novel) of the schoolboy, Stephen Dedalus. In a series of five sections, each ending in an "Epiphany," or crisis experience of enlightenment, the book traces Stephen's growth toward manhood—and away from God. He experiences both conflict with his family and challenges to his political loyalty to Ireland. He experiences his first sexual encounter and resulting religious guilt, a loss of faith and friendship, and always a desire for the beauty of art that compels him above all else to find his identity outside all the social and personal forces that shape his world. For the mature reader. **LT**

AUTHOR: **Rudyard Kipling**

TITLE: *Kim* **(1901)**

DESCRIPTION: *Kim* is the story of a half-caste Indian-Irish orphan boy who grows up totally Indian in the back streets of Lahore. He attaches himself to a wandering holy man in search of the river that will wash away his sins and immediately becomes involved in the intrigue of the secret service and counter-intelligence. Kim has to submit to the Roman Catholic schooling his father insists on, but the focus of his curiosity and intelligence is on the life of a secret agent. His adventures have captivated readers for over a century. **LT**

AUTHOR: **Charles and Mary Lamb**

TITLE: *Tales from Shakespeare* **(1807)**

DESCRIPTION: The brother-and-sister team of Charles and Mary Lamb retold twenty of Shakespeare's plays as the exciting stories they are, hoping that young people would learn to love the most famous of all British authors. Across two centuries, countless people have met the master through these faithfully told tales. You may be glad to be numbered among them. Another excellent, more recent retelling of the Shakespeare plays is by Leon Garfield. There are two volumes simply called *Shakespeare Stories.* **AA**

AUTHOR: **Harper Lee**

TITLE: *To Kill a Mockingbird* **(1960)**

DESCRIPTION: Scout and Jem Finch are growing up in Alabama during the Depression, children of the local attorney, Atticus. All sorts of odd folk, genteel and not so genteel, make life fascinating for these intelligent, curious children. But things turn ugly when their father defends a black man, Tom Robinson, who is accused of assaulting a white woman. They learn to do what Atticus advises—stand in the shoes of someone else and walk around for a while. This is one story, turning a gentle but persistent light on the soul of America, the souls of all peoples, that you would be a lesser person for having missed. **MT, LT***

AUTHOR: **C. S. Lewis**

TITLE: *Till We Have Faces* **(1956)**

DESCRIPTION: In what is probably his least known fiction, C. S. Lewis of Narnia and science fiction fame retells the ancient but most compelling Cupid and Psyche myth from the perspective of Psyche's older, ugly, and adoring sister. Psyche is the youngest daughter of a weakening king, so beautiful and so good that the jealous priest of the local deity demands she be sacrificed to The Brute to appease the gods. If you read this story carefully, especially if you are familiar with mythology, you will be greatly rewarded, not only with a great story but with discovering parallels or reverberations of the Christian gospel. But even if these are not readily apparent, the story also exposes two ancient ways of life, Greek and pagan, and the universal human heart. **LT***

AUTHOR: **George MacDonald**
TITLE: ***The Fisherman's Lady, The Marquis' Secret* (1877, 1982)**

DESCRIPTION: George MacDonald, whose children's classics *The Light Princess* and *The Princess and Curdie* and others are worth re-reading as teens and adults, is also a prolific author of historical romances. He has influenced the British Inklings (C. S. Lewis and J. R. R. Tolkien's literary crowd) and the current crop of Christian historical romance writers. One of these, Michael Phillips, has updated many of MacDonald's books for Bethany House. One of the best is *The Marquis of Lossie*, published in two volumes as *The Fisherman's Lady* and *The Marquis' Secret*. Malcolm lives a quiet life as a fisherman although he learns that he really is the new Marquis. He continues his humble persona in order to keep a promise to his father, to preserve the family honor and to live out the principle that God works good from evil. Use MacDonald as a standard by which to evaluate the spate of Christian historical fiction that he helped inspire. **MT, LT**

AUTHOR: **George Orwell**
TITLE: ***Animal Farm* (1946)**

DESCRIPTION: This story has been called an allegory, a fable, and a parable, so don't be surprised to discover people-like qualities in the animals of *Animal Farm*. The pigs and other animals take over control of Manor Farm from its incompetent, drunken owner, determined to create a utopian society of equality, respect, and adequate provisions. However, before Napoleon Pig declares himself lord of Manor Farm again, the animals come to know all too well that "all animals are equal but some animals are more equal than others." George Orwell's allegory-fable-parable has given us much to think about since World War II. **MT, LT**

AUTHOR: **George Orwell**
TITLE: ***1984* (1949)**

DESCRIPTION: Did you know that the phrase "Big Brother is watching you" comes from Orwell's satire, *1984*? Written in 1949 to "predict" what kind of a totalitarian society could develop by 1984, Orwell created the story of Winston Smith who lives in the drab world of Oceania where "Big Brother" spies on every citizen's every action by way of two-way television monitors. Winston, a writer in the Ministry of Truth who revises the government's predictions to fit what actually happened, nevertheless thinks it is safe to rebel . . . a little, anyway, with the encouragement of a bookstore owner, Mrs. Charrington, and the love of beautiful Julia. But is it? Do you see parallels to our own post–1984 world? **MT**, **LT**

AUTHOR: **Boris Pasternak**

TITLE: ***Doctor Zhivago* (1958)**

DESCRIPTION: If you are ambitious and if you are interested in the events of the Russian Revolution, then you may truly enjoy reading *Doctor Zhivago*. It is the story of Yurii, a poet-physician who gets caught up in the student riots prior to the 1917 revolution. He marries Tonia, a childhood companion; is injured while serving as a doctor on the front during World War I; is nursed back to health by the great love of his life, Lara; and is pressed into service by the various factions during the postwar turmoil both in Moscow and in the Urals to which he has fled. Through all the events of his life so torn apart by revolutionary madness, Yurii Zhivago maintains a mystical innocence that he conveys not only in his relationships with people but in his poems, published at the end of the novel. There the great theme of Christ's crucifixion and resurrection is revealed as the standard by which he judges the great sweep of history through which he has lived. **LT**

AUTHOR: **Alan Paton**

TITLE: ***Cry, the Beloved Country* (1948)**

DESCRIPTION: Alan Paton's heart-rending, poetic novel was the first to dramatize the conflict between the races in South Africa and has never been equaled in its impact around the world. It is the story of two fathers who have lost sons because of apartheid. Rev. Stephen Kumalo has a son, Absalom, who has been snared by the vice in black townships. Arthur, the son of Mr. Jarvis, a white man who has attempted to help the blacks, is accidently shot by Absalom. Kumalo and Jarvis cry not only for their sons but also for their beloved country. What makes their story so memorable is how Paton reveals through them his deep conviction that only love can overcome the hate-spawning fear that grips South Africa, a love that can redemptively spring from such sorrow as these two fathers share. This book will echo in your memory for a long, long time. **MT**, **LT***

"Jody Finds the Fawn"—illustration by N. C. Wyeth for Marjorie Kinnan Rawlings' *The Yearling* (1939); reprinted with permission of Charles Scribner's Sons.

AUTHOR: **Marjorie Kinnan Rawlings**
TITLE: ***The Yearling*** (1938)

DESCRIPTION: Pulitzer prize, 1939. As an only child, Jody longs for a pet as much as he longs to grow up. When his father kills a doe to acquire an antidote for a deadly rattlesnake bite, he is allowed to keep the fawn. They have an enchanted year together, but Flag, as a yearling, begins to destroy their crops. Jody must relinquish the pet that fed his need to share the love his taciturn family has difficulty expressing.

Perhaps you will be surprised that your emotions can be so deeply touched by a story so full of "masculine" action as this one about Jody Baxter, his father, Penny, and his mother, Ory, as they struggle against marauding wolves and bears, natural disasters, and sometimes even their untamed hard-drinking neighbors, so that they can carve out a living from the Florida scrub. **ET, MT***

AUTHOR: **Mary Renault**
TITLE: ***The King Must Die*** (1958)

DESCRIPTION: Mary Renault has no peer when it comes to bringing the ancient Greek world, both mythical and historical, to life for modern readers. *The King Must Die* is her vivid recreation of the legend of Theseus, the son of Poseidon, heir to Athens' King Aigeus, and self-offered sacrifice to the Minotaur of Crete's King Minos. Courage and wits, loyalty and treachery, love and passion, dark, blood-filled religion and airy reason all play their roles in this vivid story. If you love mythology or history, you should love *The King*. If you don't have those prerequisites, it may just crack the door open to a whole new world for you. **MT, LT**

AUTHOR: **Mary Renault**
TITLE: ***The Last of the Wine*** (1956)

DESCRIPTION: Through the life of the narrator, Alexian of Athens, you can enter the great and tragic days of the Peloponnesian War. You see all their nobility—for along with Alexian the student, you meet Socrates,

Plato, and other scholars. You see all their baseness—for with Alexis the soldier, athlete, and citizen, you are privy to the conniving, the lust for wealth and power, the sieges, the slavery, and the acceptable homosexual relationships (delicately handled by Renault). The Greek ideals of harmony, proportion, and order prevail as long as Socrates is free to be a gadfly to Athens. He is the novel's true hero, as is the Greece about which Renault writes so well. **LT**

**ET**—Early Teens
**MT**—Mid Teens
**LT**—Late Teens
**AA**—All Ages

AUTHOR: **Nevil Shute**
TITLE: *A Town Like Alice* (1950)

DESCRIPTION: A young British secretary and an Australian soldier are both made prisoners of war by the Japanese in Malaysia, meeting only briefly during their six-year ordeal. She is marched 1200 miles around the jungles, and he is tortured for stealing food for her, but both become stronger individuals than they had been. After the war they seek each other out, test whether their feelings for each other are truly love, and find mutual commitment to the undeveloped outback of Australia. Shute said that the true story of courageous women prisoners in Sumatra was more appealing to him as a basis for a novel than anything he could concoct out of his imagination. You will probably agree with him. **LT**

AUTHOR: **Betty Smith**
TITLE: *A Tree Grows in Brooklyn* (1943)

DESCRIPTION: Francie Nolan is the book-loving daughter of a good-hearted but drink-weakened father and a hard-working janitress mother. She and her brother and parents struggle against poverty and hardship to maintain a family life and gain an education in their Brooklyn tenement community at the turn of the century. Francie herself determines to read all the books in the library in alphabetical order. How she achieves her goals in such an unpromising environment, how a tree grows in Brooklyn, is her story. **LT**

AUTHOR: **Aleksandr Solzhenitsyn**
TITLE: *One Day in the Life of Ivan Denisovich* (1963)

DESCRIPTION: Ivan Denisovich Shukhov was an ordinary Russian carpenter, a man like millions of others put into Stalin's forced labor camps in the name of socialism. This remarkable book takes him through one day, from reveille to lights out, one day of the 3,653 like it in his sentence, thereby revealing the "spiritual squalor, corruption, frustration and terror" of the place, but also his "passionate outcry for dignity and justice."

Even the Soviet official who wrote a preface when it made its revolutionary appearance in the USSR said that "this novel, which is so unusual for its honesty and harrowing truth, . . . strengthens and ennobles us." **LT**

AUTHOR: **John Steinbeck**

TITLE: *The Pearl* (1945)

DESCRIPTION: You will be moved by this short novel about an Indian fisherman, Kino, whose baby son is bitten by a scorpion. Kino hunts for the Pearl of the World so that he can afford to pay the evil town doctor to treat his son. The ancient harmonious music, which Steinbeck built into the rhythms of the language and which accompany all that Kino, Juana, and the baby do, are disturbed by the Pearl that promises so much wealth. **LT**

AUTHOR: **James Thurber**

TITLE: *The Thirteen Clocks* (1950)

DESCRIPTION: Look for a new edition of this slim volume—both a fairy tale and a satire on the genre of fairy tales, about a duke frozen in time because he is such a cold creature, and the princess whom he has imprisoned, and, of course, the prince charming who rescues her. **ET***

AUTHOR: **Mark Twain**

TITLE: *Huckleberry Finn* (1885)

DESCRIPTION: This book is often assigned in English classes, but that is no reason not to want to read it! Huck, say some people, is Everyboy. His clever mind, which sees through the trickery and stupidity of others; his high but idiosyncratic ethical standards; his moral dilemmas over the slavery of his companion, the runaway Jim; his refusal to be "civilized" (by a corrupt civilization?); and his adventures on the raft floating down the Mississippi make this book an essentially American experience not to be missed. Some people feel strongly that Twain's portrayal of Jim is racist. Do you agree or disagree? Why? **LT, AA***

AUTHOR: **Mark Twain**

TITLE: *Tom Sawyer* (1876)

DESCRIPTION: How Tom Sawyer got out of whitewashing the fence, how he fell in love with the imperious Becky Thatcher, how he and Huck Finn witnessed a murder by Injun Joe, how they arrived at their own funerals, and how justice was eventually served and the boys rewarded—these are all part of the American mystique about growing up in the simpler days near the Mississippi River and should be a part of everyone's growing up today. **ET, MT***

AUTHOR: **Jessamyn West**

TITLE: ***Friendly Persuasion* (1943)**

DESCRIPTION: This gentle story is about a Quaker family. Jess, the husband, in the nursery stock business, and his wife, Eliza, the minister, live in the bounty of southern Indiana before the Civil War. Music is forbidden to the Quakers, but early on, Jess buys an organ to satisfy a longing in his soul. The outrageous organ, pacifism, suspicion of modernity, and other Quaker convictions all are important in this chronicle of three generations. **LT**

AUTHOR: **Elie Wiesel**

TITLE: ***Night* (1960)**

DESCRIPTION: *Night* is Nobel laureate Elie Wiesel's first—and most compelling—account of how his idyllic days in the village of Sighet were destroyed when the village's Jews were taken away late in World War II. Elie and his family were sent to Birkenau where his mother and sister were killed. His father, his dearest companion, died just before Buchenwald was liberated. Wiesel ultimately survived several camps and the arduous journeys between them, but his story describes what did not survive. "Never shall I forget these flames which consumed my faith forever. Never shall I forget those moments which murdered my God and my soul and turned my dreams to dust." Wiesel's writing career has been devoted to telling the civilized world "Never forget!" and to attempting to understand the role of God and God's created people in the evil and suffering of this world. **LT**

AUTHOR: **Thorton Wilder**

TITLE: ***The Bridge of San Luis Rey* (1927)**

DESCRIPTION: "On Friday noon, July the twentieth, 1714, the finest bridge in all Peru broke and precipitated five travelers into the gulf below." So begins this short, thoughtful novel about those five people whose lives intertwined and through whose stories Brother Juniper hoped that he could justify the ways of God to the people he worked with. He made his attempt because he believed that "either we live by accident and die by accident, or we live by plan and die by plan." **LT***

# Chapter 21

# Quick Reference

**A** Quick Reference list is another way to help you find the books you want to share with teens. We have gathered all the quick reference lists, including the ones scattered throughout the book, and put them together in this chapter as a convenience for our readers. We pulled out book titles from the reading categories in Chapters 12–20 to list them topically as another way of spurring interest in books. Parents, grandparents, aunts and uncles, teachers—anyone interested in young adult literature—can photocopy these lists for ideas when buying gifts or looking for books on particular subjects.

Think of what a teen could learn about the Orient by reading the books in the Quick Reference list on Asia! We can't imagine a more enlightening reading journey than the books listed under the Quick Reference to the Complexities of Race. The books in the list of Understanding Life Behind the Iron Curtain will give teens and adults alike a page-turning look at the vastness of Russia and its history.

Take advantage of a teen's particular interest by making a copy of one of these lists to facilitate further reading on a subject. One of these short lists might grab a reluctant teen's attention and inspire a whole new adventure in reading.

The potential use for these quick references is exciting. They are not meant to be a substitute for the longer annotations in Chapters 12–20, but rather an encouragement to refer back to the longer

eviews and analyses which will help the reader understand the book's
background. It is also important to notice the reading level of the
books listed. Find the books in their category listing and note whether
they are **ET**, **MT**, or **LT**. Some of the quick reference lists reflect a wide
age range; for example, in the Behind the Iron Curtain listing, a book
like *Doctor Zhivago* is for **LT** and would be hard for an early teen to
grasp, while *Night Journey* by Kathryn Lasky is a good book for early
teens. Esther Hautzig's *The Endless Steppe* could easily span all age
categories and heighten the interest in the Quick Reference to Russia's history. Take our age-ratings seriously.

## If You Like Good Romance

*Rebecca* by Daphne Du Maurier
*Pride and Prejudice* by Jane Austen
*Christy* by Catherine Marshall
*Up a Road Slowly* by Irene Hunt
*Edge of Honor* by Gilbert Morris
*Doctor Zhivago* by Boris Pasternak
*Jane Eyre* by Charlotte Brontë
*Playing Beatie Bow* by Ruth Park

## Romance, Take Two

Any book by Janette Oke
Any book by Bodie Thoene
Any book by Eugenia Price
Any book by George MacDonald
Any book by T. Davis Bunn

## Sent Out By God

*Peace Child* by Don Richardson
*Shadow of the Almighty* by Elisabeth
Elliot
*Killing Fields, Living Fields* by Don
Cormack
*Eric Liddell: Pure Gold* by David
McCasland

## If You're Intrigued
## by the Indian Subcontinent

*Shiva's Fire* by Suzanne Fisher Staples
*Shabanu* by Suzanne Fisher Staples
*Homeless Bird* by Gloria Whelan
*Kingfishers Catch Fire* by Rumer
Godden
*Kim* by Rudyard Kipling
*River* by Rumer Godden

## If You Want to Know More about Asia

*Master Puppeteer* by Katherine Paterson
*The Samurai* by Shusaku Endo
*Rebels of the Heavenly Kingdom* by Katherine Paterson
*The Good Earth* by Pearl Buck
*Killing Fields, Living Fields* by Don Cormack
*Lost Horizon* by James Hilton
*Eric Liddell: Pure Gold* by David McCasland
*Into Thin Air* by Jon Krakauer

## If You Want to go to the South Seas

*Ash Road* by Ivan Southall
*Tomorrow, When the War Began* by John Marsden
*A Town Like Alice* by Nevil Shute
*The Pearl* by John Steinbeck
*Lord Jim* by Joseph Conrad
*The Proving Ground* by G. Bruce Knecht
*Dove* by Robin Lee Graham and Derek L. T. Gill
*Moon Dark* by Patricia Wrightson

## If You're Interested in Africa

*Things Fall Apart* by Chinua Achebe
*Cry, the Beloved Country* by Alan Paton
*A Girl Named Disaster* by Nancy Farmer
*The Ear, the Eye and the Arm* by Nancy Farmer
*The African Queen* by C. S. Forester
*The Return* by Sonia Levitin
*The Baboon King* by Anton Quintana
*Born Free* by Joy Adamson

## If You Want to Understand the Complexities of Race

*Black Like Me* by John Howard Griffin
*The Autobiography of Malcolm X* as told to Alex Haley
*Dangerous Skies* by Suzanne Staples
*Monster* by Walter Dean Myers
*Roll of Thunder, Hear My Cry* and its sequels by Mildred Taylor
*White Lilacs* by Carolyn Meyer
*Cezanne Pinto* by Mary Stolz
*Go Tell It on the Mountain* by James Baldwin
*To Kill a Mockingbird* by Harper Lee
*Huck Finn* by Mark Twain
*Fallen Angels* by Walter Dean Myers
*Safe at Home* by Bob Muzikowski

## If You Want to Explore the Middle East

*A Beacon at Alexandria* by Gillian Bradshaw
*The Robe* by Lloyd Douglas
*A Hand Full of Stars* by Rafik Schami
*If You Love Me* by Patricia St. John
*Blood Brothers* by Elias Chacour
*The Plague* by Albert Camus
*The Singing Mountain* by Sonia Levitin
*The Return* by Sonia Levitin
*Tales of a Dead King* by W. D. Myers
*Masada* by Gloria Miklowitz
Zion Chronicles series by Bodie Thoene

## If You Want to Understand Life Behind the Iron Curtain

*Nicholas and Alexandra* by Robert Massie
*Doctor Zhivago* by Boris Pasternak
*Night Journey* by Kathryn Lasky
*Long Walk: The True Story of a Trek to Freedom* by Slavomir Rawicz
*One Day in the Life of Ivan Denisovich* by A. Solzhenitsyn
*The Endless Steppe* by Esther Hautzig
*Red Storm Rising* by Tom Clancy
*Last of the Breed* by Louis L'Amour

## If You Want to Visit Latin America

*Heart of a Jaguar* by Marc Talbert
*The Power and the Glory* by Graham Greene
*Green Mansions* by William Hudson
*The Shadow of the Almighty* by Elisabeth Elliot
*Bridge of San Luis Rey* by Thorton Wilder
*Dragons in the Water* by Madeleine L'Engle

## If You want a Good Laugh

*Walking Across Egypt* by Clyde Edgerton
The Mitford series by Jan Karon
*A Dog Who Wouldn't Be* by Farley Mowat
*The Ghost Belonged to Me* by Richard Peck
*All Creatures Great and Small* by James Herriot
Harry Potter series by J. K. Rowling
*A Long Way from Chicago* by Richard Peck
*The Thurber Carnival* by James Thurber
*Birds, Beasts and Relatives* by Gerald Durrell

## If You're Facing Death and Grief

*Bridge to Terabithia* by Katherine Paterson
*Walk Two Moons* by Sharon Creech
*I Heard the Owl Call My Name* by Margaret Craven
*A String in the Harp* by Nancy Bond
*Sound of Chariots* by Mollie Hunter
*The Wanderer* by Sharon Creech
*After the Dancing Days* by Margaret Rostkowski
*Yesterday's Child* by Sonia Levitin
*Memory* by Margaret Mahy
*Death Be Not Proud* by John Gunther
*Missing May* by Cynthia Rylant

## When Life Isn't Perfect

*Joni* by Joni Eareckson
*All Together Now* by Sue Ellen Bridgers
*Flowers for Algernon* by Daniel Keyes
*Stuck in Neutral* by Terry Trueman
*Lord Foul's Bane* by Stephen Donaldson
*Hang Tough, Paul Mather* by Alfred Slote
*Comeback* by Dave Dravecky
*Saint Ben* by John Fischer
*One Child* by Torey Hayden

## If You're Ready for Intellectual Stretching

Any of the Tried and Trues (pages 326–353)
*Ishmael* by Daniel Quinn
*Chris Chrisman Goes to College* by James W. Sire
*Father Elijah* by Michael O'Brien
*Red Shift* by Alan Garner
*A Wizard of Earthsea* by Ursula LeGuin
His Dark Materials trilogy by Philip Pullman
*Descent into Hell* by Charles Williams
*Pilgrim at Tinker Creek* by Annie Dillard
*Defeating Darwinism* by Phillip Johnson
*Eva* by Peter Dickinson

## If You're Feeling Left Alone

*The Great Gilly Hopkins* by Katherine Paterson
*Slake's Limbo* by Felice Holman
*Homecoming* by Cynthia Voigt
*A Door Near Here* by Heather Quarles
*Sweet Whispers, Brother Rush* by Virginia Hamilton
*Dave at Night* by Gail Carson Levine

## Civil War Stories

*Jubilee* by Margaret Walker
*Gone with the Wind* by Margaret
  Mitchell
*Edge of Honor* by Gilbert Morris
*Stranger in Savannah* by Eugenia Price
*The Civil War* by Bruce Catton
*Friendly Persuasion* by Jessamyn West
*Killer Angels* by Michael Shaara

## When Nature Is a Character

Almost any book by Gary Paulsen
*Ring of Bright Water* by Gavin Maxwell
*Pilgrim at Tinker Creek* by Annie Dillard
*To A Wild Sky* and *Ash Road* by Ivan
  Southall
*A Girl Named Disaster* by Nancy
  Farmer
*The Animals of Farthing Wood* by Colin
  Dann
*Incident at Hawk's Hill* by Allan Eckert
*Where the Red Fern Grows* by Wilson
  Rawls
*Last of the Breed* by Louis L'Amour
*Shipwreck at the Bottom of the World* by
  Jennifer Armstrong

## There's Spiritual Strength in These

*Joni* by Joni Eareckson
*The Hobbit* and the sequels by J. R. R.
  Tolkien
*North to Freedom* by Ann Holm
*The Book of the Dun Cow* by Walter
  Wangerin Jr.
*Bud, Not Buddy* by Christopher Curtis
*Saint Ben* by John Fischer
Zion Chronicle and Covenant series by
  Bodie Thoene
*Roll of Thunder* and sequels by Mildred
  Taylor
*Journey through the Night* by Anne
  DeVries
*She Said Yes* by Misty Bernall

## To Be a Slave

*Slave Dancer* by Paula Fox
*Uncle Tom's Cabin* by Harriet Beecher
  Stowe
*Anthony Burns* by Virginia Hamilton
*To Be a Slave* by Julius Lester
*The Middle Passage* by Tom Feelings

## Mother/(Younger) Daughter Read Alouds

Austin Family or Times series by
　　Madeleine L'Engle
*Anne of Green Gables* by L. M.
　　Montgomery
*Sound of Chariots* by Mollie Hunter
*The Ark* by Margot Benary-Isbert
*The Root Cellar* by Janet Lunn
*Magic Circle* by Donna Jo Napoli
*A String in the Harp* by Nancy Bond

## Mother/(Older) Daughter Read Alouds

*Christy* by Catherine Marshall
*I Capture the Castle* by Dodie Smith
Mitford series by Jan Karon
*A Tree Grows in Brooklyn* by Betty
　　Smith
*Till We Have Faces* by C. S. Lewis
*In This House of Brede* by Rumer
　　Godden
Zion Chronicle and Covenant series by
　　Bodie Thoene

## Father/(Younger) Son Read Alouds

*Walker's Crossing* by Phyllis Reynolds
　　Naylor
*A Day No Pigs Would Die* by Robert
　　Newton Peck
*Bud, Not Buddy* by Christopher Curtis
*Castaways of the Flying Dutchman* by
　　Brian Jacques
*Redwall* by Brian Jacques
*Jim the Boy* by Tony Earley
*Where the Red Fern Grows* by Wilson
　　Rawls
*Saint Ben* by John Fischer

## Father/(Older) Son Read Alouds

*Breaking of Ezra Riley* by John Moore
*Shane* by Jack Schaefer
*The Chosen* by Chaim Potok
*Northwest Passage* (and others) by
　　Kenneth Roberts
*Riding for the Brand* (and others) by
　　Louis L'Amour
*Tales of Tahitian Waters* (and others)
　　by Zane Grey
*A Bell for Adano* by John Hersey
*Eric Liddell: Pure Gold* by David
　　McCasland
Lord of the Rings trilogy by J. R. R.
　　Tolkien

## Caught in Hitler's Evil: World War II Stories

Zion Covenant series by Bodie Thoene
*The Ark* by Margot Benary-Isbert
*The Endless Steppe* by Esther Hautzig
*A Bell for Adano* by John Hersey
*The Wall* by John Hersey
*Torn Thread* by Anne Isaacs
*The Long Walk* by Slavomir Rawicz
*Journey through the Night* by Anne
    De Vries
*Guns of Navarone* by Alistair MacLean
*Anne Frank: The Diary of a Young Girl*
    by Anne Frank
*Lest Innocent Blood be Shed* by Philip
    Hallie
*Never to Forget* by Milton Meltzer
*Night* by Elie Wiesel
*The Last Mission* by Harry Mazer
*The Hiding Place* by Corrie ten Boom

## The War in the Pacific Theater

*Eric Liddell: Pure Gold* by David
    McCasland
*Under the Blood-Red Sun* by Graham
    Salisbury
*Farewell to Manzanar* by Houston and
    Houston
*Eternal Spring of Mr. Ito* by Sheila
    Garrigue
*A Town Like Alice* by Nevil Shute
*Friends and Enemies* by Louanne
    Gaeddert

## Short But Meaningful

*North to Freedom* by Ann Holm
*Holes* by Louis Sachar
*Make Lemonade* by Virginia Euwer
    Wolff
*The Magic Circle* by Donna Jo Napoli
*Cezanne Pinto* by Mary Stolz
*The Snow Goose* by Paul Gallico
*Night* by Elie Wiesel
*The Middle Passage* by Tom Feelings

## Surviving High School Life

*The Veritas Project: Hangman's Curse* by
    Frank Peretti
*She Said Yes* by Misty Bernall
*Body of Christopher Creed* by Carol
    Plum-Ucci
*Diary of a Teenage Girl* by Melody
    Carlson
*Nothing but the Truth* by Avi

# Glossary

Aestheticism—artistic beauty and taste as a basic standard; ethical and other standards are secondary.

Allegory—a story (parable, myth, or fable) that veils its deeper meaning by letting readers discover it for themselves.

Allusion—a passing or casual mention of something.

Anarchy—a society without laws or governmental control; confusion; chaos.

Animism—a belief that gives all natural objects souls or spirits.

Convivial—fond of feasting, drinking, merry company; friendly, agreeable.

Daimon—(1) a god or (2) a demon; deity, fate, fortune.

Deism—a belief that God created the world and then abandoned it.

Dualism—a theory that mind and body are the two basic realities.

Eclectic—not following one system, but taking bits and pieces from different sources.

Elemental—simple, basic.

Elitism—consciousness or pride in belonging to a select group.

Erotica—literature or art dealing with sex.

Existentialism—a belief that people make themselves who they are. It is not a full-fledged worldview. Atheistic existentialism says God does not exist; theistic existentialism has God in the equation.

Fatalistic—believing that all events are subject to fate or chance.

Genre—kind; sort; style.

Humanism—a philosophy in which human beings—their rights and interests—are the sole value.

Ideology—a defined and closed system that typifies what people believe, which allows no questions.

Illusion—something that deceives by producing a false impression.

Lyrical—having a musical quality.

Manichaeism—an ancient dualistic heresy which claims that Satan is a co-equal with God.

Metaphor—a word or phrase that suggests a likeness; as in, "A mighty fortress is our God." God is not literally a fortress; he is like a fortress.

Mores—the moral views or folkways of a group.

New Age—began with a belief that a new species will evolve. A worldview that borrows bits and pieces from other non-Christian worldviews, influenced by Eastern thought and mysticism.

Nihilism—nothingness or nonexistence; a denial of real existence.

Pantheism—identifies the universe with God—so that god is in everything that exists.

Paradoxical—something that seems self-contradictory, often two ideas that seem in opposition to each other.

Phenomenon—(1) an observable fact, occurrence, or circumstance; (2) something that impresses one as being extraordinary.

Postmodernism—the contemporary philosophy of life that claims that reality and truth are not givens but are constructed by people from their own perspectives. Postmoderns believe there are no absolutes, that what you believe is true for you while what they believe is true for them even if these beliefs are opposites.

Scientism—a belief in science as the final word on everything.

Surrealistic—a style of art or literature that stresses the sub-conscious or non-rational.

Theism—a belief in one God as creator and ruler of the universe.

Theme of a story—the idea, the general truth about life or a people brought out in a story or other literary work.

Utopia—an imaginary society that is ideal, perfect in its social and political systems. In contrast, a dystopia is one that is bad.

Vicarious—felt or enjoyed through the experience of another person.

# Index of Authors

Abanes, Richard, 95
Achebe, Chinua, 35, 259, 280
Adams, Douglas, 242
Adams, Richard, 128
Adamson, Joy, 35, 228, 280
Alcott, Louisa May, 119
Almond, David, 141, 168
Armstrong, Jennifer, 50, 61, 228, 283
Asimov, Isaac, 82, 243
Austen, Jane, 21, 259, 279
Avi, 116, 141, 219, 285

Babbitt, Natalie, 168
Baldwin, James, 54, 260, 280
Banks, Lynne Reid, 219
Barrie, J. M., 96
BeauSeigneur, James, 128, 132
Beckett, Samuel, 82–83
Benary-Isbert, Margot, 45, 93, 191,
    284, 285
Bernall, Misty, 100, 116, 229, 283,
    285
Bibee, John, 90, 169
Blake, William, 168
Blos, Joan, 110
Blume, Judy, 44
Bond, Nancy, 93, 99, 169, 282, 284
Boom, Corrie ten, 45, 111, 240–41,
    285
Bradbury, Ray, 109, 244, 260
Bradshaw, Gillian, 36, 192, 281
Brand, Paul, 229
Bridgers, Sue Ellen, 73, 192, 282
Brontë, Charlotte, 21, 260, 279
Brontë, Emily, 260–61
Brooks, Bruce, 142
Brothers Grimm, 96
Browning, Robert, 53
Buck, Pearl S., 24, 261, 280
Bunn, T. Davis, 121, 129, 279
Bunyan, John, 120, 261
Burnett, Frances Hodgson, 129

Cadnum, Michael, 193
Caldwell, Brian, 132
Calhoun, Dia, 170
Campbell, Ross, 229
Camus, Albert, 36, 261, 281
Card, Orson Scott, 109, 244
Carlson, Melody, 116, 142, 285
Carroll, Lewis, 119
Carson, Ben, 36–37, 229–30
Cather, Willa, 26, 262
Catton, Bruce, 79, 110, 230, 283
Cervantes, 120
Chacour, Elias, 36, 230, 281
Chesterton, G. K., 220
Christian, S. Rickly, 229
Christie, Agatha, 108, 220
Christopher, John, 109, 244–45
Clancy, Tom, 29, 220, 281
Clarke, Arthur C., 245–46
Cohen, Barbara, 143
Cole, Brock, 44
Coleridge, Samuel Taylor, 71
Coles, Robert, 53
Colum, Padraic, 119, 230
Coman, Carolyn, 143
Conrad, Joseph, 49, 262, 280
Cooper, James Fenimore, 106, 263
Cooper, Susan, 89, 90, 170–72, 173,
    174
Cormack, Don, 24, 75, 230–31, 279,
    280
Cormier, Robert, 44, 83, 144
Crane, Stephen, 263
Craven, Margaret, 99, 145, 282
Creech, Sharon, 99, 130, 145, 282
Crichton, Michael, 130
Curtis, Christopher, 94, 100, 193,
    283, 284
Cushman, Karen, 83, 193–94

Dana, Barbara, 194
Dann, Colin, 61, 130, 283
Davis, Ken, 229

De Vries, Anne, 45, 100, 194, 283, 285
Defoe, Daniel, 119, 253
DeFord, Frank, 254–55
Dickens, Charles, 62, 106–7, 120, 263–64
Dickinson, Peter, 66, 221, 246, 282
Dillard, Annie, 61, 66, 231, 282, 283
Dodson, Shireen, 85–86
Doherty, Berlie, 145
Donaldson, Stephen, 73, 109, 173, 282
Donne, John, 235
Douglas, Lloyd C., 36, 107, 194, 264, 281
Dow, Rosey, 221
Doyle, Sir Arthur Conan, 109, 221–22
Dravecky, Dave, 73, 254, 282
Du Maurier, Daphne, 21, 106, 264, 279
Durrell, Gerald, 91, 111, 231, 281
Dyson, Freeman, 232

Eareckson, Joni, 73, 100, 111, 232, 282, 283
Earley, Tony, 94, 195, 284
Eckert, Allan, 61, 195, 283
Edgerton, Clyde, 91, 146, 281
Eiseley, Loren, 232
Eliot, T. S., 49, 58, 65
Elliot, Elisabeth, 75, 84, 232, 279, 281
Endo, Shusaku, 24, 265, 280

Farmer, Nancy, 35, 61, 146, 246, 280, 283
Feelings, Tom, 40, 62, 233, 283, 285
Feinstein, John, 255
Felleman, Hazel, 114
Ferber, Edna, 265
Fischer, John, 50, 73, 94, 100, 195–96, 282, 283, 284
Fisk, Pauline, 173
Forbes, Esther, 110, 196
Forbes, Kathryn, 196
Forester, C. S., 35, 266, 280
Forward, Eve, 249
Fox, Paula, 62, 146–47, 196, 283
Francis, Dick, 109
Frank, Anne, 45, 233, 285
Frank, Rudolf, 197, 205
Frost, Robert, 113

Gaeddert, Louanne, 111, 197, 285
Gallico, Paul, 40, 266, 285
Garfield, Leon, 82, 110
Garner, Alan, 66, 174–75, 197–98, 282
Garrigue, Sheila, 111, 147, 285
Gaus, P. L, 222

Gilbert, W. S., 115
Gill, Derek L. T., 49, 233, 280
Gilman, Dorothy, 222
Gish, Kimbra Wilder, 94–95
Godden, Rumer, 103, 107, 266–67, 279, 284
Golding, William, 45, 267
Goudge, Elizabeth, 107, 268
Graham, Robin Lee, 49, 233–34, 280
Grahame, Kenneth, 96
Greene, Brian, 234
Greene, Graham, 84, 268, 281
Grey, Zane, 108, 109, 255, 284
Griffin, John Howard, 54, 111, 234, 280
Gunther, John, 99, 234, 282
Guthrie, A. B., 109

Haley, Alex, 54, 111, 241, 280
Hall, Donald, 114
Hallie, Philip, 45, 110, 235, 285
Hamilton, Virginia, 62, 69, 110, 222, 235, 282, 283
Harris, Joshua, 236
Hautzig, Esther, 29, 45, 110, 198, 279, 281, 285
Hayden, Torey, 73, 236, 282
Heide, Florence, 92
Hemingway, Ernest, 268
Herbert, Frank, 247
Herriot, James, 91, 108, 269, 281
Hersey, John, 45, 108, 110, 198–99, 284, 285
Hesse, Karen, 24, 148, 199
Hickman, Janet, 148
Highwater, Jamake, 200
Hillerman, Tony, 109, 223
Hilton, James, 24, 269, 280
Hinton, S. E., 44
Hirsch, E. D., 116–17
Hobbs, Will, 131
Holm, Ann, 40, 100, 131, 283, 285
Holman, Felice, 69, 148, 282
Houston, James D., 111, 236, 285
Houston, Jeanne W., 111, 236, 285
Howard, Thomas, 88
Hudson, William, 84, 269–70, 281
Hugo, Victor, 69, 107, 270
Hulme, Kathryn, 270
Hunt, Irene, 21, 110, 149, 200, 279
Hunter, Mollie, 42, 93, 200–201, 282, 284

Isaacs, Anne, 45, 201, 285

Jackson, Rachel, 214
Jacques, Brian, 23, 24, 46, 59, 94, 176, 202, 284
Jarvis, Robin, 176
Jenkins, Jerry, 50, 132
Jenkins, Peter, 236–37
Johnson, Phillip, 66, 237, 282
Jordan, Robert, 177
Joyce, James, 270
Junger, Sebastian, 256

Karon, Jan, 91, 107, 202, 281, 284
Kenyon, Jane, 114
Keyes, Daniel, 73, 149, 282
King, Laurie R., 223
King, Stephen, 35, 225
Kipling, Rudyard, 103, 271, 279
Klein, Norma, 44
Knecht, G. Bruce, 49, 255, 280
Krakauer, Jon, 24, 256, 280
Kreeft, Peter, 237
Kropp, Goran, 256

L'Amour, Louis, 29, 61, 108, 109, 132, 281, 283, 284
L'Engle, Madeleine, 44, 84, 90, 93, 143, 149–51, 177–79, 225, 281, 284
LaHaye, Tim, 50, 132
Lamb, Charles, 11, 107, 120, 271
Lamb, Mary, 11, 107, 120, 271
Lambert, Dave, 229
Landsberg, Michele, 89
Lanier, Sidney, 32
Lardner, Ring, 256
Lasky, Kathryn, 29, 202–3, 279, 281
Lawhead, Stephen, 50, 203, 247
LeCarré, John, 223–24
Lee, Harper, 26, 54, 107, 271, 280
LeGuin, Ursula, 66, 87, 90, 96, 109, 179, 248, 282
Lerangis, Peter, 228
Lester, Julius, 62, 237, 283
Levine, Gail Carson, 69, 179, 204, 282
Levitin, Sonia, 35, 36, 99, 110, 151, 204, 248, 280, 281, 282
Lewis, C. S., 11, 19, 21, 24, 39, 61, 62, 79, 88, 92, 93, 96, 107, 109, 171, 183, 185, 225, 237–38, 249–50, 271, 284
Lewis, Gregg, 257

Lincoln, Mary Todd, 214
Lipsite, Robert, 151
Little, Jean, 113
Little, Paul, 80
London, Jack, 107, 133
Longfellow, Henry Wadsworth, 112
Lowry, Lois, 83, 84, 249, 250–51
Lund, Doris, 238
Lunn, Janet, 93, 180, 284

MacDonald, George, 27, 121, 272, 279
MacIntosh, Elizabeth, 227
MacLean, Alistair, 45, 224, 285
Mahy, Margaret, 44, 83, 99, 152, 282
Mallory, Sir Thomas, 203
Marsden, John, 49, 133, 280
Marshall, Catherine, 21, 107, 204–5, 279, 284
Massie, Robert, 29, 238, 281
Maxwell, Gavin, 61, 238, 283
Mayne, William, 180
Mazer, Harry, 44, 45, 205, 285
McCasland, David, 24, 75, 108, 111, 256, 279, 280, 284, 285
McClaren, Brian, 238–39
McKinley, Robin, 108, 133–34, 180
Meltzer, Milton, 45, 239, 285
Meyer, Carolyn, 54, 205, 280
Miklowitz, Gloria, 36, 205, 281
Millay, Edna St. Vincent, 112
Milne, A. A., 51, 96
Milosz, Czeslaw, 92
Milton, John, 63, 95, 182
Mitchell, Margaret, 79, 206, 283
Montgomery, L. M., 93, 206, 284
Moore, John, 108, 134, 284
Morris, Gilbert, 21, 79, 129, 206–7, 279, 283
Morris, James, 57
Mowat, Farley, 42, 91, 207, 281
Mundle, Rob, 256
Murphey, Cecil, 229
Muzikowski, Bob, 54, 257, 280
Myers, Walter Dean, 36, 54, 152, 224, 280, 281

Na, An, 153
Napoli, Donna Jo, 40, 93, 180, 284, 285
Naylor, Phyllis Reynolds, 80, 94, 153, 284
Neal, Connie, 95

O'Brien, Michael, 66, 132, 134, 282
O'Shea, Pat, 90, 181
Oke, Janette, 59, 121, 207–8, 279
Opdyke, Irena Gut, 50
Opie, Iona, 114
Opie, Peter, 114
Oppel, Kenneth, 181
Orczy, Baroness, 135
Orwell, George, 272–73

Park, Ruth, 21, 208, 279
Pasternak, Boris, 21, 29, 273, 279, 281
Paterson, Katherine, 24, 27–28, 46–47, 69, 88, 99, 105, 119, 154–56, 208–9, 280, 282
Paton, Alan, 35, 107, 273, 280
Paulsen, Gary, 61, 83, 107, 135–37, 156–57, 283
Pausewang, Gudrun, 157
Peck, M. E., 44
Peck, Richard, 24, 30, 34, 44, 46, 91, 182, 209, 281
Peck, Robert Newton, 24, 94, 158, 284
Peretti, Frank, 116, 225, 285
Peters, Ellis, 108, 226
Peterson, Eugene, 92
Plant, Mike, 257
Plum-Ucci, Carol, 116, 157, 285
Postman, Neil, 239–40
Potok, Chaim, 49, 59–60, 108, 158–59, 284
Price, Eugenia, 79, 121, 210, 279, 283
Pullman, Philip, 66, 82, 95, 96, 182–83, 282

Quarles, Heather, 69, 159–60, 282
Quinn, Daniel, 66, 251, 282
Quintana, Anton, 35, 137, 280

Ransome, Arthur, 25
Raskin, Ellen, 226
Rawicz, Slavomir, 29, 45, 211, 281, 285
Rawlings, Marjorie Kinnan, 274
Rawls, Wilson, 61, 94, 160, 283, 284
Renault, Mary, 274–75
Richardson, Don, 75, 240, 279
Rinaldi, Ann, 211
Roberts, Kenneth, 108, 110, 211, 284
Roberts, Laura Peyton, 49
Rostkowski, Margaret, 99, 212, 282
Rowling, J. K., 91, 93, 94, 95, 96, 184–85, 281
Rylant, Cynthia, 99, 160, 282

Sachar, Louis, 24, 40, 160, 285
Sagan, Carl, 82
St. John, Patricia, 36, 212, 281
Salinger, J. D., 45, 161
Salisbury, Graham, 111, 212–13, 285
Sayers, Dorothy, 108, 227
Schaefer, Jack, 108, 137, 284
Schami, Rafik, 36, 161, 281
Schliemann, Henry, 214
Schliemann, Sophia, 214
Seuss, Dr., 112
Shaara, Michael, 79, 207, 283
Shakespeare, William, 46, 120, 172–73
Shaw, Luci, 114
Shute, Nevil, 49, 111, 251, 275, 280, 285
Siegel, Robert, 108, 186
Silverberg, Robert, 243
Silverstein, Shel, 96
Singer, Dorothy A., 33
Singer, Isaac Bashevis, 44, 48
Singer, Jerome L., 33
Sire, James W., 66, 81, 240, 282
Skurzynski, Gloria, 186
Slote, Alfred, 73, 257, 282
Smith, Betty, 107, 275, 284
Smith, Dodie, 107, 213, 284
Smith, Lillian H., 87
Solzhenitsyn, Aleksandr, 29, 62, 275, 281
Sophocles, 119
Soto, Gary, 258
Southall, Ivan, 49, 61, 108, 138–39, 161–62, 280, 283
Speare, Elizabeth George, 93, 110
Spiegel, Deborah Spector, 249
Stafford, Tim, 254
Staples, Suzanne Fisher, 54, 103, 162, 279, 280
Staudohar, Paul D., 258
Steinbeck, John, 49, 276, 280
Stevenson, Robert Louis, 26, 108, 139–40
Stewart, Mary, 203
Stolz, Mary, 40, 54, 80, 213, 280, 285
Stone, Irving, 213–14
Stowe, Harriet Beecher, 62, 120, 214, 283
Sullivan, Arthur, 115
Sutcliff, Rosemary, 89, 203, 214–15
Swift, Jonathan, 120
Swirsky, Seth, 258

Talbert, Marc, 84, 215, 281
Taylor, Mildred, 51, 54, 100, 162, 215–16, 280, 283

Tey, Josephine, 108, 227
Thoene, Bodie, 36, 45, 100, 107, 121,
   216–17, 279, 281, 283, 284, 285
Thurber, James, 42, 91, 241, 276, 281
Tinley, Scott, 257
Tolkien, J. R. R., 11, 18, 19, 20, 27, 88, 89,
   96, 100, 108, 171, 183, 187–88, 283,
   284
Tolstoy, Leo, 69
Trelease, Jim, 25
Trueman, Terry, 73, 163, 282
Turner, Megan Whalen, 140
Twain, Mark, 54, 121, 276, 280
Tyers, Kathy, 50, 252

Updike, John, 113
Uris, Leon, 217

Vande Velde, Vivian, 188
Verne, Jules, 109, 252
Voigt, Cynthia, 69, 83, 163–66, 282

Wagner, Richard, 187
Walker, Margaret, 79, 214, 217, 283
Walter, Virginia, 153
Wangerin, Walter, Jr., 80, 90, 100, 188, 283
Wells, H. G., 109, 252–53
West, Jessamyn, 79, 277, 283
Whelan, Gloria, 103, 167, 218, 279
White, John, 74, 90, 189
White, T. H., 203
Wiesel, Elie, 40, 45, 111, 277, 285
Wilder, Thorton, 84, 277, 281
Williams, Charles, 25, 66, 189–90, 282
Wilson, Dorothy Clark, 229
Wister, Owen, 109
Wolff, Virginia Euwer, 40, 167, 285
Wrightson, Patricia, 49, 190, 280

Yancey, Philip, 229
Yep, Laurence, 218

Zindel, Paul, 44

# Index of Book Titles

*1984,* 272–73
*2001: A Space Odyssey,* 245–46

*Acceptable Time, An,* 151, 178–79
*Across Five Aprils,* 110, 200
*Adventures of Sherlock Holmes, The,* 221–22
*Aesop's Fables,* 118
*African Queen, The,* 35, 266, 280
*After the Dancing Days,* 99, 212, 282
*After the First Death,* 144
*Agony and the Ecstasy: A Biographical Novel of Michelangelo, The,* 213–14
*Aimer Gate, The,* 198
*Alice in Wonderland,* 25, 119
*Alida's Song,* 135
*All Creatures Great and Small,* 91, 108, 269, 281
*All Hallows Eve,* 189
*All These Strange Hours: The Excavation of a Life,* 232
*All Things Bright and Beautiful,* 269
*All Things Wise and Wonderful,* 269
*All Together Now,* 73, 192, 282
*Amazing Mrs. Pollifax, The,* 222
*Amber Spyglass, The,* 95, 183
*American Childhood,* 231
*Amusing Ourselves to Death,* 239–40
*Andromeda Strain, The,* 130
*Angels and Other Strangers,* 154
*Animal Farm,* 272
*Animals of Farthing Wood, The,* 61, 130–31, 283
*Anna Karenina,* 69
*Anne Frank: The Diary of a Young Girl,* 45, 233, 285
*Anne of Green Gables,* 43, 93, 206, 284
*Annotated Baseball Stories of Ring Lardner: 1914–1919,* 256
*Anpao: An American Indian Odyssey,* 200
*Antar and the Eagles,* 180
*Antarctica: Journey to the Pole,* 228

*Anthony Burns: The Defeat and Triumph of a Fugitive Slave,* 62, 110, 235, 283
*Arandel,* 211
*Ark, The,* 45, 93, 191, 284, 285
*Arm of a Starfish,* 150
*Arthur,* 203
*Ash Road,* 49, 61, 138, 280, 283
*At Home in Mitford,* 202
Austin Family series, 93, 149–50, 284
*Autobiography of Malcolm X, The,* 54, 111, 241, 280

*Baboon King, The,* 35, 137, 280
*Baseball in April,* 258
*Baseball Letters: A Fan's Correspondence with His Heroes,* 258
*Beacon at Alexandria, A,* 36, 192, 281
*Bearkeeper's Daughter, The,* 192
*Beauty,* 134
*Beekeeper's Apprentice, The,* 223
*Before the Darkness Falls,* 210
*Beginning of Sorrows, The,* 129
*Bell for Adano, A,* 45, 108, 198–99, 284, 285
*Beloved Invader, The,* 210
*Beowulf,* 187
*Best Loved Poems of the American People, The,* 114
*Best of Frank Deford: I'm Just Getting Started,* 254–55
*Best of Zane Grey Outdoorsman,* 255
*Between Heaven and Hell,* 237
*Beyond the Burning Lands,* 244
*Beyond the Chocolate War,* 145
Bible, the, 41, 47–48, 77–78, 82, 85, 91–92, 97–103, 118
*Bicentennial Man and Other Stories,* 243
*Big Sky, The,* 109
*Birds, Beasts and Relatives,* 91, 111, 231, 281
*Black Like Me,* 54, 111, 234, 280

*Blessing Way, The,* 223
*Blood Brothers,* 36, 230, 281
*Blood of the Prodigal: An Ohio Amish Mystery,* 222
*Body of Christopher Creed, The,* 116, 157–58, 225, 285
*Book of the Dun Cow, The,* 80, 100, 188–89, 283
*Book of the Lion, The,* 193
*Born Free,* 35, 228, 280
*Boy Meets Girl,* 236
*Boy's King Arthur, The,* 32
*Breaking of Ezra Riley, The,* 108, 134, 284
*Breath,* 83
*Brian's Return,* 137
*Bridge of San Luis Rey, The,* 84, 277, 281
*Bridge to Terabithia,* 99, 154–55, 282
*Broken English,* 222
*Bronze Bow, The,* 110
*Brothers Karamazov, The,* 121
*Bud, Not Buddy,* 94, 100, 193, 283, 284
*Burned Onion,* 258
*Byzantium,* 50, 203

*Call of the Wild, The,* 107, 133
*Captain Horatio Hornblower,* 266
*Castaways of the Flying Dutchman,* 24, 94, 202, 284
*Castle on the Hill, The,* 268
*Catcher in the Rye, The,* 45, 161
*Catherine, Called Birdie,* 193–94
*Cezanne Pinto,* 40, 54, 80, 213, 280, 285
*Charlotte's Web,* 23, 42
*Chasing Redbird,* 145
*Cheaper By the Dozen,* 42
*Child from the Sea, The,* 268
*Chocolate War, The,* 144
*Chosen, The,* 108, 158–59, 284
*Chris Chrisman Goes to College,* 66, 240, 282
Christ Clone trilogy, 128, 132
*Christy,* 21, 107, 204–5, 279, 284
*City of Gold and Lead, The,* 245
*Civil War, The,* 79, 230, 283
Clearwater Crossing series, 49
*Clouds without Rain,* 222
*College and Adult Reading List, The,* 117
*Come a Stranger,* 163–64, 165
*Comeback,* 73, 254, 282
*Completely Alive,* 229
*Contender, The,* 151

*Cross by Day, The Mezuzzah by Night, The,* 249
*Crossing, The,* 136
*Crown of Fire,* 252
*Cry, the Beloved Country,* 35, 273, 280
*Crystal Cave, The,* 203
*Crystal Prison, The,* 176
*Cultural Literacy: What Every American Needs to Know,* 116
*Cure, The,* 248–49

*Dangerous Skies,* 54, 162, 280
*Danzig Passage,* 217
*Dark is Rising, The,* 170–71
*Dark Portal, The,* 176
*Daughter of Time, The,* 227
*Daughter of Zion, A,* 216
*Dave at Night,* 69, 204, 282
*David Copperfield,* 106, 120
*Day No Pigs Would Die, A,* 24, 94, 158, 284
*Dean's Watch, The,* 268
*Death Be Not Proud: A Memoir,* 99, 234–35, 282
*Death Comes for the Archbishop,* 262
*Defeating Darwinism by Opening Minds,* 66, 237, 282
Deptford Mice trilogy, 176
*Descent into Hell,* 25, 66, 190, 282
*Diary of a Teenage Girl,* 116, 142–43, 285
*Dicey's Song,* 42, 164
*Disturbing the Universe,* 232
*Doctor Zhivago,* 21, 29, 51, 273, 279, 281
*Dog Who Wouldn't Be, The,* 42, 91, 207, 281
*Dogsong,* 108, 135–36
*Don Juan McQueen,* 210
*Don Quixote de la Mancha,* 120
*Door Near Here, A,* 69, 159–60, 282
*Dove,* 49, 233–34, 280
*Dragons in the Water,* 84, 281
*Dreadful Future of Blossom Culp, The,* 182
*Dune,* 247

*Eagle of the Ninth, The,* 214–15
*Ear, the Eye and the Arm, The,* 35, 246–47, 280
*Earthfasts,* 180
*Edge of Honor,* 21, 79, 206–7, 279, 283
*Elegant Universe, The,* 234
*Elidor,* 174
*Ella Enchanted,* 179–80
*Elske,* 165

Empyrion, 247–48
Endeavor, 24
Ender's Game, 109, 244
Endless Steppe, The, 29, 45, 110, 198, 279,
    281, 285
Eric, 238
Eric Liddell: Pure Gold, 24, 75, 108, 111,
    256–57, 279, 280, 284, 285
Eternal Spring of Mr. Ito, The, 111, 147–48,
    285
Ethan Frome, 121
Eva, 66, 246, 282
Every Pitcher Tells a Story: Gathered by a
    Devoted Baseball Fan, 258
Exodus, 217
Eye of the World, The, 177

Fahrenheit 451, 260
Fall-Out, 157
Fallen Angels, 54, 152, 280
Farewell to Arms, 268
Farewell to Manzanar, 111, 236, 285
Farewell to the Island, 218
Farthest Shore, The, 179
Fatal Storm, 255
Father Brown, 220
Father Elijah: An Apocalypse, 66, 132, 134,
    282
Father Figure, 44
Fearfully and Wonderfully Made, 229
Fellowship of the Ring, The, 19–20, 187
Final Reckoning, The, 176
Finding Faith, 238–39
Firebird, 50, 252
Firebird series, 252
Firegold, 170
Fisherman's Lady, The, 272
Flip-Flop Girl, 156
Flowers for Algernon, 73, 149, 282
Football's Best Short Stories, 258
Foundation, 243
Foundation Empire, 243
Friendly Persuasion, 79, 277, 283
Friends and Enemies, 111, 197, 285
Friendship, The, 216
Fusion Fire, 252

Gaal the Conqueror, 189
Gates of Excellence, 154
Gates of Zion, The, 216
Gathering Blue, 251

Gathering of Days, A, 110
Get a Life, 49
Getting a Clue in a Clueless World, 229
Ghost Belonged to Me, The, 91, 182, 281
Ghosts I Have Been, 182
Giant, 265
Gift of Asher Lev, The, 159
Gifted Hands: The Story of Ben Carson,
    36–37, 229–30
Girl Named Disaster, A, 35, 61, 146, 193,
    280, 283
Giver, The, 84, 249, 250–51
Go Tell It on the Mountain, 54, 260, 280
Golden Compass, The, 95, 182
Golden Fleece and the Heroes Who Lived
    Before Achilles, The, 119, 230
Gone with the Wind, 79, 206, 283
Good Earth, The, 24, 261, 280
Good Master, The, 11
Good Walk Spoiled: Days and Nights on the
    PGA Tour, 255
Grail, 203
Granny Reardun, 198
Granny Was a Buffer Girl, 145–46
Great Divide, The, 129
Great Expectations, 263
Great Gilly Hopkins, The, 46–47, 69, 155,
    282
Great Train Robbery, The, 130
Greek Treasure, The, 214
Green Mansions, 84, 269–70, 281
Greenwich, 172
Grey King, The, 171–72
Gulliver's Travels, 120
Guns of Navarone, The, 45, 224, 285

Hamlet, 46, 120
Hand Full of Stars, A, 36, 161, 281
Hang Tough, Paul Mather, 73, 257–58, 282
Hardy Boys series, 59, 108
Harry Potter and the Bible, 95
Harry Potter and the Chamber of Secrets, 184
Harry Potter and the Goblet of Fire, 185–86
Harry Potter and the Prisoner of Azkaban,
    184–85
Harry Potter and the Sorcerer's Stone, 184
Harry Potter series, 59, 91, 93–94, 96,
    184–86, 281
Hatchet, 137
Heart of a Jaguar, 84, 193, 215, 281
Heart of the Family, The, 268

*Heidi*, 11
*Hero and the Crown, The*, 134
*Hiding Place, The*, 45, 111, 240–41, 285
*His Dark Materials series*, 66, 95, 182–84, 282
*Hitchiker's Guide to the Galaxy*, 242
*Hobbit, The*, 18, 100, 187, 283
*Hold on to Love*, 43, 201
*Holes*, 24, 40, 160–61, 285
*Hollow Hills, The*, 203
*Home is the Sailor*, 234
*Homecoming*, 69, 164, 166, 282
*Homeless Bird*, 103, 167, 279
*Honey for a Child's Heart*, 11, 12
*Horses of Heaven*, 192
*Hound of the Baskervilles, The*, 109
*Hounds of the Morrigan, The*, 181
*House Like a Lotus, A*, 44, 150–51, 178
*Huckleberry Finn*, 54, 121, 276, 280

*I Capture the Castle*, 107, 213, 284
*I Heard the Owl Call My Name*, 99, 145, 282
*I Kissed Dating Goodbye*, 236
*I Remember Papa*, 42
*Ice at the End of the World*, 186
*If You Love Me*, 36, 212, 281
*Iliad, The*, 119
*In His Image*, 128–29, 229
*In My Hands: Memories of a Holocaust Rescue*, 50
*In the Beginning: Creation Stories from Around the World*, 235
*In the Grip of Winter*, 131
*In This House of Brede*, 107, 266, 284
*Incident at Hawk's Hill*, 61, 195, 283
*Into the Wild*, 256
*Into Thin Air: A Personal Account of the Mt. Everest Disaster*, 24, 256, 280
*Iron Sceptre, The*, 189
*Iron Will: The Triathlete's Ultimate Challenge*, 257
*Ishmael*, 66, 251, 282
*Island of Doctor Moreau, The*, 252–53
*Island of Ghosts*, 192
*Island, The*, 156–57
*Islander, The*, 160
*It's My Life*, 143

*Jackaroo*, 165
*Jacob Have I Loved*, 155–56

*Jane Eyre*, 21, 120, 260, 261, 279
*Jason's Gold*, 131
*Jericho*, 148
*Jerusalem Interlude*, 217
*Jim the Boy*, 94, 195, 284
*Johnny Tremain*, 110, 196
*Joni*, 73, 100, 111, 232, 282, 283
*Journey through the Night*, 45, 100, 194, 283, 285
*Jubilee*, 79, 206, 217–18, 283
*Julie*, 205
*Julius Caesar*, 120
*Jumper Fables*, 229

*Key to Zion, The*, 216
*Kidnapped*, 108, 139–40
*Killer Angels*, 79, 207, 283
*Killing Fields, Living Fields*, 24, 75, 230–31, 279, 280
*Kim*, 103, 271, 279
*King Lear*, 120
*King Must Die, The*, 274
*King of Shadows*, 172–73
*Kingfishers Catch Fire*, 103, 267, 279
*Kit's Wilderness*, 141
*Know What You Believe*, 80

*Land, The*, 216
*Last Amateurs, The*, 255
*Last Enchantment, The*, 203
*Last Mission, The*, 45, 205, 285
*Last of the Breed*, 29, 61, 132–33, 281, 283
*Last of the Mohicans, The*, 106, 263
*Last of the Wine, The*, 274–75
*Leaving the Land*, 134
*Left Behind*, 132
*Left Behind series*, 49–50, 132
*Left Hand of Darkness, The*, 248
*Legend of Luke, The*, 176
*Lest Innocent Blood Be Shed*, 45, 110, 235, 239, 285
*Let the Balloon Go*, 161–62
*Let the Circle Be Unbroken*, 216
*Life, the Universe and Everything*, 242
*Light Beyond the Forest*, 203
*Light in the Window*, 202
*Light in Zion, The*, 216
*Light Princess, The*, 272
*Lion, the Witch and the Wardrobe, The*, 62, 93
*Little Women*, 119

*Long Walk: The True Story of a Trek to Freedom,* 29, 45, 211, 281, 285
*Long Way from Chicago, A,* 24, 46, 91, 209–10, 281
*Lord Foul's Bane,* 73, 173, 282
*Lord God Made Them All, The,* 269
*Lord Jim,* 49, 262–63, 280
*Lord of the Flies,* 45, 133, 139, 267
*Lord of the Rings, The,* 27, 89, 108, 187–88, 284
*Lost Horizon,* 24, 269, 280
*Lost Prince, The,* 129–30
*Love Comes Softly,* 207
*Love is Eternal,* 214
*Love's Enduring Promise,* 207
*Love's Long Journey,* 207
*Lust for Life,* 214
*Lyddie,* 209

*Macbeth,* 120
Magic Bicycle series, 90
*Magic Bicycle, The,* 169
*Magic Circle, The,* 40, 93, 180–81, 284, 285
*Magnificent Obsession,* 107, 264
*Make Lemonade,* 40, 167, 285
*Making Up Megaboy,* 153
*Mama's Bank Account,* 196
*Man Who Was Poe, The,* 219
*Many Stones,* 143, 151
*Many Waters,* 143, 177–78
*Mariel of Redwall,* 176
*Marquis of Lossie, The,* 272
*Marquis' Secret, The,* 272
*Martian Chronicles, The,* 244
*Mary Poppins,* 11
*Masada: The Last Fortress,* 36, 205–6, 281
*Master Puppeteer, The,* 24, 208, 280
*Mattimeo,* 176
*Meet the Austins,* 149
*Melusine: A Mystery,* 219–20
*Memory,* 99, 152, 282
*Merchant of Venice, The,* 120
*Merlin,* 203
*Middle Passage, The,* 40, 62, 233, 283, 285
*Midnight Blue,* 173
*Midnight Hour Encores,* 142
*Midsummer Night's Dream, A,* 120, 172
*Miranda's Last Stand,* 218
*Misérables, Les,* 69, 107, 121, 270
*Missing May,* 99, 160, 282
*Mississippi Bridge,* 216

Mitford series, 91, 107, 281, 284
*Moby Dick,* 121
*Monster,* 54, 152–53, 280
*Moon by Night,* 149, 178
*Moon Dark,* 49, 190, 280
*Moon of Gomrath,* 174
*Moonlight Man, The,* 146–47
*Morbid Taste for Bones, A,* 226
*Morte d'Arthur,* 203
*Mossflower,* 176
*Mother-Daughter Book Club, The,* 86
*Mother Goose Rhymes,* 118
*Mr. Lincoln's Army,* 230
*Mrs. Pollifax,* 42
*Munich Signature,* 217
*Murder on the Orient Express,* 220
*Music of Dolphins, The,* 148
*My Ántonia,* 26, 262
*My Family and Other Animals,* 231
*My Name is Asher Lev,* 60, 159

Nancy Drew series, 59, 108
Narnia Chronicles series, 11, 24, 61, 62, 89, 93
*Never Call Retreat,* 230
*Never to Forget,* 45, 239, 285
*New Song, A,* 202
*Nicholas and Alexandra,* 29, 238, 281
*Night,* 40, 45, 111, 277, 285
*Night Journey, The,* 29, 202–3, 279, 281
*Nightfall,* 243–44
*Nine Tailors,* 227
*No Hero for the Kaiser,* 197, 205
*North to Freedom,* 40, 100, 131, 283, 285
*Northwest Passage,* 108, 211, 284
*Nothing but the Truth,* 116, 141–42, 285
*Nothing Else Matters,* 212
*Nun's Story, The,* 270

*Odyssey, The,* 105, 106, 119, 164, 166
*Oedipus Rex,* 119
*Oh, the Places You'll Go,* 112
*Oliver Twist,* 106
*Oliver Wiswell,* 110, 211
Omega trilogy, 129
*On Fortune's Wheel,* 165
*On the Beach,* 251–52
*Once and Future King, The,* 203
*Once on This Island,* 218
*One Child,* 73, 236, 282

*One Day in the Life of Ivan Denisovich*, 29, 62, 275–76, 281
*One-Eyed Cat*, 147
*Only Game in Town, The*, 169
*Other Wind, The*, 179
*Otherwise: New & Selected Poems*, 114
*Out of the Dust*, 199
*Out of the Silent Planet*, 249
*Out to Canaan*, 202
*Outlaws of Sherwood, The*, 108, 133–34
*Outsiders*, 44
*Over Seas, Under Stone*, 170
*Owl Service, The*, 175
*Oxford Book of Children's Verse in America, The*, 114
*Oxford Book of Children's Verse, The*, 114

*Paradise Lost*, 182, 183
*Parents in Pain*, 74
*Park's Quest*, 156
*Parsival*, 156
*Peace Child*, 75, 240, 279
*Pearl, The*, 49, 276, 280
*Pearls of Lutra*, 176
*Pendragon*, 203
Pendragon Cycle series, 203
*Perelandra*, 249–50
*Perfect Storm: A True Story of Men Against the Sea*, 256
*Peter Rabbit*, 55
*Pied Piper of Hamelin, The*, 53, 55
*Pigman*, 44
*Pilgrim at Tinker Creek*, 61, 66, 231, 282, 283
*Pilgrim's Progress*, 120, 261
*Pirates of Penzance, The*, 115
*Plague, The*, 36, 261, 281
*Playing Beatie Bow*, 21, 208, 279
*Pool of Fire, The*, 245
*Portrait of the Artist As a Young Man*, 270
*Power and the Glory, The*, 84, 268, 281
*Prague Counterpoint*, 217
*Preacher's Boy*, 156
*Present Darkness, This*, 225
*President's Lady, The*, 214
*Pride and Prejudice*, 21, 120, 259, 279
*Prince and the Pauper, The*, 121
*Prince in Waiting, The*, 244–45
*Princess and Curdie, The*, 272
*Promise, The*, 159
*Proving Ground, The*, 49, 255–56, 280

*Quest for the King*, 189

*Rabble in Arms*, 211
*Read-Aloud Handbook, The*, 25
*Reading for the Love of It*, 89
*Reaping the Whirlwind*, 221
*Rebecca*, 21, 106, 264, 279
*Rebels of the Heavenly Kingdom*, 24, 209, 280
*Red Badge of Courage, The*, 121, 263
*Red Shift, The*, 66, 174, 175, 282
*Red Storm Rising*, 29, 220, 281
*Redwall*, 23, 94, 176, 284
Redwall series, 46, 59, 176
*Rescue, The*, 239
*Restaurant at the End of the Universe, The*, 242
*Return of the King, The*, 20, 187
*Return, The*, 35, 36, 110, 204, 280, 281
*Return to Hawk's Hill*, 195
*Return to the Island*, 218
*Return to Zion, The*, 216
*Reversed Thunder*, 92
*Riding for the Brand*, 108, 284
*Ring Cycle*, 187
*Ring of Bright Water*, 61, 238, 283
*Ring of Endless Light, A*, 150
*River, The*, 103, 267, 279
*Road to Camlann*, 203
*Road to Memphis, The*, 216
*Robe, The*, 36, 107, 194, 281
*Robin Hood*, 25
*Robinson Crusoe*, 119, 253
*Roll of Thunder, Hear My Cry*, 51, 54, 100, 215–16, 280, 283
*Romeo and Juliet*, 46, 120
*Root Cellar, The*, 93, 180, 284
*Rowan Farm*, 191
*Rumplestiltskin Problem, The*, 188
*Runner, The*, 164

*Safe at Home: The True and Inspiring Story of Chicago's Field of Dreams*, 54, 257, 280
*Saint Ben*, 50, 73, 94, 100, 195, 282, 283, 284
*Saint George and the Dragon*, 55
*Samurai, The*, 24, 265, 280
*Sanctuary Sparrow*, 226
*Sand Reckoner*, 192
*Savannah*, 210
*Scarlet Letter, The*, 121

Scarlet Pimpernel, The, 135
Screwtape Letters, The, 225, 237–38
Second Bend in the River, The, 211
Second Foundation, 243
Secret Garden, The, 11
Sentries, The, 136
Seventeen Against the Dealer, 165
Seventh Raven, The, 221
Shabanu: Daughter of the Wind, 103, 162, 279
Shadow at Hawthorne Bay, 180
Shadow of the Almighty, 75, 84, 232–33, 279, 281
Shakespeare, 11
Shakespeare Stories, 110, 271
Shane, 108, 137–38, 284
She Said Yes: The Unlikely Martyrdom of Cassie Bernall, 100, 116, 229, 283, 285
Shiloh, 80
Shipwreck at the Bottom of the World, 61, 228, 283
Shiva's Fire, 103, 279
Siege of Dome, The, 248
Silence, 265
Silver on the Tree, 172
Silverwing, 181
Singing Mountain, The, 36, 151, 281
Skellig, 168
Slake's Limbo, 69, 148, 282
Slave Dancer, The, 62, 196, 283
Snow Goose, The, 40, 266, 285
So Big, 265
So Long and Thanks for All the Fish, 242
Socrates Meets Jesus, 237
Solitary Blue, A, 166
Song for a Dark Queen, 215
Song of the Trees, 216
Sons from Afar, 165, 166
Sound of Chariots, A, 43, 93, 99, 200–201, 282, 284
Space trilogy, 249–50
Spindle's End, 134
Spy Who Came in from the Cold, The, 223–24
Star Fisher, The, 218
Step from Heaven, A, 153
Stillness at Appomattox, A, 230
Stone Book, The, 197–98
Stone Quartet, 174, 197–98
Stowaway, 24, 199
Stranger in Savannah, 79, 210, 283

String in the Harp, A, 93, 99, 169, 282, 284
Strong Poison, 227
Stuart Little, 91
Stuck in Neutral, 73, 163, 282
Subtle Knife, The, 95, 182–83
Summer of the Monkeys, The, 160
Sunwing, 181
Sweet Valley High series, 49
Sweet Whispers, Brother Rush, 69, 222–23, 282
Swiftly Tilting Planet, A, 177
Sword and the Circle, 203
Sword at Sunset, 203
Sword Bearer, The, 189
Sword of the Spirits, The, 244

Taggerung, 176
Tale of Two Cities, A, 62, 106, 107, 120, 263–64
Tales from Earthsea, 179
Tales from Shakespeare, 107, 120, 271
Tales of a Dead King, 36, 224, 281
Tales of Tahitian Waters, 108, 255, 284
Taliesin, 203
Ten Fingers for God, 229
Terrible Swift Sword, A, 230
That Hideous Strength, 249, 250
These High, Green Hills, 202
Thief, The, 140
Things Fall Apart, 35, 259, 280
Thirteen Clocks, The, 42, 276
Thirty Thousand on the Hoof, 109
Thomas Covenant Unbeliever, 109
Thurber Carnival, The, 91, 111, 241, 281
Till We Have Faces, 107, 271–72, 284
Times Quartet series, 93, 149, 177, 284
Timothy Twinge, 92
To a Wild Sky, 283
To Be a Slave, 62, 237, 283
To Kill a Mockingbird, 26, 54, 271, 280
To See Your Face Again, 210
To the Wild Sky, 61, 139
Tom Fobble's Day, 198
Tom Sawyer, 121, 276–77
Tombs of Atuan, The, 179
Tomorrow, When the War Began, 49, 133, 280
Torn Thread, 45, 201, 285
Tower of Geburah, The, 90, 189
Town Like Alice, A, 49, 111, 275, 280, 285
Toy Campaign, The, 169

*Tracker*, 135
*Treasure Island*, 26, 55, 108, 140
*Tree Grows in Brooklyn, A*, 107, 275, 284
*Troubling a Star*, 150
*Tuck Everlasting*, 168–69
*Twenty Thousand Leagues Under the Sea*, 252
*Two Towers, The*, 187

*Ultimate High: My Everest Odyssey*, 256
*Unaborted Socrates, The*, 237
*Uncle Tom's Cabin*, 62, 120, 214, 283
*Under the Blood-Red Sun*, 111, 212–13, 285
*Unicorns in the Rain*, 143
*Universe Next Door, The*, 81, 240
*Up a Road Slowly*, 21, 149, 279

*Veritas Project, The: Hangman's Curse*, 116, 225, 285
*Vienna Prelude*, 217
*Villain by Necessity, A*, 249
*Virginian, The*, 109
*Voyage of the Dawntreader, The*, 79
*Voyage to the Land of the Brobdingnags*, 120
*Voyage to the Land of the Lilliputians, The*, 120
*Voyages of Dr. Doolittle, The*, 42

*Waiting for Godot*, 82
*Walk Across America, A*, 236–37
*Walk Two Moons*, 99, 145, 282
*Walk West, The*, 237
*Walker's Crossing*, 94, 153, 284
*Walking Across Egypt*, 91, 146, 281
*Wall, The*, 45, 110, 199, 285
*Wanderer, The*, 99, 130, 282
*War of the Worlds, The*, 109, 253
*Warrior Scarlet*, 89
*Warsaw Requiem*, 217

*Watership Down*, 128
*Watsons Go to Birmingham, The*, 193
*We All Fall Down*, 132
*We Didn't Mean to Go to Sea*, 25
*Weirdstone of Brisingamen, The*, 174
*Well, The*, 216
*Westing Game, The*, 226
*Whalesong*, 108, 186
*What About Tomorrow*, 139
*What Happened in Hamelin*, 186
*What's a Christian to Do With Harry Potter?*, 95, 185
*Wheel of Times* series, 177
*Where the Red Fern Grows*, 11, 61, 94, 160, 283, 284
*White Lilacs*, 54, 205, 280
*White Mountains, The*, 245
*White Whale*, 186
*Wicked Day, The*, 203
*Wind in the Door, A*, 177
*Wind in the Willows, The*, 25, 42, 46
*Wings of a Falcon, The*, 165
*Witch of Blackbird Pond, The*, 93, 110
*Wizard of Earthsea, A*, 66, 179, 282
*Wrinkle in Time, A*, 90, 177
*Wuthering Heights*, 120, 260

*Year Down Yonder, A*, 24, 46, 209–10
*Yearling, The*, 42, 274
*Yesterday's Child*, 99, 151, 282
*Young Joan*, 194
*Young Unicorns, The*, 149–50

*Zebra and Other Stories*, 159
Zion Chronicles series, 36, 100, 107, 216–17, 281, 283, 284
Zion Covenant series, 45, 100, 107, 217, 283, 284, 285

## Share Your Thoughts

**With the Author:** Your comments will be forwarded to the author when you send them to *zauthor@zondervan.com*.

**With Zondervan:** Submit your review of this book by writing to *zreview@zondervan.com*.

## Free Online Resources at

## www.zondervan.com

**Zondervan AuthorTracker:** Be notified whenever your favorite authors publish new books, go on tour, or post an update about what's happening in their lives.

**Daily Bible Verses and Devotions:** Enrich your life with daily Bible verses or devotions that help you start every morning focused on God.

**Free Email Publications:** Sign up for newsletters on fiction, Christian living, church ministry, parenting, and more.

**Zondervan Bible Search:** Find and compare Bible passages in a variety of translations at www.zondervanbiblesearch.com.

**Other Benefits:** Register yourself to receive online benefits like coupons and special offers, or to participate in research.